To Tuxtepec

Guelatao de Juárez

Ixtlan de Juárez

Calpulalpan de Mendez

El Punto

190

175

Oaxaca

Monte
Albán

Santa Maria el Tule

190

Teotitlan del Valle

San Mateo Macuilxochitl

Tlacochahuaya

Dainzu

Santa Ana del Valle

Mitla

Ruinas de
Lambityeco

Yagul

San Bartolo
Coyotepec

Tlacolula

San Pablo

Zaachila

San Martin Tilcajete

Villa de
Mitla Xaaga

175

San Tomas Jalieza

San Antonio Castillo Velasco

190

Ocotlán

SIERRA MADRE DEL SUR

To Tehuantepec 126 miles

The Food and Life of Oaxaca

Traditional Recipes from Mexico's Heart

Zarela Martínez

Edited by Anne Mendelson
Photographs by Laurie Smith

Macmillan • USA

MACMILLAN
A Simon & Schuster Macmillan Company
1633 Broadway
New York, NY 10019-6785

Macmillan Publishing books may be purchased for business or sales promo-
tional use. For information please write: Special Markets Department,
Macmillan Publishing USA, 1633 Broadway, New York, NY 10019.

Library of Congress Cataloging-in-Publication Data
Martínez, Zarela.
    The food and life of Oaxaca, Mexico / by Zarela Martínez.
        p.   cm.
    Includes index.
ISBN: 0-02-860350-8 (alk. paper)
     1. Cookery, Mexican. 2. Cookery—Mexico—Oaxaca. 3. Oaxaca
(Mexico)—Social life and customs. I. Title.
TX716.M4M3757   1997
641.5972'74—dc21   97-3202
                            CIP

ISBN: 0-02-860350-8

Book design by Amy Trombat

Manufactured in the United States of America
10 9 8 7 6 5 4 3 2 1

To the People of Oaxaca

Contents

Acknowledgments

During my twelve trips to Oaxaca since 1985 many people have opened their hearts and their homes to me. Some have cooked with me—letting me grind chocolate on their own metate, having me stir a traditional dish for hours, or helping me pack the ingredients for a Barbacoa de Cabrito (goat barbecue) into a huge earthenware pot. Some have marched at dawn with me at town fiestas and others have taken me to markets and pointed out ingredients previously unknown to me. Others have told me stories and shown me the ways of their people.

On my first trip I was lucky enough to meet and cook with María Concepción Portillo de Carballido, author of a cookbook that I had picked up at a bookstore. That was my first taste of Oaxacan home cooking. She also helped me make sense of the wonderful but mysterious panoply of ingredients in the markets.

Hugo Antonio Santiago of the Oaxacan Tourism Office spent hours on the telephone with me, tracked down elusive information, and arranged some of my most valuable encounters. Best of all he introduced me to his family in Teotitlán del Valle and especially his sister, Zoyla Mendoza, who taught me the wonderful cuisine of the Valley Zapotecs.

Venancia Toledo Hernández and her son Luis Armando Hernández gave me hours, or rather days, of their time helping me discover the intricate and dazzling cuisine of the Isthmus of Tehuantepec.

Also helpful were Martha Toledo and Julio Bustillos, proprietors of Bar Jardín in Juchitán, and their chef, Odilia Román.

In Oaxaca City Lucila Zárate de Fuentes, Olga Martínez of Case de la Abuela, and Nicolasa Ramírez of La Pereñita provided their favorite recipes and much information.

Behind any book there is a good editor. This book would not be what it is without the effort, enthusiasm, and encouragement of Anne Mendelson.

At Macmillan I sincerely thank Jennifer Griffin, who has been a joy to work with and who has always been there for me when I have needed her. Chris Dreyer spent many hours working with us comma by comma.

The vision of this book owes much to the photographer, my friend Laurie Smith, who shared so many of my journeys and loves Oaxaca as much as I do.

My mother, Aida Gabilondo Desouches, who carefully tested most of the recipes, offered good suggestions and most importantly gave me support when I was discouraged and overwhelmed.

Laurel Gonsalves, another frequent travel companion, attended countless tasting dinners and patiently listened to me, always giving me sound advice.

To my agent, Jane Dysstel, for service above and beyond the call of duty.

To everyone else who in small or big ways helped me along the way.

Young girl drinking Chocolateatole
(ritual foamed drink)

Preface

I present this ofrecimiento (offering)
to thank you for helping us to celebrate
this special occasion, for you know that alone
we cannot share life. Others must be there.

These simple words sum up all I have ever wanted to say about the life and food of Oaxaca. The speaker is a middle-aged Mixe Indian, Diego Vázquez Pacheco, addressing the guests at his son's vocational-school commencement banquet in the dusty mountain village of Tlahui (officially Santa María Tlahuitoltepec). He stands holding out a tiny pottery bowl of *tepache*, an immemorial Oaxacan fermented ritual drink, before the whole company and ceremonially asking them to receive the offering.

The deputy mayor of the town rises to accept on behalf of everyone. We all drink from our bowls of *tepache* and then proceed with a delicious lunch, for which a whole cow has been butchered and cooked. The banquet is held in a low, dark building filled with long benches in front of tables covered in shiny turquoise oilcloth stamped with red and yellow roses.

I have returned to the scene in memory a hundred times since. So many different worlds coming together in a moment—the unexpectedness of it is just what you learn to expect in Oaxaca. Yet what moved me most was Mr. Vázquez's invitation. "Offering"—is it not a beautiful word? In modern societies we have almost forgotten how to consecrate food and drink to something larger than ourselves while we fill our shopping carts or plates. But the concept of offerings still resonates everywhere in Oaxacan life. Rooted in the old pre-Hispanic world where humans and gods spoke to each other every day, it is at the heart of the culture and especially the food culture.

In the markets I have seen elderly men and women at their regular spots setting out a few little bunches of herbs or a handful of squash blossoms with as much dignity and grace as prosperous tradespeople selling mountains of colorful produce. On particularly sacred days of the year I have seen simple, courteous, but solemn exchanges of fruit and bread between families and friends marking the meaning of the occasion. At the big annual pan-Oaxacan festival called the Guelaguetza, I have watched as representatives of many Indian peoples who don't even speak the same language come to place their own region's food and—through ceremonial dances—their distinctive living history before all the rest of Oaxaca.

It is fitting that the literal meaning of *guelaguetza* in the Zapotec language is "offering" and that in the villages the same word refers to a system of offering time, labor, and money to help out one's neighbors. The whole society is filled with different manifestations of this belief: "Alone we cannot share life."

A gesture of respect to the patron saint of a church

The Life of Oaxaca

What is Oaxaca? Answers crowd into my mind, but I have trouble keeping to straight and narrow factual descriptions. Though there is much to say about history, geography, and folkways, my memory always strays back to particular scenes . . .

I am wandering about an enormous, flat grassy plaza, just below the summit of a great hill set in a vista of majestic mountains and spacious valleys under a boundless, shining sky. How the huge rectangular surface was squared and leveled boggles the imagination. It is about a thousand feet long—nearly a fifth of a mile—and all around its sides are weathered gray stone buildings of a scale to put any merely human visitor in awe.

Even without knowing the details of how they were aligned by astronomical sightings, I sense the mathematical precision of the tremendous structures. Stepped platforms, pyramids, walls, staircases, terraces, inset patios; sundials and sacrificial altars; stone slabs carved all over with intricate hieroglyphs or violently contorted human figures; the remains of a ceremonial ball-court; rows of stone columns left standing with no roof to support—even today these seem filled with the ancient builders' knowledge and power.

Standing in the center of the plaza, I look up to the immense blue sky. The grass under my feet is thick and a little breeze caresses my skin. I have a sensation of light and space formally contained and structured by the high ramparts that surround the square to the north, south, east, and west. For some reason, it makes my heart soar and inside my head I hear a line from a popular Mexican song, "El cielo tengo por techo"—I have the sky for my roof.

The great, mysterious expanse that I was exploring for the first time was the central square—what modern Mexicans call a *zócalo*—of the ancient city of Monte Albán, close to the center of Oaxaca State. If the story doesn't absolutely begin with Monte Albán, it's one of our earliest glimpses of the past.

Thousands of years ago, possibly by 8000 B.C., people began moving into a remote area of southeastern Mexico near where the two coastlines—Gulf and Pacific—narrow to a slender neck of land called the Isthmus of Tehuantepec while beginning an eastward swerve. Because the terrain is incredibly chopped up by huge, rugged mountain ranges, many cultures developed their own languages and customs. Some of the larger ones grew into complex civilizations. And none was more brilliant than that of the Zapotecs, the people who found their way to a cluster of sweeping, fertile valleys close to the center of the jumbled mountain systems. In the end they established an empire covering an area about the size of Indiana, though considering the extreme geography, it might be more like the size of Texas if it were ironed out! This realm roughly matches the borders of the modern Oaxaca State.

The other peoples in the area did not yield to the Zapotec expansion willingly and always kept their separate ways even when forced to pay tribute. The Zapotecs successfully took over only two main regions for their own homes. But these were the most desirable farmland of the empire: the rich, sheltered Central Valleys—especially the Valley of Oaxaca in the flood plain of the Atoyac River—and much of the little available arable land about a hundred miles to the south, along the Pacific coast in the Isthmus of Tehuantepec. In the Central Valleys they built several settlements that today are magnets for archeology buffs visiting the state. The greatest of all was Monte Albán.

Monte Albán began its transformation into a major city at least three centuries before Christ and went from stage to glorious stage for more than a thousand years. The ruins I visited were once administrative buildings, palaces, temples for sacrifices, houses of prayer. At Monte Albán there was also an astronomical observatory where priests skilled in reading the heavens carried out a major responsibility of all pre-Hispanic societies: interpreting a highly intricate calendar that governed every part of people's lives from choosing days for planting to naming children. (Time was actually measured by *two* overlapping calendars based on different systems of calculation. Astonishingly, some Oaxacan villages are still using these reckoning methods to plan important activities.)

At its height the city had perhaps as many as 30,000 inhabitants, and may have been the greatest trading center south of Tenochtitlan—the site of modern Mexico City, some 300 miles away. The vast plaza was among other things a marketplace where people bought or sold cloth, dyes, grains, fruits, spices, salt, all manner of pottery, herbs for medicine, rare feathers of tropical birds, precious stones, gold, and the substance as good as gold—cacao beans, which were actually exchanged as money in several parts of pre-Conquest Mexico.

Monte Albán's glory ended at some point after A.D. 750 for reasons no one has ever certainly explained. The vast hilltop site was abandoned and at last swallowed up by shrubs and trees, while for more than half a millennium the Zapotecs continued to dominate the region from other strategic cities in the valleys. Then toward the start of the fifteenth century two catastrophes arrived in short succession. The Mexica (as they called themselves) or "Aztec" people established a powerful empire in the north and gathered most of the former Zapotec empire under their sway through battles and canny alliances. The region was still reeling from this change when the conquering Spanish marched in.

Hernán Cortez, fresh from pillaging and destroying Tenochtitlan, had heard that the Oaxacan mountains were rich in gold. In 1521 he sent an expeditionary force to claim the region for Spain. In a bloody struggle lasting for generations, the invaders set out to obliterate the existing culture and recreate the land in their own image. In most of the new province of Oaxaca they were amazingly unsuccessful. Though they destroyed ancient temples, erected big buildings of their own, and imposed a new faith, they were unable to conquer the spirit of these people. They had to learn to live with them, and from the centuries-long process have come things of great beauty. For example . . .

I sit under the shade of graceful whitewashed Spanish arches lingering over a bottle of mineral water and a shot glass of mezcal, the smokier, gutsier southern Mexican cousin of tequila. The air on my skin feels as if some alchemist high up in the radiant sky had taken the best parts of spring and summer and mixed them to perfection.

Blackbirds are chattering in the branches of the green laurel trees that fill the square in front of me. Here people sit at their ease on lovely ironwork benches in this shady but light-filled sanctuary. An ensemble of musicians—indeed, the official state band—is assembling in a matching ironwork bandshell, tuning up for a medley ranging from operatic arias to cha-cha-chas.

Late afternoon is passing into evening, and throngs of vendors spring up as if on cue. Their features speak of mixed or, very often, pure Indian ancestry, a dramatic contrast to the unmistakable Spanish character of the ornate baroque buildings that I can see in every direction. Many times the clothes and headdress identify a distant home town, and they sell crafts their home towns are known for—black pottery with a satiny, lustrous finish; intricate carvings following the fanciful windings of the copal tree branches that they are sculpted from; delicately embroidered dresses and blouses; woollen weavings done on the spot by women in long, square striped red and white tunics who bend over small looms that they carry strapped around their waists.

Grownups or teams of children are proffering colorful woven yarn bracelets or handmade sarapes. Five or six balloon vendors appear with their bouquets of Mickey Mouse figures, snakes, balls, and airplanes bobbing in the breeze. Different tantalizing smells announce the food vendors—a man who sells chile- and lime-seasoned corn kernels (esquites), the one who has jot kekis *("hot cakes" in phonetic Spanish), and his neighbor selling hot dogs wrapped in bacon. Last will come the sweet potato vendor whose special whistle signals that it is almost time to turn in for the night.*

Everyone in sight, from dignified elderly couples strolling hand in hand to young Swiss tourists in army boots, seems carried along by the delicious music of the marimba band that just made its appearance and the mariachis who soon follow. The scent of roses and gardenias fills the air. How can one single spot combine so many enchantments?

This is the heart of modern-day Oaxaca City, which is the heart of Oaxaca State. It is the beautiful *zócalo* or town square—the human-size counterpart to the god-size one at Monte Albán—that sits at the hub of all life in Ciudad Oaxaca de Juárez surrounded by government buildings, hotels, and outdoor cafés, enveloped in the most absolute air of serenity I have ever known in any city. But an effervescent serenity, not a glassy land-that-time-forgot calm.

No trace of this charmed spot existed when the Spanish armies came into the former Zapotec territory. On the Atoyac river in the main central valley, about five miles east of the then undiscovered Monte Albán ruin, they found an Aztec fort called in Nahuatl (the language of the Aztecs) "Huaxyacac." The name referred to a kind of *huaxe* or *guaje* (acacia) that grows abundantly in the region. The conquerors decided to set up local headquarters here and christened it "Villa de Antequera de Guaxaca" after Antequera, a town in Andalusía. After a time, just plain "Oaxaca" won out, in various early spellings.

The beautiful surrounding valley—obviously the best local farmland—was given the same name, and Cortez lost no time appropriating it for himself along with the title "Marqués del Valle de Oaxaca." He isn't remembered here with much love, though today the outdoor café of the Hotel Marqués de Valle—the very spot where I was seated in front of the square—is one of the favorite leisure spots in the city. Oaxacans prefer to recall the city's association with a later arrival, Benito Juárez. This great Mexican president and contemporary of Abraham Lincoln's was a Oaxacan village Zapotec who served as governor of the state from 1847 to 1852. In his honor the city now bears the official name of "Oaxaca de Juárez."

In the early days of the colonies, the paradisiacal location of the new town attracted Spanish settlers in large numbers. It was a natural choice for the capital of Oaxaca province. Most of the existing city was built between the late sixteenth and eighteenth centuries, predominantly using a wonderful muted greenish stone that glistens after the rain or glows in the late evening sun. (People here call it simply *cantera*, or "quarry stone.") Vast amounts of money were spent on erecting the imposing and elaborate churches that today are among the main tourist sights, even now testifying to the zeal of the many different Catholic missionaries in colonial times. The Dominican order of friars—officially the chief missionaries in the region—left the most flamboyant architectural statement of all the region's settlers and missionaries in the fantastic gilded stucco work of Santo Domingo church. Dedicated to the founder of the order, it was finished in the seventeenth century and has a gaudy majesty that makes visitors gasp—or, as I once saw done by an awestruck woman wrapped in a black rebozo, burst out spontaneously into the "Ave Maria."

The town grew to be one of the most prosperous cities of "New Spain." In the time of Oaxaca's greatness it was beautifully laid out by Alfonso García Bravo, the sixteenth-century architect who also designed Mexico City. As the architect's vision grew to reality, the early Spanish aristocrats, government officials, and prosperous tradespeople built handsome, dignified houses of quarry stone or pretty painted stucco—pink, indigo, faded gold—with wrought iron grillwork. Lining the well-proportioned grid of spacious, tree-shaded cobbled streets, islands of greenery or swirls of bright bougainvillea in shocking pink, orange, magenta, and red greet you everywhere.

Can you wonder that this is the city of my heart? I have been falling more and more in love with it since my first visit there a dozen years ago. It seems to be a perfect size—the population is roughly 330,000—and I know no place more civilized. Small wonder that the Mexican government has designated the entire city a national historic monument, or that in 1987 UNESCO named it part of "the cultural patrimony of humanity."

People who are usually unromantic use words like "magical" and "enchanting" to describe Oaxaca City. The light has a special quality, as caressing as the air. Most of the region's blessings are concentrated here—from the climate, which is lovely and refreshing at all times of the year, to the greater part of Oaxaca State's wealth. Yet just for that reason, it is not typical of the state as a whole. Once you have left the haven of the Central Valleys and the crown-jewel city, your ideas of Oaxaca can change rapidly. An indelible image:

I stand in a muddy, tired-looking marketplace, gazing at a meager selection of vegetables that seem to have given up the struggle for life and flyspecked hunks of meat. The vendors in shabby blue jeans are no happier-looking than the wares. The lack of selection here is ironic, because beyond the neglected, featureless white-painted buildings that enclose the market, trucks are unloading and reloading the most glorious produce.

None of these beautiful fruits and vegetables grew here, and few will be eaten here. The spot happens to a be a distribution point for produce coming from and going to luckier places.

The ground rises to a view of low brown hills, barren except for an occasional scattering of stunted oak trees. But all else that I see is eclipsed by a gigantic inflated vinyl replica of a Coca-Cola can. The ground is almost shaking under my feet because at the center of the square an obnoxious salesman is yelling into a microphone connected to six powerful yard-high speakers.

I close my eyes and try to remember the descriptions I've read of this area before the Conquest—a nexus of great trade centers to which merchants came from as far away as Tenochtitlan to the north or Peru to the south, selling or seeking gold, rare feathers, and precious cacao beans. This glorious and brilliant past contrasts sharply with its forlorn present.

Here is yet another *zócalo* or town square, one that tells a sadly different story from the great *Zócalo* of Oaxaca City or the ancient Monte Albán market plaza. It is the center square of Tlaxiaco, one of the larger towns of the upland region called the Mixteca Alta for its principal ethnic group, the Mixtec Indians. Once they were known as the "Cloud People" or "Raingod People." What happened to them and their land—a high-lying, badly damaged terrain located west of the plenteous Central valleys—is all too typical of the lot of the indigenous Oaxacan peoples.

The Mixtecs were one of the great early civilizations and proud rivals of the conquering Zapotecs. Most of the surviving codices (illuminated manuscripts) and gold work of ancient Oaxaca were their beautiful creations. This once was a great agricultural center of the region. But when the Spanish came they carved up the land into large ranches distributed to the officers of Cortez's army or attached it to the many convents of the missionary friars. Ignoring the local peoples' ways of choosing different vegetables, grains, and tough succulents to plant in careful arrangements on the most suitable portions of the steep, difficult ground, they plowed up the fragile hillsides for their own wheat crops and brought in large herds of cattle. The subdued

Mixtecs were forced into servitude as farm laborers for the big convent farms.

In a few generations the land was horribly eroded and impoverished. Today it produces almost nothing beyond scanty local subsistence crops. Now the descendants of the Mixtecs live in great poverty while tourists are shown through the baroque churches and convents that the friars built all over the Mixteca Alta.

Not all areas or ethnic groups suffered equally, but many went through some version of this disaster. Today Oaxaca is one of the poorest states of Mexico—but in many ways it is one of the richest. It has kept an ethnic heritage that is generally agreed to be the most diverse and colorful of any Mexican state. This fantastic cultural wealth is vividly seen as one travels among the villages. At least sixteen or seventeen distinct Indian peoples—Amuzgos to Zoques—have retained their own names, languages, dress, and proud sense of selfhood. Though the state population is tiny compared to Mexico's (about 3,300,000 to 90 million), it includes more than one fifth of the unassimilated indigenous people in the nation. The reason lies both in the stubborn individuality of the different Oaxacan peoples, with their fierce pride in their customs and culture—to this day, no Mixe could stand to be taken for a Zapotec—and in the geography.

Even today parts of Oaxaca State are hard to reach overland from Mexico City, and the area was many days' march away before the era of trains and cars. Thus some regions were long able to resist conquerors and colonizers. Within its boundaries, the landscape includes every kind of ecosystem between the misty high-altitude rain forests of the north and the barren, insect-ridden coastal deserts of the far southeast. Numberless jumbled ranges of forbidding mountains separate all of these. The natural result was resolute independence.

The many pockets of culture that evolved in isolation from each other never had much reason to conform to someone else's ideas. The Zapotecs, Aztecs, and Spanish in turn failed to make one people out of all the diverse groups ensconced in their own well-protected corners. European diseases had ravaged other wealthier and better-populated Mexican regions within the first century after the Conquest. Oaxaca was hard hit too—but the relatively small, scattered communities of the province could not be as efficiently wiped out by infections.

Far from the main strongholds of power and wealth, the region never fully shared in the general *mestizaje* (mingling) of races and cultures in Mexico, the hybrid Spanish-Mexican fusion that gradually took hold in most of "New Spain," blurring the old lines of race and culture. The most thoroughly *mestizo* community of the state is the prosperous Oaxaca City, which is a magic kingdom to itself. Everywhere Oaxaca became a treasury of independent identities and elusive complexities. The lovely town square of the capital city isn't the whole story—but neither is the dreary town square of Tlaxiaco.

In most of Oaxaca State, Old World and New World elements did not so much mingle as manage to get permanently juxtaposed. They exist together in ways that aren't always beautifully harmonious but can be very moving. I recall one flash of illumination that humbled my preconceptions . . .

Imagine the clean-washed morning light spreading over a little town dizzyingly perched in a nearly vertical, incredibly green wonderland of towering heights and bottomless drops, tremendous climbing vines and gigantic ferns. It is a site I've dreamed of visiting for many years, enchanted by the tales of adventure-seeking friends. This spot has a reputation not just for marvels but for magic. But now that I am here I feel puzzled and disappointed—the mountains all around are so glorious, but the town itself is a drab little scattering of cinderblock boxes and tin-roofed sheds. What kind of magic can such colorless dwellings hold? And then I turn to my companion. With his first few words the scene starts to redraw itself before my eyes.

The town I was viewing as a letdown was Huautla de Jiménez in the Sierra Mazateca, the cloudy mountain home of the Mazatec Indians. For a while it enjoyed fame throughout world hippiedom because of the hallucinogenic mushrooms that are gathered in the surrounding rain forest and used in traditional Mazatec healing ceremonies. Then, my companion told me, it was mostly forgotten. As far as he was concerned, it was no loss.

Valeriano García Rojas is a dignified, open-faced man in his early fifties, with the innate courtesy of the village people. He has lived in Huautla all his life and served a term as mayor. As he described it to me, the community has been content to stay true to itself without trying to impress anyone else. What I found a drab exterior is not drab to the people who see this same town from inside. A rich inner life exists here with very little in the way of monetary riches.

Don Valeriano explained that the crucial local source of income is coffee, the principal cash crop of the Sierra Mazateca. A fall in world prices always leaves many families unable to support themselves. The only insulation against market seesawing is the ancient village ethos of mutual help. A wedding party coming down the street at that moment provided a concrete example of the community's generosity.

Weddings are traditionally lavish and even exorbitant. In this one, the town band had been hired to accompany the procession, playing in the plaintive, oddly haunting mode of all Mexican town bands. The bridesmaids were outfitted in magnificent embroidered turquoise and shocking pink *huipiles*, the tunic-like Mexican garments. The sight of the bride in her white wedding dress was a shock— an unbelievably slight, frail girl, so tiny that for a minute I thought I was watching a first communion. How could such heartbreakingly young people afford to set up a household? How could their families even manage to pay for the celebration in these uncertain economic times, with all the world taking about the Mexican crisis? Don Valeriano's answer was that the local community always pitches in like one family.

Many friends and neighbors would help defray the cost of the big wedding, believing that no one should be denied a celebration for such a memorable passage. (In the course of time any necessary baptisms and funerals would be handled in the same spirit.) The newlyweds would not be expected to set up a house of their own for several years. Until then they would remain with the groom's parents, who would teach the bride their ways. When the couple was ready to move out of the groom's parents' home and start their own, it would not be a matter of buying a house or hiring a builder. Every man of the town would show up to help cut down trees from the nearby forest and prepare the lumber for a simple wooden hut. Not another concrete building like the ones in downtown Huautla—to be able to afford anything as durable and sound as that is one of the definitions of success in the villages! If the "debt" to helpful neighbors cannot be repaid within the lifetimes of the young husband and wife, the obligation will be inherited by their children.

I realized that a society bound by such powerful loyalty isn't going to be endangered by superficial or stylistic gaps between old and new ways. We talked and talked about the different cultural amalgams that make up Huautla—how the Mazatec language and a special "whistling language" developed to carry over mountain abysses still coexist with Spanish, how the medicine of the mushroom healers still coexists with modern medicine. I saw that the town belongs very much to both worlds—on its own terms. The one adjustment between traditional and modern ways that no one seemed prepared to accept was in the arena of politics, and here I would say that Huautla represents hundreds of other isolated villages in the state of Oaxaca.

The town reacted angrily to the idea of allowing the unloved federal government in Mexico City to abolish the village's own customary ways of handling community responsibilities. There is a staunch traditional meritocracy that calls for public-minded men (almost never women) of the village to assume increasing responsibilities, starting as *topiles* (street constables) in their teens and moving on up through different unpaid posts until they reach the rank of mayor and then join the council of senior advisors. Some version of this system goes back to a time before the Conquest, and no villager is willing to see it meddled with. Don Valeriano proudly announced that Huautla (population 8,300) had recently forced Mexico City (population more than 18 million) to partly retrench on a plan to get rid of the autonomous locally elected officials and impose some alien bureaucrat on the town as mayor.

By the time we left Huautla, my sense of incongruity between the charmless semblance of the town and its majestic mountain setting had dissolved. I saw a community spanning two cultures and close to five centuries with tremendous stability. It was something that I would recognize again and again in the Oaxacan villages—an intense solidarity that has held these hard-pressed places together even when Mexico as a nation has been going through political and economic disarray. This is the other side of Oaxaca's poverty and apartness: it has held onto values that are hardly a memory in some more affluent parts of Mexico.

The Spanish conquerors and missionaries also noticed that the various Indian groups of the ex-Zapotec empire had a strong sense of community and citizenship. People were expected to help their neighbors by the same system of reciprocal aid that Valeriano García Rojas described to me. Known in Zapotec as *guelaguetza*, this concept of mutual obligation—including obligations carefully passed down from parents to children—has survived for nearly five hundred years along with another part of the Indian village culture called by the Nahuatl word *tequio*. Most of Mexico knows some form of *tequio*, and the tradition remains especially strong even now in Oaxaca State. The idea is for every able-bodied man to contribute one day's labor every week to tasks organized by the township (*municipio*, in modern usage). The job may be cleaning the town square, planting certain fields owned in common as municipal assets, repairing a bridge, or even building a school. Whatever the business of the day, everyone shows up at the call of the *tequitlato* (town crier), intent on the communal goal.

This is self-government as most people would like it to be in the villages. It depends on everyone knowing everyone else. Outside influences are not welcomed. People from elsewhere usually are not allowed to buy land in the *municipio* and are discouraged from trying to become permanent village residents. The villagers will not allow anyone to interfere with their affairs or especially to assert a superior authority over them. The indigenous people prize their own brand of self-determination above well-meant measures to counter their poverty and isolation. Even the state government in Oaxaca City is often seen as coercive and alien.

Today many Oaxacans have had to leave the security of their villages in search of employment, for their own communities are often growing poorer rather than richer. They may travel as far as Mexico City or Washington State, yet still they consider the village their spiritual home. Migrant laborers or construction workers living hundreds or thousands of miles away, and often providing their home town's principal source of income through money orders they wire back to their families, will return home every year to renew their ties.

Many people relocate abroad for a time until they can return permanently with a nest-egg to set themselves up in a small business. I know a family from the weaving town of Teotitlán del Valle who did just that, transplanting themselves to Chicago where they owned a successful butcher shop for years. Their daughter, Zoyla Mendoza, spent all her adolescence in Chicago but at the end of her teens gladly came back to Teotitlán to marry and become the perfect Valley Zapotec village wife—hard-working, quietly self-contained, and completely dedicated to her work on the loom and the domestic tasks like preparing *masa* (the dough for tortillas and tamales). This gives you an idea of the powerful stability of the culture.

The ancient sense of shared communal duty is one of the biggest factors in the survival of the ancient Oaxacan Indian peoples as strong, well-defined societies, even on the eve of the twenty-first century with widespread unrest clouding the whole future of Mexico. But it isn't the only factor. The *indígenas*—as they are always called in Mexico—need something more to claim as their own, and they have it. They hung onto it generation through generation through every kind of persecution that the Spanish could invent. Today it still belongs to the land as much as the mountains and rivers: their religion. My memory returns to one astonishing afternoon . . .

The low bedroom, unadorned except for a saint's picture on the wall, is all in shadow behind closed wooden shutters. But it glows wildly with colors—pinks, blues, purples, oranges, and above all red, red, red. In my black outfit I'm the only thing not adding to the brilliance.

The medley of different colors belongs to a bevy of young women crowded into the square, plain room in stunning, riotously embroidered huipiles and bright skirts. The red that overwhelms them all comes from a mass of red primroses piled on a white sheet on a small bed. Underneath the heaped crimson bouquets lies a young woman. Only her face is visible, framed by her streaming black hair and a red bandanna scarf bound around her forehead.

She smiles and responds like a triumphant hostess as more girls come in to kiss her and deposit their flowers. Even though I understand not a word of the lively Zapotec banter, I can't miss the sense of excitement and congratulation.

The scene was an ordinary neighborhood of Juchitán, the largest city of the Isthmus of Tehuantepec in the far south of Oaxaca State. What I was watching was the sort of observance that goes by the name of *costumbre*—meaning a practice rooted in Oaxacan pagan tradition that coexists with Christian rituals. In this case it was the aftermath of the *rapto* or make-believe abduction, a Juchitecan custom by which an engaged couple stages a ritual elopement and he proves her virginity by breaking the hymen with his finger. The next day she lies in state to receive good wishes and blood-red flowers from all her friends. I had been invited by a girl who said she was going to make an offering to the "god of women."

This is the kind of *idolatría* that caused the Spanish missionaries much vexation when they started trying to claim the souls of the people for the holy faith. What fooled the priests at first was that the people were quite eager to be baptized and to say that they believed what any Christian wanted them to believe. The lofty pageantry of Church rite struck a responsive chord with the highly ceremonious *indígenas*. Besides, they thought accepting other people's gods was a good general precaution—had they not done it before when somebody in the region conquered them? But accepting a new god *exclusively* in a dangerous world while abandoning acts of respect to old ones through whom they had always worshipped the physical forces of nature struck them as unreasonable. No one was about to give up the traditional offerings to their gods—the spirits of mountains, seas, and sky.

The colonists had believed that the work of conversion was done when they had finished destroying the great Zapotec and Mixtec temples, burning copies of the old calendar, and christening everyone with new Spanish names. When they realized their mistake, noisy turf wars broke out within the Church. The Dominican friars who came into the area as missionaries tended to take a practical view of the situation, allowing people to be baptized and continue in the faith when they said they believed in the true God without inquiring too closely into what else they believed. The Dominicans actually had much feeling for the suffering of the people under the oppressive Spanish provincial government—though they themselves at times had added to the oppression—and took their side when the parish clergy and the see in Mexico City started screaming about *idolatrías* such as turkey sacrifices or the continued use of the pre-Hispanic calendar with days sacred to different gods. It is ironic that the official inquiries into seventeenth-

Preparing for the regada de frutas ("fruit throwing") at the celebration of Santa Rita de Casia in the Isthmus of Tehuantepec

century *idolatrías* now furnish some of the most priceless surviving records of the Zapotec religion.

In the end the Church had to accept the situation. Throughout Mexico, Catholicism as a whole became stubbornly imbued with elements of the pre-Hispanic religion—but nowhere more so than in Oaxaca. Today all the indigenous people here celebrate betrothals and marriage with a mixture of accepted Catholic rituals and their own observances, cure children's ailments by touching them with talismans, or pray to unseen presences of the seas and mountains. They bury magic objects to the accompaniment of Christian prayers and calculate the most auspicious days for important events by the old reckoning. Above all they make offerings. Sometimes these are blood sacrifices of animals to propitiate higher powers, sometimes ceremonial gifts presented to the living or—on November 1 and 2, the Catholic All Saints' Day and All Souls' Day—to the dead, who are also believed to be able to intercede with higher powers. (These sacred days happen to fall close to the date of an older autumn pre-harvest ceremony for honoring and communing with the departed; nowadays families busily make ready to bring deceased loved ones their favorite foods, cigarettes, and beer.)

The composite pre-Hispanic-Catholic religion has yet another function in Oaxacan life: it brings each village and each parish an annual supreme, extravagant, tumultuous moment of patriotic glory and emotional release that echoes for a long time in memory—even a chance visitor's memory . . .

On a usually quiet street of simple adobe houses I endeavor to find a path through a dense, eager crowd of people and horses, all outfitted in stunning colors and preparing to form themselves into a procession.

The air is crackling with anticipation, and there is an interval of excited bustle until a dignified middle-aged man and woman appear outside one of the front doors. Despite the sweltering May afternoon she wears a long black velvet gown intricately embroidered with a whole garden of flowers, an enormous gold medallion, and a headdress that looks like (and is) a starched lace child's dress framing her face like ones in Frida Kahlo paintings. He is in black dress trousers and an immaculate starched white shirt. The riot of humans and animals composes itself into formal, solemn ranks. The parade begins.

Ahead of everyone else runs a young man, also attired in black pants and white shirt (it is practically the Mexican male dress uniform), setting off firecrackers. Then comes a small band of brass instruments together with flute-like bamboo pipes and wooden drums hollowed from logs. Playing a hymn, they lead the way for the stately husband and wife. Behind the couple march many elaborately costumed waves of people. As they walk they sing the same hymn that the band is playing, repeating it over and over again like a mantra. Clusters of bystanders line the route, some also singing.

There are twenty men following the husband, each carrying an olive-green beeswax candle four feet high; fifty ladies in black velvet gowns like the wife; a group of radiant young girls in extraordinary costumes embroidered in yellow and red chain-stitching, led by a female marshal with a proud Zapotec face and escorting a satin banner stenciled "BEATRIZ I" in gilt letters; another group of older women. A group of young men in black and silver charro outfits (the showy Mexican cowboy regalia) appears. They are riding horses adorned with both paper and real flowers, led by a male marshal who bears a great burgundy velvet standard embroidered in gold letters with the name "SANTA RITA DE CASIA."

Another brass band leads the way for a vast, elaborate float carrying the chosen queen of the event along with a mariachi band. Today the queen is a pretty teenager in charro costume, the "Beatriz" of the banner.

The sounds of the three bands and the singing marchers overlap in competing waves, but there is no sense of rowdiness. The deep seriousness in the midst of boundless joy is obvious. The procession winds and redoubles back through all the dusty unpaved streets, growing ever larger, until no corner has been overlooked. At last we turn out onto a paved highway for the short final stretch that brings us to a modest church with a plain whitewashed stucco façade.

In front of the church the procession halts. Since the start of the parade nearly all the marchers have been carrying some present. Now the scene explodes into a frenzy of gift-giving—in fact, a barrage of brightly-colored plastic bowls and buckets, paper-wrapped candies, beans, pottery mugs, bags of rice, bars of Palmolive soap, clear plastic cups, and cans of pickled chiles being actually thrown by the celebrants.

After this spectacular display of largesse the high celebration shifts to another key. Some of the marchers quietly slip into the flower-filled church before the whole group collects in the tin-roofed meeting hall to sit in its ceremonial ranks and talk—reaffirming the just-completed act of homage to the community.

The hot, dusty town was Ixtaltepec, a smaller neighbor of Juchitán in the Isthmus of Tehuantepec. What I had seen was the culmination of the village fiesta.

No one can understand the power of the Spanish/ Indian culture in Oaxaca without understanding fiestas. The ones of the Isthmus are confusingly called by their local name—*velas*, or "candles," and have other regional distinctions as well. (The word *velas* probably refers to the candles that are an important part of the occasion—among other things, fiestas are marked by the presentation of candles that will be used to light the parish church for the next year.) The hailstorm of presents at the end of the parade is an Isthmian custom called *la regada de frutas* (the fruit-throwing) that used to involve all the delicious regional fruits in season around May, the time for most of the *velas*. The name persists but nowadays fruit has been replaced by more practical gifts.

Local distinctions or not, this joyous observance, the annual May celebration of Santa Rita de Casia (or Cascia), Ixtaltepec's patron saint, was a true Oaxacan fiesta. These events are not about cavorting in the streets. They have a real context. To see fiestas in a proper light, you must realize that centuries ago the Spanish missionaries decided to forgo some priorities—like higher theology—for the sake of Christianity's biggest success among the Mexican people: the idea of the saints.

They parceled out the villages into parishes, assigning each a saint's name along with another name picked from Nahuatl (unfortunately, the names in most of the original Oaxacan languages were lost). They explained that the saint, as depicted by an image in the parish church, was a holy being who would specifically dedicate himself or herself to this one community's welfare and intercede with other high powers on its behalf. In return, the parish must honor its patron through prayers and offerings. The day assigned to the saint in the Church calendar was like the whole village's birthday—its own fiesta.

This was greeted with total enthusiasm. It matched what the Oaxacans had done for thousands of years, appealing to the people's love of ceremony and their sense of duty and gratitude. It confirmed their age-old belief in spirits of place who had special purlieus in their keeping. Through the exquisite visual trappings of the colonial churches—the rich gold or gilt decorations, the elegantly sculpted and painted images of the saints, and their wardrobes of jeweled satin garments—the missionaries also deepened the emotional bond between parishioners and parish.

Paying the patron saint due respect came to mean paying the community due respect, and it turned into an expensive business. Eventually a system developed where most of the lay work of the parish (for example, bell-ringing, cemetery upkeep, furnishing the church) as well as the saint's fiesta was paid for each year by one volunteer from the congregation, the *mayordomo*. The imposing couple I saw leading the procession at the Ixtaltepec *vela* were that year's *mayordomo* and his wife. Probably they planned and saved for many years to be able to afford the honor. Today some of the expenses may be shared with others who undertake to be *padrinos* or *madrinas* (literally, godfathers and godmothers) overseeing certain responsibilities, but still the *mayordomo* must pay for many gifts, candles, banners, musicians, and food on a lavish scale. And not just for the one day!

Most of the really important fiestas span nine days. They are kicked off with a *convite* ("invitation"), a procession from the church through the parish streets bidding everyone to the feast. The whole town may then get decked out for a street fair through the balance of the *novenario* (nine-day period), which features special evening masses and prayers. The Isthmians hold evening dances and parties that for some are the main business of the *velas*. On the eve of the actual saint's day, there is a procession called the *calenda* (similar to the *convite* but more vivid, elaborate and emotionally charged), bringing the whole community together and climaxing in a night of fireworks and revelry followed by a solemn early mass. The saint's image may accompany the *calenda* through the streets. For their *velas* the Isthmian villages add yet another procession that ends in the *regada de frutas*.

Oaxaca City has more and bigger fiestas than anywhere else. Probably the loveliest is the annual celebration of La Virgen de La Soledad (The Virgin of Solitude) in early December. (She is the patron saint of all Oaxaca State, and her beautiful wooden image—consisting only of the exquisitely carved face and hands—was according to legend carried to the city by a mysterious donkey that inexplicably appeared in a seventeenth-century mule train bound for Guatemala.) Probably the most famous is the Guelaguetza, the pan-Oaxacan celebration that state authorities conduct every year in July on a hill overlooking the city. It amounts to a kind of secular fiesta, with all the peoples of the state coming together as everyone born in a village comes together for the town's religious fiesta. The fiesta processions here feature amazing, brilliant balloon-like inflated cloth or paper globes (*marmotas*) carried on tall poles and proclaiming the name of church or community, and surreal papier-mâché figures of walking giants (*gigantes* or *monos de calenda*) that dwarf the people inside manipulating the arms and legs. The Oaxaca City street food, already the best in Mexico, surpasses itself during these celebrations. But fiestas are equally moving in poorer towns where

the food may not be as diverse. The feeling of the village—even the state—as an extended family always shines through.

What can you call these vibrant occasions? For the peoples of Oaxaca living often difficult lives, they are civic memorial, fashion show, stage play, reunion, circus carnival, and holy offering to gods who still only half-intersect with the Christian God. To me they are an inimitable art form and a consummation of feeling.

The great poet and essayist Octavio Paz has written at length about fiestas in Mexican life—he has a priceless anecdote about a Oaxacan village mayor explaining that the budget was always stretched to the limit because the town had to pay for *two* patron saints. For him, the passionate communal outpouring of fiestas shows up something about richer Western societies' public occasions that he calls "the absence of people, in the sense of *a* people." In his view, even when Parisians or New Yorkers assemble for a big celebration "they never form a living community in which the individual is at once dissolved and redeemed." This, Paz asserts, is just the need for which fiestas exist, not despite the frequent poverty of the revelers but *because* of the poverty.

This insight leads us back once more to the central importance of offerings in Oaxacan life. Each people, each church, each village in this very poor state has its own jealously guarded identity separate from its neighbors, symbolized in the way it honors its own saint. And always the members of even the remotest community know how to reach into themselves and give to each other with dignity through work, belief, and especially rejoicing.

Through the clouds I can just glimpse the majestic gorges of the Sierra Madre de Oaxaca. Then the plane emerges over clear space and slowly, slowly floats around the magnificent stone bowl formed by lower mountain ranges, sunlit and purple, framing a fruitful expanse of cropland. Here is the sight I have been longing for—the Valley of Oaxaca, surrounded by the summits of the Sierra Madre del Sur with silvery arroyos snaking down their sides. It is summer, the sky is an incomparable blue, the green world below glistens from the daily afternoon rain of this season. A great flat tabletop appears, carved out high on a hill—Monte Albán, seen close up in imposing detail. We seem to be floating weightlessly above the Valley. I realize that the pilot is deliberately taking his time to let us take in the beauty of the approach. My heart starts to race. As if by gravity I am pulled back into the magic that is Oaxaca, the land fifteen hundred miles from my own Mexican birthplace that has deeply altered my sense of what it means to be Mexican.

Family lunch in Teotitlán del Valle

The Food of Oaxaca

When I say that Oaxaca has redefined my whole understanding of Mexico, I am speaking as both a Mexican person and a trained Mexican cook. My mind and heart have been deeply enriched by my contacts with this unique culture. My culinary awareness has been truly kindled and transformed in the twelve years that I've known Oaxaca.

Just as the state's remote location and diverse terrain have helped keep alive many distinctive cultural traditions, so they have allowed the cuisine to keep its own unique character. The glory of the food begins with the land, even allowing for those parts of it that were despoiled by the Spanish landowners.

All Oaxaca State lies in the tropics, but because it includes almost every imaginable habitat, it can produce almost every imaginable food. On one level, the ubiquitous corn, beans, tomatoes, squashes, and chiles are necessities that will grow virtually everywhere. Nearly every village family in the state can manage to raise them for itself even in badly eroded locales. These indispensable pre-Hispanic foods are the backbone of a very simple, basic cuisine that doesn't vary a lot from one remote hamlet to another. (The deputy mayor of Tlahui where I went to the graduation banquet told me that Mexico's widely publicized economic ups and downs had not meant any more hardship than usual for the townspeople, since they just went on raising and eating the same subsistence fare as ever.)

Some areas from one end of the state to another are more suitable for various tropical cash crops. Depending on the local altitude and rainfall, they can grow such foods as first-quality pineapples, sugarcane, cacao beans, avocados, maguey, bananas and other plantains, rice, coffee, tamarind, different kinds of citrus, and a wealth of other tropical fruits from mangos and guavas to gorgeous cactus fruits. In the south, the torrid coast of the Isthmus of Tehuantepec, divided between areas of steamy humidity and windswept desert, is the region that supplies every area of Oaxaca with fish and shellfish, most often in dried form—parts of the cuisine would hardly exist without the crucial accent of intensely flavorful dried shrimp. Lastly, there are a few blessed spots that have the soil and climate to support some livestock while growing both tropical produce and all sorts of temperate crops like cabbages, carrots, apples, pears, quinces, table grapes, almonds, walnuts, pecans, and wheat for world-class flour. These lucky places also furnish superb cheeses and other dairy products. Naturally these rich and versatile agricultural areas—chiefly the Central Valleys of Oaxaca and some fertile parts of the Isthmus—are where the most exciting culinary flowerings took place. They are the regions where Zapotec cooking intersected with the influences of the conquering Spaniards, and sometimes with later Old World influences such as French and Lebanese cuisine.

Before the Spanish came, the Zapotecs and other indigenous peoples of Oaxaca enjoyed a cuisine of much color and refinement that probably would have delighted modern nutritionists. People lived on a nearly fatless diet of lime-treated corn—bred with great sophistication for different purposes—together with beans, squash, tomatoes, many aromatic herbs and wild greens, and fresh fruit. Few sweetenings were available (mostly, the honey of some bee-like insects). Almost the only domesticated source of meat was the turkey, though venison and other game were hunted. Already Oaxacans had raised the skill of seasoning to a high art, using a huge range of fresh and dried chiles for different culinary effects. There was a magnificent repertory of sauces—often very complex—that were considered to be dishes in themselves. Frying was unknown because the people did not extract cooking fats from any food, animal or vegetable. The cooking methods were direct and healthful, and included simmering in liquid, steam-baking in leaf wrappings, dry-baking on clay griddles, and pit-barbecuing.

The ingredients and other cooking resources brought by the Spanish—especially the meat and fats—triggered a huge process of culinary redefinition. They made possible whole new (to the native peoples) categories of food like the confections made with sugar and eggs, or the excellent breads that sometimes supplanted the original daily bread, corn tortillas. The new spices (cinnamon, cloves, pepper, nutmeg, coriander) turned out to have a wonderful affinity for the native chiles and cacao. So did the European herbs and aromatics (cilantro, thyme, globe onions, garlic).

What is interesting to a student of culinary history is that many of the new ways didn't take hold uniformly in all places. By far the most sophisticated cooking today is found in Zapotec towns of the Central Valleys, Zapotec parts of the Isthmus, and the state capital, Oaxaca City. These three areas are the source of most of my recipes—but I would have to say that all three are special cases.

The Valley Zapotecs are a somewhat austere people, and their cooking reflects this. Probably they are closer to the foodways of their ancestors—and to some of the unassimilated indigenous peoples in other parts of the state—than the other two. Usually they are sparing in their use of cooking fats, and they have preserved many nearly fatless dishes from earlier eras. Even when they can afford to eat meat they tend to view it as an occasional pleasure, not everyday fare. The Isthmian Zapotecs are a taller, lusty stock with striking presences and a passion for the richest of the European-derived foods. They are known for eating a lot of meat and cooking everything in vast amounts of lard, which was introduced when the conquerors brought in pigs and became *the* Oaxacan cooking fat. They love aggressive combinations of sweet and sharp flavors featuring things like raisins together with capers or pickled onions.

Oaxaca City, that oasis of gracious streets and evening music, is also an oasis of perfectly harmonious *mestizo* (hybrid Spanish/Indian) cuisine that is more full-bodied than the Valley Zapotec but less extravagant than the Isthmian Zapotec cooking. It is truly the state's gastronomic as well as political capital, the center from which the Spanish/Mexican fusion spread out somewhat unevenly to other areas of Oaxaca. When people generalize about "Oaxacan cuisine," it's almost always that of the city that they are talking about.

The influences and patterns you find here aren't invariably *different* from the ones in other parts of Mexico. They just seem to be *more*—there's a heightening and refinement that everyone senses in the great Oaxacan dishes, with the Old and New World elements even more deeply intermarried than in most Mexican cooking. The many different chiles of the area seem to have sparked the Spanish imagination from the first. Here is a late seventeenth-century recipe that I found quoted in Ana María Guzmán de Vásquez Colmenares' fascinating book *Tradiciones Gastronómicas Oaxaqueñas*. The author is none other than the great colonial Mexican poet Sor Juana Inés de la Cruz.

Clemole de Oaxaca

For a medium-size cooking pot: A handful of toasted coriander seed, four roasted garlic cloves, five cloves, six peppercorns, about a tlaco's [a Mexican coin] worth of cinnamon, ancho or pasilla chiles as you prefer; all this very well ground and put on to fry, then pork, chorizos, and chicken are added. The chiles are toasted in lard and then add toasted sesame.

This is a recipe—with many details left to the user's own knowledge—for a *mole*, something that is still almost synonymous with Oaxaca. Of course it would be an incredibly simple *mole* by modern Oaxacan standards. (The state is called "the land of the seven *moles*," and everyone knows that the real *mole* map is much more complex than this catchword would indicate.) But already three centuries ago this cook is using the pre-Hispanic spice, dried chile, to heighten and color a collection of Old World seasonings in a New World-type sauce for Old World meats. She also presupposes that the user knows different chiles and their nuances. She casually refers to the techniques of toasting and roasting the crucial flavorings as something well-known. She not only cooks the chiles in fat—the European method of deepening and enriching flavors—but apparently double-cooks them, once by themselves and once with the other seasonings. So we already see some of the key elements from which the magic of Oaxacan cooking has flowered.

In Oaxaca City especially, the great main-dish Mexican sauces like *moles* and *pepianes* were raised to their highest glory over the centuries. Today they range from simple purées based on fresh green herbs to incredibly elaborate mixtures of Old World spices, many different chiles, and nuts or seeds for thickening (like the sesame in Sor Juana's "clemole").

The food of poor districts in the countryside is often another story from Oaxacan food as you encounter it even at little street stalls in the capital city. In many of these villages the everyday cooking is extremely simple, demanding absolutely fresh, flavorful ingredients. This aspect of the cooking is nearly impossible to capture in a cookbook. Giving "recipes" for something like a very minimalistic vegetable stew using average U.S. commercial produce will only make it seem dull and tasteless—especially if the original is made in the pre-Hispanic manner with little or no added fat. I sadly had to accept that many good things I had tasted in Oaxaca as the simple, ordinary fare of the land could never be reproduced in this book. Often it will be a town's few ceremonial dishes such as some special kind of tamales served at weddings and the saint's fiesta that are easiest to explain through recipes.

One thing that is true of Oaxacan cooking from its plainest and thriftiest to its richest and most exciting is that it is a real cooking of the people. Everybody understands the same principles of the cuisine—for example, that you choose various strains of corn for separate purposes like giving body to a soup or making tamal dough, or that some ingredients must be toasted to the point of charring in order to give a black *mole* the right intensity. (Oaxaca has a particularly wide spectrum of corn varieties and is known for favoring "burnt" flavors.) Individual cooks will vary the seasonings or proportions to their own liking but do not change the basic formulas. The cooking expresses the stability and strength of the culture. It seems fitting, then, that some of the best dishes are cheaply available on street corners and that everyone can afford to shop at treasuries of the glorious ingredients that go into them. In fact, what I find most exciting about Oaxacan food is embodied in its street food and markets.

These two things overlap but are not identical. The markets do have food stands where you can get a quick and very inexpensive bite. But there are also prepared foods sold in the streets and plazas that are not connected with markets, and the biggest cookstands or *fondas* at the markets can be quite substantial—not at all limited to a quick bite. At the best ones you can ask for the day's *comida corrida* (sort of a blue-plate special) and get a meal of several courses rivaling anything in more elaborate establishments.

When I say "street food" I am mostly thinking of food sold from vending carts, small booths, or even baskets. On this fare alone anyone can eat as sumptuously and sample as grand a range of dishes as in the most distinguished restaurants of New York.

At their simplest the vendors' wares consist of one specialty—for example, toothsome charcoal-roasted sweet potatoes, or roasted fresh ears of corn eaten with a jolt of lime juice and powdered red chile. The local version of salted peanuts, sold hot, fresh, and piquantly seasoned, can't be bettered. Spicy pickled vegetables or fruits served up with "rocks" (*piedrazos*—actually dense chunks of coarse, flavorful bread to absorb the pickling liquid) are a perennial streetside favorite. In the summer everyone flocks to the sellers of fried *chapulines*, a kind of tiny cricket that turns crisp and nutty in cooking and is also given the popular lime juice-chile treatment. (After one bite I guarantee you will forget any prejudice against eating bugs.)

The beverage-sellers generally have a choice of drinks. Some specialize in *tejate*, a slightly fermented corn-based frothy beverage served in colorful painted gourds. Others sell the exquisite fresh fruit drinks called *aguas frescas*, made out of all kinds of fruits that grow in Oaxaca, from melons to prickly pears. Just as heavenly are the famous ices (*nieves*) of Oaxaca City. Sold in dozens of fascinating flavors from fresh corn to "burnt milk," they are better than any gelati or sorbets I have ever found, and like the *aguas frescas* their secret is complete purity and simplicity.

Most of the great Oaxaca corn dishes can be bought as easily as you'd get a hot dog in this country. Often they are a meal in themselves. Always they have the rich, satisfying flavor of the wonderful local corn. The big, chewy round *clayudas* or *tlayudas*, spread with a slather of the grainy bottom layer from home-rendered lard and topped with ingredients like beans and shredded cheese, are like no other tortillas, just as the "empanadas" made of slightly smaller tortillas folded around a yellow *mole* filling are like no other empanadas. So many sorts of tamales and other leaf-wrapped foods are sold on the streets that a whole book could be written on the subject alone.

The streets always provide a big selection of sweets and pastries, anything from chile-spiked balls of tamarind paste to rich, eggy rolls for eating with your morning hot chocolate or *atole* (hot corn gruel, which goes back to pre-Hispanic times). Often sweet things have some seasonal association. During the Days of the Dead preparations the candy-sellers have a riotous selection of luridly tinted skulls and costumed skeletons. *Buñuelos*, the renowned platter-shaped fritters, are especially popular in Oaxaca City at the season of the Guelaguetza and the many celebrations stretching from early December (with the preparations for the Soledad fiesta) to Three Kings Day on January 6. At this monthlong time of rejoicing, the whole area close to the Oaxaca City *Zócalo* resembles an outdoor party. Phalanxes of street booths called *chachacuales* supply toys, games like the ever-popular *lotería* (a sort of bingo played with stylized picture-cards), and of course food in unstinting bounty. As Christmas approaches, *turrones* (a nougat-like candy) and *tortitas de Nochebuena* (pastries with a coconut filling and a royal icing topping) appear at the stands together with *jamoncillo* (a caramelized milk candy) and *nenguanitos* (little stacked pastries in syrup).

In this way the cuisine takes the form of a movable feast, and many of its high points are possessions casually shared in the public spaces of the community. We in the United States have little to compare with this rich culinary life of the streets. We have even less to compare with the Oaxacan markets.

Anywhere I visit in Mexico, the first thing I want to see is the markets. They are my window into the unique character of the place, whether hamlet or city. This is especially true in Oaxaca State with its intense sense of local identity.

The market may be no more than a large open lot or shed with people sitting on the floor, but it is where most of the important economic give and take of the community occurs, on a one-to-one basis. Vendors may have to walk miles to a town on market days to sell their wares, bringing the whole family with them. (Often the older children will interpret for parents who speak no Spanish.) In remote areas the market may be open only one day a week and may be all a village possesses in the way of general store, restaurant, butcher shop, dairy, drugstore, doctor's office, yard goods and clothing shop, and hardware store. No matter where, it is a microcosm of everyday life, an internal village-within-the-village where people from all levels of society are brought together. The markets truly express the being of the community, rich or poor.

I think of the market in the town of Teotitlán del Valle, where the shoppers greet friends by touching their cupped hands in a lovely traditional gesture. (After a few visits I was honored when my Teotitlán acquaintances started offering me the same welcome.) The place is well matched to the straightforward dignity of the Valley Zapotec people who frequent it. Inside a plain, utilitarian adobe building the stands are neatly arranged and everything is of scrupulously good quality. Here are the freshest of limes and avocados from people's home trees; wonderful tomatoes, beans, and squash; excellent fresh and dried chiles; handmade corn tortillas; green herbs like thyme (much used here) and *chepil*; beautiful mounds of spices. As is usual, there are small commercial mills in or close to the market where you can take the ingredients for a *mole*, freshly bought in the proportions you like best, and have them ground to order once you have toasted or fried them. (People commonly do the same with the cacao and flavorings for the chocolate used in cooking.)

This market well mirrors a prosperous though thrifty community where cooks appreciate the nuances of simple, good ingredients. In fact, Teotitlán del Valle is wealthy as Oaxacan towns go. It is a magnet for foreign visitors seeking the famous though sometimes commercialized Teotitlán rugs, shawls, blankets, and other weavings. Yet the shape of people's lives still is not distorted by hucksterism. As shown

in the market, Teotitlán belongs very much to the Valley Zapotec world rather than the tourists.

The market of San Mateo del Mar in the poorest and most distant part of the eastern Isthmus of Tehuantepec has another story to tell. My friends from the main Isthmian towns could not imagine why I would want to visit such a godforsaken place. The answer was simply that I wanted to see the lives of the Huave people who dwell in this remote sandspit, keeping a unique language unrelated to any of the other Oaxacan languages and struggling to make a living from the lagoons and bays of the Pacific coast.

I happened to arrive at the San Mateo market (by chance, not design) at the time of the semi-annual shrimp harvest. I walked through the front door of a low, oppressive shed-like building into another time, another world. The place was almost unlit, the only light coming through some broken ceiling beams. Women dressed in magenta and purple and other bright colors chattered rapidly among themselves or loudly at any potential customer as they pushed their wares. I was at once accosted by ten different women vying to sell the local version of fish tamales. The produce displays were forlorn little mounds of shriveled potatoes, chiles, and a few other vegetables. Picking my way through large buckets of water and other hazards lurking on the dark, muddy floor, I found smoked salted fish—the fresh ones seldom make it to market—arranged artistically in large, shallow baskets. Even the fish was overpowered by the one product that was visible everywhere: pile after pile of salmon-pink shrimp, their sea-smell assaulting the nose.

I wandered for a while through the dank maze until I'd seen all the wares, and at last got to the back door of the market. I stepped out into an open-air clothing department that was a throng of makeshift stands selling Levis, cowboy shirts, and underwear, with a man shouting a sales pitch into a large speaker reverberating with static.

This market makes as much sense in San Mateo as Teotitlán market does in its well-ordered village. The only real sources of income for the Huave people are the shrimp and fish, which are mostly sold dried except at the time of seasonal gluts like the ones I was seeing. The village and its even smaller neighbors have never pushed any of their local crafts in a manner to attract tourists or create a sales niche in other parts of the state. I was introduced to a local activist who was organizing a weaving cooperative to try to do just that. But meanwhile, the men harvest steadily dwindling stocks of fish and shrimp. The women prepare the catch for sale and bring it not only to the grubby San Mateo market but to larger markets in other parts. (Earlier in the day I had seen stately Huave women walking—almost floating, really—along the road to the Juchitán market, six hours' journey on foot, their bright cotton skirts blowing in the wind, carrying baskets or enamelware bowls of shrimp and fish on their heads.) All know that the future is uncertain, but for now the people devote every effort to the work their seas and lagoons have given them.

If the San Mateo market speaks of a now-threatened traditional way of life, the market of Juchitán, the most thriving city of the Isthmus, bears out everything people say about the vibrant, colorful Juchitecan culture. In the first place, visitors will find—as I have found on repeated occasions—almost no men in sight in the open-air stalls around the *zócalo* or in the white colonial building that houses the indoor part of the market. The buyers and sellers are all take-charge women. (The men play a distinctly subordinate role.) Big and tall, they wear their girth proudly, swinging and sauntering at the same time. These women are a byword in all Oaxaca. When *juchitecas* are gathered together, they don't just sit there, they inhabit the chair or booth or any chosen space. No wonder that this region has the reputation of a matriarchy!

Everywhere is something that makes you say, "What's that?"—the dented ping-pong balls that to my dismay turned out to be the eggs of endangered sea turtles; the tethered armadillos; the live iguanas fastened like Medusa's snakes in the hair of promenading iguana-sellers; or the brilliant, startling magenta-red-yellow hues of the delicious cactus fruit called *pitahaya*. Floral scents and colors seem to overfill the market from one corner to another. Every woman walking past has a flower in her hair, usually a bright hibiscus. The air is laden with the aroma of tropical blossoms such as the waxy frangipani (called *guie' chaachi'* in Zapotec) or the cloying plumy *corozos*, which are like perfumed feather dusters growing out of enormous boat-shaped pods. "Everything to excess" is the feeling. When mangos are displayed, they come in a dozen varieties from a two-inch-long yellow kind to gigantic red and green Manila mangos. Where cooked chickens are sold, they are split open to reveal startling red-tinted flesh (from an achiote marinade) and the unborn eggs.

The showy, exotic products of the rich tropical coast near Juchitán are guaranteed to disconcert, intrigue, captivate—as are the lush, dashingly costumed women with their air of command. This is a scene that you leave with your senses saturated almost to the point of dizziness. Once again the market is the perfect expression of a little world, this time the generous flamboyance of the Isthmian Zapotec culture.

It goes without saying that the markets of Oaxaca City also sum up the soul of that community. As ever, the capital city is a richer, more varied scene than anywhere else in the state. It receives a tremendous food-and-crafts traffic from other parts. This is where anybody who can manage it travels—often on foot—to sell his or her wares. Indian villagers who live far away sometimes establish little roosts here in order to be close to the several great or many lesser city markets. At all times, the life of Oaxaca City is enriched by these clusters of people wearing their own regional costumes and speaking their own languages, taking advantage of sales opportunities that don't exist in their isolated towns.

Some of the small city "markets" are just spillovers from official market buildings or ad hoc locations in the streets. At the other extreme are two supreme markets known to all visitors who have ever plunged into the

Food stand at the Mercado de Abasto

adventure of Oaxacan food. They are the vast Mercado Central de Abasto in the western part of the city and the Mercado Benito Juárez just a block south of the big central *Zócalo*. The two are very different experiences. The Mercado Central is an immense sprawl housing many counters or stands serving prepared foods, interspersed among the hundreds of produce- or food-related crafts vendors; it turns into an even more gigantic bazaar on Saturdays when additional Indian sellers trek to Abasto from villages all over the state. Juárez was reorganized along simpler lines a number of years ago. Today Juárez market proper holds mostly produce and a few prepared specialties, together with a limited number of regional crafts and clothing departments, while a satellite building across the street called the Mercado 20 de noviembre has most of the *puestos* or *fondas* (stands, little eating places) for cooked dishes. For me, no markets in all of Mexico—and I've gone to many—can compare with the Mercado Central and Juárez.

The beauty of the produce is beyond belief. All is arranged with a proud and tender artistry that once again brings to mind the word "offering." And it isn't necessarily a matter of great plenty. You may see a prosperous-looking sales force supervising mountains of glorious produce at a big stand right next to a very old man with gray hair neatly parted in the village Indian fashion, presiding courteously over a tiny stock of ground toasted chickpeas or black beans. The one is contributing something of as much worth as the other.

As is sometimes seen in the older village markets, everything is grouped in a logical manner that is reported to reflect a pre-Hispanic tradition of arranging like things together. The aisles of different chiles are next to the spice counters followed by tomatoes, onions, and herbs, so that the buying of ingredients for a *mole* can be done in a practical sequence. The flowers are next to the candles, which are next to the stations of the *curanderos* or healers, with their potions and amulets. This makes sense since both candles and flowers are used in votive offerings, while the candles also may be burned in connection with healing rituals. All is supremely efficient—and nothing here is wasted! In a bravura of conservation, people have actually set up little spots to sell carefully washed Nescafé jars, the pretty baby-blue Chocomilk cans, and piles of old copper wire. The sellers of bottled drinks thriftily empty the bottles into plastic bags fitted with straws and save the bottles for another use or return them to the bottler.

In these dazzling aisles one encounters every color, smell, and taste. Even if you buy nothing the market is a feast for the eyes—the almost blinding orange of squash blossoms, the many lush greens of fresh herbs and leafy vegetables, the brilliant shades of the shimmering *gelatinas* (clear jelled desserts) and *nicuatole* (blancmange-like desserts jelled with hand-extracted cornstarch). As you make your way through the stands and another stratum of sellers parked directly on the floor, your nose distinguishes ripe guavas, fresh cheese, pungent dried chiles, heady tuberoses, new-made leather sandals or saddle bags, coffee beans being roasted, chocolate being ground, shoes being shined.

Because of the tropical location the produce is not as limited by the season as it would be in North American farmers' markets. The main times when something arrestingly different shows up are before fiestas—especially the Days of the Dead, when people make ready for the most important offering of the year. The markets everywhere in Oaxaca are filled with fruits, breads, and greenery that will be placed at the home altar or carried to the cemetery. Most of all, the markets are ablaze with fuschia-red cockscombs and stunning mountains of *cempasuchil*, the yellow and orange marigolds used to decorate the altars and graves. If I could pick one moment to show the markets in their greatest glory, this would be it.

At all times the markets of Oaxaca offer profound food for thought. Here you find represented every economic activity and occupation. Here you look at some object and glimpse both the person who made it and the person who will use it—the artisan who sculpted the stone *molcajete*, the woman who will grind spices on it for a *mole*. This is what I miss most when I go to shop for food and necessities in a big supermarket or even a fine gourmet store: the sense of direct interconnectedness between maker and buyer, grower and consumer. In the Oaxacan markets one can feel the lifeblood of the society coursing. They are the highest glory of a land where food can truly express dignity, generosity, and grace.

Grinding corn on a metate

Basics of Oaxacan Cooking

Equipment and Techniques

Oaxacan cooking does not depend on a elaborate *batterie de cuisine* and feats of technical wizardry. The saucepans and tools of any moderately well-equipped U.S. kitchen will be more than adequate for most dishes. However, it is a good idea to understand that certain pieces of equipment will be used again and again for particular cooking processes that are integral to the cuisine.

For griddle-roasting (see sidebar), a **griddle** or **large cast-iron skillet** are absolutely essential. (The authentic Oaxacan griddle, the *comal*, is made of clay and has a fairly short life span.) You should also have **tongs** and/or **long-handled spatulas** for turning the food on the griddle.

The lengthy grinding and puréeing techniques for making the rich Oaxacan sauces are carefully outlined in the introduction to the chapter *Moles and Pepianes* (pages 135 to 172). The original pre-Hispanic tools used for those purposes were a bowl-shaped volcanic stone mortar (*molcajete*) with a pestle (*mano*) of the same material and the sloping table-shaped *metate* (also paired with a *mano*). These still do the best job for puréeing or grinding, but have mostly yielded to electric devices even in Oaxaca. Modern cooks rely on a **heavy-duty blender** to supply the muscle and one or two **medium-mesh sieves** to finish the sauce to the right texture. A **food processor**, though it can be a useful aid, is no substitute for the all-important blender-sieve combination. I find the **electric coffee or spice grinder** helpful in preparing dry spices, though a large, stout **mortar and pestle** will also do the job.

A tortilla press is a must for shaping corn tortillas. The inexpensive cast-aluminum ones sold in Mexican neighborhood stores are fine for basic tortillas; unless you travel to Oaxaca, you may have a hard time finding the larger ones used for some special tortillas (pages 100 to 101). A large steamer is invaluable for tamales, but you don't necessarily have to buy a special one if you can improvise a steaming arrangement as suggested on page 98.

Oaxacan Ingredients: An Overview

To bring Oaxacan food to life in your kitchen, you must not only find the right ingredients but welcome the challenge of discovering them. I could try to skim over this crucial fact, but I would only be misleading you. My recipes will repeatedly call for seasonings or sometimes basic materials that U.S. cooks may never have seen before in a cookbook, even a Mexican cookbook.

Griddle-Roasting: The Secret of Flavor

What gives so many Oaxacan sauces their richness and intensity? As you'll see from dozens of recipes, the answer is a long one. But it nearly always begins with roasting some crucial ingredients on a griddle. In Oaxaca this would be a flat, round clay *comal* treated with slaked lime and often placed right over an open fire on the ground. In my New York kitchen I use either a griddle or a cast-iron skillet. A heavy cast-aluminum or cast-iron griddle is the simplest thing. You may want to search for one with a non-stick coating. (I have one and enjoy the ease of cleaning it). But be sure to ask if it is heat-resistant. It should be able to tolerate 45 minutes of cooking over medium heat. Models with flimsier coatings will hardly last a week.

The idea of griddle-roasting is to sear the food by direct contact with a heavy, evenly heated surface. Searing under the broiler or blackening over an open flame are just not the same technique and will not produce the same taste. What you want is a special kind of charring that not only makes it easier to peel some ingredients but brings out the natural sugars of the food in order to deepen the flavors.

Oaxacan cooks are known for their love of intensely charred flavors—sometimes actually burnt, in the case of chile seeds and tortillas ground into some *moles*. The basic technique of griddle-roasting is less extreme and is usually applied to onions, garlic, tomatillos, and tomatoes. It is also used for green chiles (page 42). The more you work with Oaxacan food, the more automatic it will become to reach for the griddle or skillet as soon as you reach for the ingredients.

To Griddle-Roast Onions and Garlic

Heat a heavy ungreased griddle or cast-iron skillet over medium-low heat until a drop of water sizzles on contact. Place the unpeeled onion and individual unpeeled garlic cloves on the griddle. Cook, turning frequently, until somewhat softened, about 15 to 20 minutes for small onions, 20 to 25 minutes for medium onions, and 8 minutes for garlic cloves. With large onions I usually cut them in half crosswise (leaving the skin on) and roast, turning frequently, for about 20 minutes. The cut side will char, but the black bits are easily scraped off. Remove the onions or garlic cloves from the griddle; when cool enough to handle, peel them over a bowl to catch the juices.

To Griddle-Roast Tomatoes

Heat the griddle or skillet over medium heat until a drop of water sizzles on contact. Place the tomatoes on the griddle stem side down. (Started this way they lose less juice.) Cook, turning frequently, until the skin is blackened and blistered all over, about 10 to 15 minutes for small to medium and 15 to 20 minutes for larger tomatoes. Remove from the griddle to a bowl that will hold the juices. When they are cool enough to handle, peel

I hasten to reassure you that what this cooking requires is within your powers. In the first place, many of my recipes require only familiar materials and simple preparations. Secondly, and more excitingly, dozens of ingredients that may sound remote and difficult to find are now regularly coming into the country with waves of immigrants from southern Mexico and other tropical regions.

When I wrote about the food of Oaxaca in my first book, *Food From My Heart*, the only way I could get my hands on some of the best chiles and herbs like *chepil* was to travel there. What a difference the past few years have made! Believe it or not, you probably do not live far from a good source of savory dried shrimp, fragrant banana leaves, the true cinnamon we call *canela*, fresh Mexican cheese, and corn *masa* for tortillas and tamales. You can even find Oaxacan chiles in shops and markets in large cities like New York and San Francisco. Also, the range of retail and mail-order offerings continues to expand. So I feel justified in presenting a book of Oaxacan food that rests on genuine ingredients.

There are only a few cases where I had to admit defeat. I could not discover a domestic source for *yerba de conejo* ("rabbit grass"), a slightly tart fresh herb with grass-like blades that Oaxacan cooks add to simmering pots of beans. The frangipani flowers (*guie' chaachi'*) and other agents that help make the famous frothed toppings for some traditional beverages are not exported. I'm convinced that the delicious crunchy street snack of fried *chapulines* (a kind of tiny grasshopper) would find avid fans here if people could get past the Eurocentric taboo against eating insects, but meanwhile I regretfully had to leave them out. (Though I hear that *chapulines* are becoming a favorite bar snack in Chicago!)

Only twice did I indulge myself by offering a recipe requiring something I know is totally unavailable outside of Oaxaca—the Salsa de Gusanitos (page 261) that is the perfect sauce for so many dishes, and the Chocolateatole (page 281) that it would be almost a betrayal to leave out. I'm not so secretly banking on the crucial ingredients for these dishes becoming available in the U.S. in the next few years as cooks here continue to discover Oaxacan food.

When I speak of Oaxacan culture I am speaking of something with many layers. The ingredients of the cuisine reflect this. Oaxaca stands out among the states of Mexico for preserving both an overall Spanish-Mexican fusion (with smaller Lebanese and French additions) and many regional ethnic strongholds that had separate languages and traditions centuries before the Spanish came.

These barely Hispanized Indian communities still refuse to surrender their identities. It is possible to eat meals there containing hardly a single European ingredient.

The two most prosperous and also most Europeanized regions—the best-known Oaxacan culinary centers—are the fertile central Valleys of Oaxaca near the capital, Oaxaca City, and the Isthmus of Tehuantepec on the southeastern coast. In both these areas there is a strong Old World flavor to the cooking. *Canela* (page 30), **cumin**, and **cloves** are prominent in the spice mixtures, combining magically with the native American **chiles** (pages 42 to 47) and **allspice**. Herbs brought by the Europeans such as **bay leaf, parsley, cilantro, marjoram,** and **thyme** are also very much used. Thyme has a special place. People in Oaxaca call it *yerba fina* instead of the standard Spanish *tomillo*. In some dishes that my local guides and mentors shared with me, thyme was used in amounts that I found almost overwhelming. (If you have qualms about the amounts in some recipes, feel free to experiment with less.) This is clearly a southern Mediterranean touch that struck a responsive chord in Oaxaca.

I also feel a Mediterranean aura in the heavy use of **capers** and **olives**, especially in the food of the Isthmus. The olives are invariably a brine-cured green variety, sometimes stuffed with pimientos like the familiar U.S. supermarket product. The sharp accent is often contrasted with the sweetness of **raisins**, another Spanish import. Use only the intense dark kind; golden sultana raisins are not used in Oaxaca.

Most of the favorite aromatic and table vegetables are also European, including **globe onions, scallions, garlic, carrots, cauliflower,** and **cabbage**. They marry happily with **beans, squashes, tomatoes, tomatillos, potatoes, sweet potatoes,** and other New World vegetables. In just the same way, the fruits of Oaxaca come from all sorts of origins—the Old World temperate zones (**apples, quinces**) and warmer regions (**citrus fruits, mangos, tamarind, bananas**) as well as the American tropics (**papayas, guavas, sapotes** and **mamey sapotes, pineapples,** various **cactus fruits.**) The beauty of the produce is breathtaking, especially in the Valley markets. Whenever I go back there I feel that I am entering a valley of the blessed where all good things of the world are meant to meet and flourish together.

The following list of major ingredients is not intended to be exhaustive. I have singled out those that are least likely to be familiar to U.S. audiences or

off the charred skin. If some tiny blackened bits remain, they will just add to the flavor. Be sure to save all the delicious juices and add them to the dish.

To Griddle-Roast Tomatillos

These are handled differently from tomatoes because of the papery husks and the sticky skin underneath. I prefer to roast them in the husk. There is less sticking and less loss of juices. Heat the griddle or skillet over low heat until a drop of water sizzles on contact. Add the tomatillos and cook, turning frequently to guard against scorching, until they are lightly softened all over, about 10 to 15 minutes. Handle them delicately so as not to squeeze them and pierce the skin. Carefully remove from the griddle to a bowl in order to catch any juices that escape. When cool enough to handle, remove the husks. It is not necessary to peel them further.

that may be misinterpreted without special guidance (for example, *canela*, oregano, lard).

A List of Important Oaxacan Ingredients

Achiote. The tiny brick-red and also brick-hard seeds of a tropical American tree (*Bixa orellana*), also called "annatto" or "achuete" and sold in many Latin American and Filipino stores. By itself achiote has a mild, rather clay-like flavor. It is more of a coloring agent than a spice. When finely ground to a paste, the seeds give a beautiful orange-yellow color to other foods.

To make Achiote Paste (*Pasta de Achiote*): Working in three batches, process 1/2 cup achiote seeds to a fine powder in an electric coffee or spice grinder. (Don't try to do more than this at once—they are so hard it's best to work in small quantities.) In a small bowl, mix the ground achiote to a paste with the freshly squeezed juice of 1 1/2 oranges (about 6 tablespoons) and 1/2 lime (about 2 tablespoons) and 2 tablespoons vegetable oil. Taste the mixture. If it is overly bitter, mix in up to 2 teaspoons sugar, adding 1/2 teaspoon at a time and tasting for balance. It will keep indefinitely in the refrigerator, tightly sealed. Yield: about 2/3 cup.

Commercial pastes are available in Latin American stores, but they may contain a mixture of seasonings not suitable to Oaxacan food.

When a recipe call for achiote as part of a *mole* or sauce, always grind it first, separately from the other ingredients. This is also because of the extreme hardness of the seed.

Avocado Leaves and Avocados. Though avocado trees grow in many parts of Oaxaca, the anise-scented leaves are more important in the cooking than the fruit itself. The leaves are wonderful when freshly plucked, but growers in the U.S. don't seem to have discovered their use as an herb. **Don't** try to gather your own if you live in an avocado-growing region—the leaves from some of the commercial U.S. avocado strains are poisonous. Buy the dried imported avocado leaves sold in packets in Mexican groceries. Though sizes are not standardized, they generally come in 1/4-ounce packets, sometimes with the contents fairly broken up. Some brands are sun-dried; these have a more intense flavor than those dried in dehydrators, but tend to be more curled up and irregular-looking. One ounce of dried avocado leaves is usually equivalent to about 30 leaves.

Dried avocado leaves are often briefly toasted in a skillet to release their flavor and aroma before being used in a recipe.

I feel strongly about making every effort to obtain avocado leaf because it is such a crucial ingredient. It is essential to Barbacoa de Carnero con Masita (page 210) and Barbacoa de Cabrito (page 212), Frijoles Negros Colados (page 235), and countless sauces. There is one barely acceptable substitute for cooks who absolutely can't find avocado leaves: **Anise Tea** (*Te de Anís*). In a small saucepan, combine aniseeds and boiling water in the ratio of 1 teaspoon seeds to 1 cup water. Boil over high heat until reduced by half, strain out the seeds, and let cool to room temperature. Use in place of avocado leaves, substituting the tea for part of any liquid a recipe calls for.

When my recipes call for avocados, always use the buttery Hass or Fuerte varieties, never the big green monsters from Florida and Puerto Rico.

Banana Leaves. A fragrant wrapper for tamales and steamed fish (see Pescado en Hoja de Plátano, page 222), containing just enough natural oils to help the wrapping peel away from the contents after steaming. Luckily you will not be called on to deal with a whole banana leaf, which can be twice the height of the cook. Pre-cut rectangles of the leaves are sold in most tropical groceries, usually frozen in convenient packets. See Basic Tamal Procedures, page 106.

Cacao and Chocolate. See pages 277 to 280 and also Mail Order Sources (page 320).

Cactus Paddles (Nopalitos and Nopales). The cactus plants of Mexico can be not only edible but very valuable in cooking. The most important are nopalitos or nopales, the fleshy oval "leaves"—they're about the shape of ping-pong paddles—from plants of the *Opuntia* genus. (This is the same type of cactus that is host to the tiny cochineal insect, source of a beautiful red dye that once furnished one of the major Oaxacan industries.)

I have had some difficulty providing reliable cooking directions for the nopalitos generally available in this country. I kept coming up with thick, tired old specimens that took three or even five times as long to cook as the tender, thin young paddles always readily available in Oaxaca. Please use some flexibility in all recipes calling for nopalitos. Those commonly sold here may be as large as 6 to 8 inches long and 1/4 inch thick, compared to perhaps 4 inches long and less than 1/8 inch thick for nice young nopalitos. The larger ones also tend to retain a somewhat papery, chewy skin even when thoroughly cooked, and it is a nuisance to remove it.

The general approach I suggest is as follows: Wear rubber gloves to handle cactus paddles, which always have hard-to-see spines unless they have been pre-cleaned. (Once cleaned, cactus paddles should be used immediately because they tend to go bad quickly.) Carefully cut out all the spines with a small, very sharp knife or the tip of a potato peeler. If many spines are clustered along the edges, cut all around the paddle to detach the entire rim; otherwise cut and dig out one by one. Usually I cut the nopalitos into 1/2-inch dice before cooking. If they seem tough, cut in larger dice or strips so that the skin can be peeled off after cooking; with tenderer ones this won't be necessary. Have ready a small saucepan of boiling water; add the diced or cut-up nopalitos and cook for about 3 to 4 minutes before draining in a colander and rinsing under first hot and then cold running water. (This helps remove some of their sticky juices.) Use the cooking time suggested in the recipe as an approximate rather than exact guide, starting to test for doneness 15 minutes after adding them to the other ingredients and allowing as much as 40 minutes if necessary.

Cactus Fruits also belong to the treasures of the Oaxacan table, but I have had little luck finding them here. *Jiotilla*, the exquisite fruit of *Escontria chiotilla*, is not grown in the U.S. Prickly pear (which comes from the *Opuntia* cacti and is called *tuna* in Mexico) is widely sold, but is sadly tasteless and mealy compared to the vibrant fruits of Mexico. I don't even try to cook with it in this country.

Cal. Calcium hydroxide, a fine white powdered substance that is mixed with water to make an alkali bath for corn kernels (page 92). It is also the astringent used to keep preserved pumpkin firm-textured (see Calabaza en Tacha, page 312). *Cal* is sold as "slaked lime" at pharmacies and building-supply stores in the U.S. One ounce equals about 1/4 cup.

Canela. I have given up using the word "cinnamon" in my recipes because it seems impossible to convince U.S. cooks that the product they buy under that name is not true cinnamon at all—it is a harsher spice properly called cassia. In Mexico we cook exclusively with the delicately flavored bark of *Cinnamomum zeylanicum*, which can be easily identified by its soft, splintery texture and loose concentric layers. By contrast cassia (*Cinnamomum cassia*) is rolled up into a tight hard scroll. At herb and spice stores, ask for "soft-stick cinnamon" or "Ceylon cinnamon." This is our *canela*.

Like good black pepper, *canela* should not be bought pre-ground. Because it is so soft, it can easily be ground in an electric coffee or spice grinder or even in a blender just before use. Or in *moles* and other seasoning pastes it can be directly puréed in a blender along with the other ingredients. Never try this with cassia, the hard-stick "cinnamon" you probably have in your spice rack! It is so hard that it may break the blades.

A 1-inch piece of *canela* yields about 1 teaspoon freshly ground.

Cheeses. The abundant grasses of the central Oaxacan valleys produce wonderful, slightly herb-flavored milk that yields delicious cheeses. In the last few years some commercial approximations of the main types have been made in the U.S. Look for them in Latin American markets.

The youngest of the classic Mexican cheeses is called *queso fresco* and usually comes in squares or ovals of about 8 ounces. It is delicate, still somewhat milky-tasting, and just slightly acid. The texture is crumbly. The older cheeses are very similar in basic type but drier and more pungent. *Cotija* or *queso cotija* is usually made in large blocks and cut into pieces on request by the retail grocer. It is a harder, saltier cheese than *queso fresco*, firm enough to be grated. *Queso añejo* is the general name applied to any aged cheese including *cotija*. Often the terms *cotija* and *queso añejo* are used interchangeably. It takes about 4 ounces of either to produce 1 cup of grated cheese.

I cannot agree with the authorities who suggest feta as a good substitute for any of these cheeses. Instead I prefer to use a young Italian ricotta salata to replace *queso fresco* and an aged ricotta salata for *queso añejo*. Parmesan is an acceptable stand-in for aged ricotta salata, but not ideal. For *cotija* I have sometimes used aged ricotta salata, but a better approximation would be a mixture of a young ricotta salata and an aged goat cheese.

The most specifically Oaxacan type of cheese is *quesillo de Oaxaca*, also known as *queso de hebra* (string cheese) or *queso de bola* (ball cheese). As these names suggest, it consists of long strands wrapped into a flattened ball. It may have been brought by Lebanese immigrants trying to reproduce their traditional braided string cheese. But it is less salty and much lower in fat than the Middle Eastern kind—and better for cooking. *Quesillo de Oaxaca* has to be one of the most versatile cheeses in existence. It can be fried, shredded in a sort of salad, or melted into a fondue-like dish called *queso en salsa*. As an excellent melting cheese, it is used as a topping for many *botanas* (snacks) and other dishes. It is widely available in Latin American groceries in the U.S.

Chepil. My New York friends have been intrigued trying to decide just what this seductive Central American herb (*Crotolaria longirostrata*) resembles. Most think it tastes a little like sorrel. It is tart and refreshing, with an intense herbal aroma. It is used in soups, tamal fillings, and rice dishes.

Even a whiff of *chepil* makes me feel I am in Oaxaca. We can't buy it here fresh. However, I am pleased with the frozen *chepil*—also called *chipilín*—imported from Guatemala, though it is closer to the large-leafed variety found in Chiapas State than to the kind I have eaten in Oaxaca. It is sold here in Latin American groceries, in 6-ounce packages. The contents should be thawed and the leaves stripped from the fibrous stems before using.

Chickpeas. It may seem like a lot of bother, but Mexicans always remove the skins of cooked chickpeas before adding them to a dish. Rub the cooked peas between your palms to loosen the skins. Like other dried legumes, chickpeas are often toasted and ground into flour in Oaxaca (see page 86).

Chiles. See pages 42 to 47.

Chocolate. See pages 277 to 280 and also Mail Order Sources (page 320).

Cooking Oils. Since the Spanish came, lard has always been more central than vegetable fats to Oaxacan cooking, but olive oil is sparingly used for some purposes—one of the Mediterranean influences that turn up especially in the cooking of the Isthmus. It is used only in salads, escabeches, and fish dishes. Olive oil is expensive in Oaxaca, and the extra-virgin grade barely exists. People would generally use something close to our "pure" or at the most "virgin" grades. However, I definitely prefer to use extra-virgin olive oil, especially in dishes like Escabeche de Pescado (page 224) where there is a crucial oil-vinegar balance. Be guided by your taste.

Of the other vegetable oils used in Oaxaca, corn oil and safflower oil are the most popular. Some cooks perfume these tasteless oils by slowly frying garlic cloves (peeled or unpeeled) or sliced onions and then straining them out before using the oil for further cooking. (See Frijoles Negros Colados, page 235, and Manchamantel, page 160.) The technique adds depth and dimension of flavor.

Corn. See pages 90 to 95.

Corn Husks. Tamales just don't taste the same if wrapped in aluminum foil or parchment paper. Often in Oaxaca they are folded in the green husks from fresh ears of corn, or sometimes the actual leaves stripped from the cornstalk. But the usual, most versatile wrappers are dried corn husks. Packaged dried husks, available in any Latin American grocery, also turn up in crafts stores as the material for "corn dollies," but in that case make sure they have not been treated with dyes or fixatives. See pages 105 to 109 for the usual soaking and wrapping procedures.

Crema. This is not just cream any more than *canela* is just cinnamon. It is ripened with a bacterial culture like sour cream or crème fraîche, but neither is a true substitute. *Crema* is a little more liquid than other cultured creams and the flavor is warmer and nuttier. Excellent *crema* is sold in sturdy plastic bags at market stalls in Oaxaca. Several commercial U.S. brands now show up in many Latin American groceries catering to Mexican and Salvadoran shoppers. Look for names like *crema criolla*, *crema salvadoreña* or *mexicana*, or just *crema*; experiment with different brands if possible to find the one with the most flavor and the fewest preservatives.

Dried Beans. See page 234.

Dried Shrimp. These are one of the major ingredients in the cooking of the indigenous peoples of Oaxaca. Centuries before the Spanish came, the Huaves and other coastal peoples were harvesting shrimp from southeastern bays and lagoons. Most of the catch was boiled, salted, and dried whole in the shells, for transport to the interior regions.

Today the flavor is still beloved everywhere in Oaxaca, but I have had a hard time selling it to some of my U.S. friends. Only Thai food enthusiasts take to it readily. It is penetrating and briny, with the insistent overtone of the dried shells. But I remember that many people here didn't like cilantro either, until they learned to appreciate its magical chemistry with other flavors. Dried shrimp is another of those flavors that seem to mingle with many kinds of ingredients. It combines wonderfully with such Oaxacan accents as pumpkin seeds, dried chiles, beans, *masa*, *chepil*, or epazote.

Whole Mexican dried shrimp is available in Latin American groceries everywhere in the U.S. It is usually sold in 1- or 2-ounce packets. One ounce

The Valley of Oaxaca;

maguey plant in foreground

roughly equals 10 to 12 large dried shrimp, or about 1/2 to 2/3 cup. But there is no standardization of sizes between different brands. The shrimp are brittle and easily crushed, so look for packets with the contents as intact as possible. Usually the heads will still be attached. They are the most delicious part, but Oaxacan cooks are absolutely adamant about one detail: Always remove the two bitter-tasting black bits that are the eyes.

Unless I will be toasting them, I generally give dried shrimp a brief soaking in several changes of cold water to remove some of the salt. Do not worry about removing the thin, delicate shells except in puréed dishes where they are easily removed by forcing the purée through a sieve.

Mexican dried shrimp are also sold ground to a fine powder (*camarón molido*). Though this is more convenient, I usually prefer the flavor of the whole shrimp.

Epazote. In my native part of Mexico, the north, this ubiquitous herb (*Chenopodium ambrosioides*) was most often used dried. But for most Oaxacan cooking fresh epazote is definitely preferable. The slightly bitter taste and unique medicinal odor mellow in cooking. Epazote is always used in cooking dried beans, and goes into various green *moles* as well as other stews and soups. It can be gathered as a roadside weed in many parts of the country (even New York City) and is sometimes sold fresh in farmers' markets. Dried epazote is available in most Latin American groceries, usually in 1/4-ounce packets equivalent to about 5 to 6 tablespoons. To substitute dried for fresh epazote in recipes, allow 1 tablespoon of the dried herb to the leaves of about four 8-inch sprigs of fresh epazote. (The stems are tough unless the plant is gathered young, so discard them after stripping the fresh leaves.)

Gusanitos de maguey (maguey worms). People in this country seem prejudiced against the idea of eating insects—until they taste the haunting, smoky Salsa de Gusanitos (page 261). Unfortunately you will not be able to find these delicious tidbits unless you travel to Oaxaca or ask a friend to bring them back from there. They are the specially dried, smoked larvae of a tiny insect that lives on the maguey plants. I have not given up hope that an importer will recognize the value of *gusanitos* as a seasoning and make them available to a wider public. Meanwhile, travelers should look for them in herbal remedy stalls in the market. They are sold in strings of 100.

Hoja Santa. I have been trying to bring true Mexican flavors to the U.S. for almost fifteen years and have had many ups and downs with crucial ingredients. At times this essential herb (*Piper auritum* or *P. sanctum*) has been difficult to find in the fresh rather than dried state. Now its importance is being recognized and the fresh herb is much more available. (See Mail Order Sources, page 320.) It is as preferable to the dried variety as fresh basil is to dried basil.

The heart-shaped fresh leaves are a beautiful dark green and have a vivid herbal flavor that reminds me a little of anise, though *hoja santa* is more complex. The leaves are usually between 6 to 8 inches long, big enough to make small wrapped packets enclosing pieces of food. But in addition to being used as wrappers they are often puréed with other ingredients in sauces. The brittle dried leaves can be used for the latter purpose but are too fragile for wrappers.

Dried *hoja santa* can be found in most Latin American groceries. The usual packet, which weighs 1/8 ounce and contains about 6 dried leaves (often in a fairly crumbled state), is equivalent to about 2 large (8-inch) fresh leaves.

If unable to obtain either fresh or dried *hoja santa*, you can make a crude substitute from Anise Tea (see above, page 29), using 1/2 cup of tea to replace 3 to 4 large fresh leaves and substituting the tea for part of any liquid called for in the recipe. I have to say that this should be only a last resort.

Lard, Asiento, Pork Cracklings. Lard, the classic Mexican cooking fat since the Spanish introduced pigs in the sixteenth century, is an ingredient that I learned to view differently after visiting Oaxaca and especially the Isthmus of Tehuantepec. Of course we always had lard at hand at my parents' ranch in the north, but it did not have the nearly liquid consistency and nutty flavor I found in Oaxaca. It is true that many cooks there are switching to tasteless vegetable oils for some purposes. This means a sacrifice of flavor that is noticeable but acceptable in some of the major *moles* and *pepianes*, but absolutely disastrous in tamales. To lighten and mellow the corn *masa* for tamal fillings, you need real lard—preferably home-rendered or made at a small butcher shop catering to a Latin American or Eastern European clientele. The home method also gives you good cracklings (traditionally ground into a coarse paste called *sorrapa*) and a tasty, grainy residue known as *asiento* that makes a wonderful spread for tortillas.

Home-rendered Lard (Manteca Hecha en Casa) and *Asiento.* This recipe involves rendering pork fat in two stages. Neither stage will give you a lard resembling the fluffy, firm product commonly found in U. S. markets. Both, and especially that from the second stage, are closer to the semi-liquid, light brown lard of the Isthmus that is sold in plastic bags at the markets.

Please note that the pork fat must be fresh, not salted or smoked. Not all pork fat will produce *asiento*—try to get some with a little meat attached.

Cut 3 pounds fresh pork fat into 1/2-inch dice. This is a messy job that will be easier if the fat is deeply chilled or partly frozen.

For the first stage of the rendering process, place the diced pork fat in a large, deep roasting pan or shallow Dutch oven with thick sides. (I use a 12- by 3 1/2-inch Dutch oven with a cover.) Make sure that the bits are somewhat separated, not all clumped together. Place on the stove over low heat and cook, uncovered, stirring often, for 20 to 30 minutes or as long as it takes for the fat to have partly rendered out and the diced pieces to be somewhat (not fully) crisp. Remove the pan from the heat and let cool slightly. Pour the contents of the pan into a tall, narrow container. Set aside the half-finished cracklings and any grainy residue (*asiento*). You will now have about 3 cups clear, pale tan lard and 1/4 cup grainy residue. Refrigerate the lard until solid, cover tightly, and store up to a week in the refrigerator or indefinitely in the freezer.

To proceed with the second stage of the rendering process, place the half-done cracklings in the same pan or in a large cast-iron skillet. Cook, covered, stirring occasionally, over low heat for another 20 to 30 minutes, or until the cracklings have yielded all their fat. Watch carefully toward the end, reducing the heat as low as possible to avoid scorching. Let cool and strain as instructed above. When the lard has cooled and settled, carefully transfer into another container and separate the sediment (*asiento*) that has collected on the bottom of the container. You will have about 3 to 3 1/2 cups of crisp cracklings, another 1/3 cup of *asiento*, and 1 cup of a darker, more intensely flavored lard called *manteca amarilla* ("yellow lard"). Use this in cooking when you want an especially rich, nutty favor. (In Oaxaca it is used to make a hearty-textured bread called *pan amarillo*.)

Add the second batch of *asiento* to the first and place in a tightly covered container. It will keep in the refrigerator for up to a week or the freezer for several months. The cracklings can be eaten out of hand (sprinkle with a little salt and powdered red chile, if desired) or ground in a mortar or food processor until barely crumbly (not a paste) and added to tamal fillings; see Tamales de

Camarón (page 128) for one suggested use. They will keep up to a week in the refrigerator but are always best eaten fresh.

Limes and Oranges. Lime rather than lemon is the citrus fruit of choice used to add a dash of acidity in Oaxacan cooking. The local variety is closer to Key limes than to the large Persian limes sold in most parts of the U.S., but I find the Persian variety acceptable. I also use our Persian limes or a combination of lime juice and orange juice to replace the *naranja agria* or "bitter orange" often used in Oaxaca. Despite the name, it isn't really bitter—it just has a more interesting acidity than our sweet oranges. If you can find *naranja agria* (also sometimes called "Seville orange") in Latin American stores, by all means use it.

Masa. See pages 92 to 96.

Nixtamal. See pages 92 to 96.

Onions. Oaxacan cooks use white onions rather than the sweeter yellow ones more popular in U.S. supermarkets. It's not a big difference in flavor, but it is a difference.

Please familiarize yourself with the griddle-roasting procedure for onions described on page 26—an important prelude to many recipes.

Oregano. This is a name that seems to have gotten stuck to more than a dozen different Mexican herbs, none botanically related to the true Mediterranean oregano used in the U.S.

Two kinds are important in Oaxacan cooking. "Mexican oregano," which can be found in Latin American groceries and (in a version packaged by McCormick & Co.) many U.S. supermarkets, has a little resemblance to the true oregano, though it is more full-flavored. "Oaxacan oregano," on the other hand, does not look or taste anything like any oregano I know. The leaves are larger, and it has a subtle grassy, lemony flavor that can't be duplicated here. I love this crucial herb and am delighted to have finally found a U.S. supplier after years of frustration (see Mail Order Sources, page 320). Be sure to order at least 2 ounces, as you will use it in larger amounts than regular oregano.

My recipes call for both Oaxacan oregano and (usually as a second choice) Mexican oregano in the dried form. However, there are dishes in which the vividness of fresh herbs is important. Here I prefer to use fresh Mediterranean oregano. It may not be authentic, but it blends better with other fresh green accents than any dried herb.

Plantains. Our familiar yellow bananas represent the sweetest, softest type of plantain. Actually plantains come in many other gradations of size, color, and sweetness or non-sweetness. Oaxacan use them as a starchy vegetable in soups and stews and add them to certain *moles*.

Plantains, as we know them in the U.S., are tougher-skinned and usually larger than bananas. Different varieties may be green or yellow at the same stage of ripeness. Look for them in Latin American markets and when possible, try to choose ones that have turned partway from green (or yellow) to black. Sometimes they are used semi-ripe (only blackened in spots), sometimes at the highest stage of ripeness (black nearly all over), but seldom when they are green. If you have to buy them green you may need to plan ahead, as they take a few days to ripen.

To peel a plantain, cut off the ends with a sharp knife. Slit through the skin from end to end, and work it free until it comes off like a glove. Trim away any remaining fibrous bits. They can also be griddle-roasted in the skin to make a wonderful dessert (page 305).

Pumpkin Seeds (Pepitas). In pre-Hispanic cooking these played a role somewhat like almonds in medieval Spanish or Moorish cooking—contributing some fat as well as a thickening action when ground to a paste and used in sauces. They are still important in Oaxacan *pepianes*. In Oaxaca the whole toasted seeds, hulls and all, are ground up and eaten in some dishes. Because the hulls of U.S. pumpkin seeds are thicker and harder, I have not included any dishes with this authentic touch. But see Pepián Zapoteco (page 156) for a delicious sauce in which the seeds are toasted and partly crushed in the hulls, which are then strained out. I find that toasting in the hulls definitely gives better flavor.

One cup of hulled pumpkin seeds weighs about 4 ounces, 1 cup of seeds in the hull a little less than 3 ounces.

Rice and Rice Flour. The rice brought to Oaxaca during the colonial period and still used today resembles our standard long-grain white rice. Do not use converted rice, which will not cook to the right texture. Rice is soaked, dried, and ground (sometimes by hand at home) into a fine starchy flour that is used in cakes (especially in the Isthmus). I have found that Oriental brands of rice flour are totally dissimilar. Look for a Latin American brand in ethnic groceries.

Squash. This ancient pre-Hispanic vegetable flourishes throughout Oaxaca and is not known only for its fruit. The blossoms of the plant are used in soups and vegetable stews, or stuffed with savory cheese fillings, deep-fried, and served with a simple tomato sauce like Caldillo de Tomate (page 259). Even the tender young vines (*guías*) are cooked in a marvelous soup that I regretfully had to leave out because we have nothing corresponding to the good, starchy corn that gives body to the soup in Oaxaca.

Two summer squash varieties are especially important. Apparently they are really one variety at different stages of maturity. When young it is a delicate summer squash that is nearly globe-shaped and measures about 4 inches across. Farmers' markets in New York carry a similar squash under the name "roly-poly." In Oaxaca it is simply called *calabacita* and is much used for stuffing (see Calabacitas Rellenas, page 244). Later it grows into a large squash called *chilacayota*, which contains a mass of fine filaments like spaghetti squash. This is the source of an unusual, refreshing cold drink (Agua Fresca de Chilacayota, page 272).

The classic winter squash is a form of pumpkin (*calabaza*) that is smaller and firmer than our Halloween pumpkins, usually with a variegated green-yellow-and-white skin.

Sugars and Sugarcane (Panela and Piloncillo). Sugar was and is an important cash crop in Oaxaca. The most popular sweetening used in the cooking is a form of unrefined loaf sugar locally called *panela*. It is an intensely flavored brown sugar formed into a rounded platter weighing about 10 to 12 ounces and measuring about 4 to 5 inches across and 1 inch high. U.S. shoppers can usually find *panela* in Latin American markets. It is very much a tradition of southern Mexico and the Central American nations. If no *panela* is in sight, ask whether the store has *piloncillo*, a similar type of brown loaf sugar that is common in the north of Mexico. *Piloncillo* is made in the shape of truncated cones large or small—there is no standard size. *Piloncillo* is somewhat milder and less molasses-y than *panela*, but it is the closest thing you will find. Dark brown sugar is a blander but acceptable substitute.

Both *panela* and *piloncillo* are rock-hard and have to be broken up or grated before use. The simplest thing is to break off a chunk with a hammer and beat it into smaller pieces that will easily dissolve in cooking. Or for more careful measurement, grate the sugar on the medium-coarse side of a four-sided grater, or pulverize it (after breaking into small pieces) in a food processor.

Fresh sugarcane is sold everywhere in the markets, especially during the Days of the Dead. I have experimented with it as a cooking ingredient (for example, as a bed for the simmering pumpkin pieces in Calabaza en Tacha, page 312). In this country, long stalks of cane are often sold in tropical groceries, and Frieda's in California distributes shorter chunks to supermarkets and retail stores nationwide. To reduce the tough stalk to manageable (6- to 12-inch) lengths, chop it with a heavy cleaver or break it across your knee.

Tomatillos. In Oaxaca, these tomato-shaped berries in papery husks are called *miltomates*. Roasted (page 27) or unroasted, they add a refreshing tartness to many sauces. The interior seedy pulp tends to set to a jelly after cooking; when this effect is not desired it is sometimes discarded. The husks are not eaten directly, but are sometimes saved and boiled in water to make an infusion like the one that goes into Buñuelos (page 302).

I don't recommend canned *tomatillos* now that fresh ones have become so easy to find.

Tomatoes. Oaxacan tomatoes are vibrant and gorgeous. Please do your best to avoid using pallid, grassy supermarket tomatoes in any of my recipes calling for ripe tomatoes! When I say "ripe" I mean dead-ripe and very juicy.

Please read the directions for griddle-roasting and peeling tomatoes on page 26. This is a procedure you will be repeating dozens of times before beginning a recipe. Cooks in Oaxaca do it so automatically that it may be only casually alluded to in a recipe with a terse "tomate asado."

Vinegar. Oaxacan cooks often make this at home and the commonest type is from pineapple trimmings. Someone is missing a great opportunity to market pineapple vinegar in the U.S! I usually substitute a clean-tasting cider vinegar or distilled white vinegar. Wine vinegars are not appropriate.

Wheat Starch. This is the starch that remains when the gluten has been extracted from wheat flour. It serves as a fine flour in some cakes (see Marquesote, page 289, and Panque de Almendra, page 292). I have successfully substituted cornstarch. But wheat starch, available in Chinese groceries where it is sometimes misleadingly labeled "wheat flour," gives a more authentic texture.

Preparing Fresh Chiles

Griddle-Roasting

This is the preferred method for chiles that are to be chopped and puréed in sauces. The principle is the same as for griddle-roasting onions or tomatoes (page 26)—the flavor is deepened but also mellowed by searing on a hot surface. Don't try to work with too many at a time; if you crowd the griddle you will not have enough room to roast properly.

Heat a griddle or cast-iron skillet over medium-high heat until a drop of water sizzles on contact. Add the chiles, a few at a time, and cook, turning occasionally with tongs, until the skin is blackened and blistered on all sides, about 5 to 7 minutes depending on the size of the chiles. Remove from the griddle as they are done and place in a plastic or brown paper bag. Let sit for about 5 minutes, until the skins soften enough to be easily removed. Remove the chiles from the bag; using your fingers and a small sharp knife, peel and scrape off as much of the blackened skin as possible. (A few black specks don't matter.) Cut off and discard the tops with the main part of the seedy core; slit the chiles lengthwise from top to bottom and scrape out any remaining seeds. I usually do not cut out the membranes (the hottest part), but if you want to tone down the heat this is an easy way to do it.

Note: When I want to keep chiles crunchy to use them in salads or cut them in *rajas* (strips), I like to char green chiles over an open flame by

Chiles

Oaxaca has traditionally been home to a wealth of different chile varieties, especially ones raised for drying. The cuisine was known for a symphony of distinctive chile flavors, with cooks skillfully choosing and blending many kinds that are not grown in other parts of Mexico. I remember first coming to the great Benito Juárez market of Oaxaca City in 1985 and staring at whole arrays of red, yellow, or black dried chiles I had never seen before, realizing how much more I still had to learn about the classic Mexican spice.

All this is sadly changing as more and more cooks in the state take to substituting readily available, cheaper varieties like ancho chiles that are known everywhere in Mexico for the rarer, more expensive local kinds such as chilhuacle negro and chilhuacle rojo. The result is that Oaxacan food is inevitably beginning to lose some of what makes it Oaxacan. Yet I see other more hopeful signs as well. Quite late in the preparation of this book I was overjoyed to find U.S. mail order—and even retail—sources for some of the best Oaxacan dried chiles. I believe that this heritage will not only survive in corners of Oaxaca but spread wherever Oaxacan flavors are cherished.

My recipes do not call for any irreplaceable type of Oaxacan fresh chile. With dried chiles I follow a case-by-case policy on substitutions. Often I give common multipurpose chiles and the unique local ones as alternatives, figuring that it is better to make the dish with a slightly less characteristic chile than not to make it at all.

Before you begin looking for chiles, it is good to understand why they are used in the first place. I hope that anyone cooking from this book has graduated from the idea that chiles just make a dish hotter. This is an oversimplification, especially in the case of Oaxacan cuisine.

The truth is that the variable hotness of chiles (some are no hotter than bell peppers) goes along with the range of other effects. There are times when they are used very simply, others when they add deep complexity. For example, Oaxacans do not like a lot of fussy flavors in fresh uncooked salsas. Here something with a fresh green taste and clean, direct heat like the excellent local jalapeños and serranos should predominate. Dried chiles, however, are valued for a spectrum of flavor possibilities. They are meant not just to detonate on the palate but to add particular notes that are beautifully brought out in drying—sweet, sharp, fruity, nutty, woodsy, and so forth. When rehydrated and puréed, dried chiles also add body to *moles* and other sauces. In very simple cooked sauces they may almost be the only thickening.

In the following lists of fresh and dried chile varieties used or mentioned in this book, the more unusual Oaxacan chiles are marked with an asterisk*. Most of the others are known throughout Mexico and are fairly easy to find in this country in Latin American groceries or specialty food shops.

Note: Handle both fresh and dried hot chiles with respect for the stinging substance called capsaicin *that gives them their bite. Be sure to wear rubber gloves when working with any really hot chiles. If your bare fingers touch them, wash your hands carefully before touching your face and* especially your eyes!

Fresh Chiles

In cooking, these are most often used in the green state, when fully matured but not allowed to ripen to red, yellow, or another color. Look for bright green chiles with smooth, firm, glistening skin. Jalapeños and serranos may have small brown striations on the surface.

Plan to use fresh chiles within a few days of buying them. If they are very fresh you can sometimes make them last up to ten days or two weeks by storing in the refrigerator in tightly closed plastic bags. However, they will be better if used quickly.

Anaheim Chile. My preferred U.S. substitute for chile de agua (see below). Chiles of this type—a long, fleshy, fairly mild green chile big enough for stuffing or trimming into strips—can also be found under the names of "long green" or "New Mexico" chiles.

Chile de Agua. The most popular Oaxacan chile for cutting into *rajas* (strips) for use as a vegetable. They are also the usual choice of Oaxacan cooks for stuffed chile recipes such as Chiles Verdes Rellenos (page 56). They are cone-shaped, fleshy chiles, a little fatter and wider at the top than Anaheims—perhaps similar to Italian frying peppers (though the flavor is different). Chiles de agua can range from quite mild to slightly hot.

impaling them at the stem end, one at a time, on a long-handled fork or skewer and holding directly in the flame, turning to blacken them evenly on all sides. Place in a bag and peel as directed above.

Note: I rarely griddle-roast chiles when I want to leave them whole for stuffing; the frying method suggested below gives better texture. If you prefer to griddle-roast, leave the tops on after roasting and peeling; cut a small (1- to 1 1/2- inch) lengthwise slit in each chile and carefully pull out the seeds without further tearing the flesh.

Frying

This produces a firmer, less fragile texture when the chile is to be stuffed and batter-fried or baked. (Griddle-roasting makes them very soft.) Rinse the chiles under cold running water and dry very thoroughly. Make a short (1- to 1 1/2- inch) lengthwise slit in each chile to allow steam to escape during frying. Pour vegetable oil into a medium-size skillet to a depth of about 1/2 inch; heat over high heat until almost smoking. Add the chiles two at a time; cook, turning frequently with tongs, until they puff up and take on an olive-beige color on all sides. Remove the chiles to a platter as they are done, let cool slightly, and carefully peel under cold running water. Pull out the seeds through the slit, working very gently to avoid tearing the flesh.

Women dancing together at the vela
of Santa Rita de Casia

Chile Jalapeño. The best-known fresh hot variety in the U.S., and also widely used in Oaxaca—though the flavor there is crisp, delicious, and vivid compared to some of the ones I've eaten in New York. Oaxacan jalapeños can be quite hot. If the ones in your local markets seem unusually dull you can try substituting chiles serranos (see below).

Jalapeños are often eaten in pickled form. They are an especially important flavor note in the cuisine of the Isthmus of Tehuantepec, where people love the combination of spicy heat and briny tang. Home-pickled jalapeños are the best (page 247). Canned commercial varieties can also be useful, but please look for Mexican brands—the U.S. ones tend to be extremely vinegary, with an unpleasant aftertaste.

Chile Poblano. In the U.S. this is one of the most readily available chiles for stuffing (see Chiles Rellenos de Pollo, page 62, and Chiles Rellenos de Carne, page 60) or making into *rajas* (cooked strips of green chile). Poblanos vary in color from a medium green to a sort of purple-black. I find that the larger ones sold here tend to be on the bland side. The smaller heart-shaped ones are usually better, and seem to be more used in Oaxaca.

Poblanos are dried to produce two important types: the chile ancho and chile mulato (see below).

Chile Serrano. Very similar to the chile jalapeño in use, but bullet-shaped and slightly smaller. Serranos are probably the fresh hot chile of choice in Oaxaca, and I often recommend them as an alternative to jalapeños in recipes calling for medium-hot to decidedly hot fresh chiles.

Dried Chiles

The more types you can experiment with, the better. But I must caution against buying any variety in too large a quantity. Experience has taught me that when kept for more than 2 to 3 weeks in my kitchen cabinets, they develop unwelcome crops of little insects. (For some reason, I've had better luck keeping them in the basement.) Store at room temperature in tightly closed containers, and check every so often to make sure the bugs haven't invaded.

*****Chile Amarillo or Chilcosle.** This small, very hot yellow-red chile is one of the true Oaxacan varieties. Though less common than it was, it is still required for a really authentic Mole Amarillo (page 142) or Chileajo (page 52).

Preparing Dried Chiles

This simple procedure is almost always the prelude to using dried chiles for my recipes. Very tiny chiles are toasted or blanched whole before cooking, and I have seen Oaxacan cooks fry larger chiles before soaking them, but the following method is the one I find best for chiles to be used in sauces.

Griddle-Drying

Unless otherwise directed in a recipe, remove and discard the tops and seeds of the chiles. I leave in the veins (the hottest part), but you can cut them away if you want to tone down the heat. Rinse the chiles under cold running water and shake off the excess moisture, but do not dry them. Heat a griddle or cast-iron skillet over medium-high heat until a drop of water sizzles on contact. A few at a time, place the chiles on the griddle and let them heat, turning occasionally with tongs, just until any clinging moisture is evaporated and the aroma is released. Allow approximately 30 to 45 seconds in all per chile for most kinds, slightly less for guajillos (which are very thin-skinned). The chiles should just become dry, hot, and fragrant; do not allow them to start really roasting or they will have a terrible scorched flavor. Remove from the griddle as they are done. Most recipes will call for placing them in a deep bowl, covering generously with boiling water, and letting stand for about 15 to 20 minutes, then draining well.

Chile Ancho. The name means "broad chile," from the shape. This is the most common dried form of chile poblano (see above), and is one of the most important in all Mexico. The chile is large and vaguely heart-shaped, with a wrinkled reddish-brown skin. Anchos are probably the most versatile dried chile. When rehydrated by soaking they become fleshy, a little sweet, and semi-hot. In the food of Oaxaca they are often the main chile giving body to a sauce while other rarer chiles contribute fire and more unusual flavors. Powdered ancho chile, available from some suppliers, is useful for purposes like homemade Chorizo (page 208).

Chile de Árbol (also called chile árbol). A small, skinny, pointed reddish chile that is one of the hottest varieties available. I have called only for the dried form (which is fairly easy to find here), but in Oaxaca they are also eaten fresh, either green or red.

Chile Chipotle. This brownish, wrinkled chile is a smoke-dried version of the chile jalapeño (see above). Smoke-dried chiles (as opposed to air-dried or oven-dried ones) develop a complex, haunting flavor. The kind that is really preferred in Oaxaca is not chipotle but the chile pasilla de Oaxaca (see below), but it can be hard to find whereas chipotles are readily available.

When I call for chipotles I usually mean the plain smoke-dried version. These chiles are also sold in cans in a thick, pungent *adobo* (spice-paste sauce), and occasionally I suggest the canned chipotles in a recipe.

*Chile Costeño. As the name implies, this small chile is native to the coastal regions of Oaxaca. Dark yellow to orange in color, it can be fairly or very hot and is used in sauces similar to the Salsa de Chile Pasilla on page 254.

*Chilhuacle. This type includes several characteristic Oaxacan chiles that are seldom found in most other parts of Mexico. The name means "old chile" in Nahuatl (the Aztec language). Chilhuacles are about the size and shape of small bell peppers when fresh and remain smooth when dried, with intense heat and robust flavor. There are different-colored strains. The very dark, spicy chilhuacle negro is integral to both the color and the flavor nuances of traditional *mole negro*. More and more cooks in Oaxaca are now using chile ancho instead, so I suppose the substitution is legitimate—but now that chilhuacle negro is imported into the U.S. (see Mail Order Sources, page 320) I would certainly try to use it. Chilhuacle rojo is also increasingly available and is used to make Coloradito (see page 158).

Chile Guajillo. A long, thin, smooth-skinned variety that can be dark red to maroon. In terms of quantity, guajillos are the most used chile in Oaxacan cooking, though they are common in most of Mexico, not unique to Oaxaca State like some other kinds. The guajillos sold in the U.S. usually are not as hot as the Oaxacan strain, which can be really fiery.

Chile Morita. A less known variety of smoked chile that can be used in place of Oaxacan pasilla chiles.

Chile Mulato. Closely related to chile ancho (page 46). The mulato is also a form of dried poblano, but it ends up much darker, nearly black. Since the color can be a good match for the elusive chilhuacle negro (page 46), I sometimes use them to make Oaxacan *mole negro*, though the flavor is less vivid than chilhuacle.

Chile Pasilla de Oaxaca. *Pasilla* is one name for small raisins, and the term has gotten very confusedly applied to chiles. In most parts of Mexico chile pasilla refers to an important type of air-dried chile. Never use this where a recipe calls for Oaxacan pasilla chiles! They are smoke-dried, like the more common chipotles that are the closest substitute. The Mixe people are the preeminent producers of Oaxacan pasilla. The chiles are redder and shinier than chipotles, with deep flavor. Sometimes they are prepared whole for stuffing; they also lend their smoky flavor to sauces like Salsa de Gusanitos (page 261) or the pickled vegetable snack Verduras en Vinagre (page 54).

Chile Pequín or Chile Piquín. (also "chiltepín," "chiltepe," and several other spellings.) These tiny, bitingly hot peppers are thought to be close to the wild ancestors of most hot peppers. You will probably find them only dried, though they are also eaten fresh throughout Oaxaca.

Woman making totopos in Ixtepec in the Isthmus of Tehuantepec

Little Dishes and Appetizers

"Appetizer" is not a strictly accurate term for any traditional Mexican dish. What we have are *snacks*, ranging from bite-size to meal-size and really meant to be eaten hot from the streetside vending cart. When you put them in the context of a home-cooked meal they are thought of quite differently.

There are different names for different kinds of snacks. The category of *antojitos* (whims) includes the sort of *masa* specialties you will find in the Corn Dishes chapter, such as Empanadas de Amarillo (page 104) or Clayudas (page 102). The name *botanas* usually refers to little nibbles corresponding to cocktail snacks; Botana de Cacahuates and Bocaditos de Papa are good examples. Oaxacans put some other unusual twists on the street snack idea—the pungently seasoned paste called Chintextle, the great garlicky fricassee known as Chileajo, or pickled vegetables or fruits eaten with hunks of robust bread.

With an eye to U.S. menu expectations, I've brought together in this chapter a selection of snack-type dishes that would make good first courses.

Botana de Cacahuates
Peanut Snack

This is one of the perennial street snacks sold all around Oaxaca City. Eventually I was able to reproduce it from memory. The peanuts used there are a larger variety, but the taste is identical. Be sure to use a medium-coarse salt like kosher salt. The garlic is peeled and eaten along with the peanuts.

Though strictly speaking this should be served hot, I confess that when I started nibbling on a bunch of room-temperature leftovers, they were so delicious I couldn't stop.

About 2 1/2 cups

4 tablespoons lard (preferably home-rendered; pages 36 to 38) or vegetable oil

2 1/2 cups shelled raw peanuts, with skins on

1 head of garlic broken into cloves, unpeeled

2 tablespoons chile pequín (page 47) or other tiny chiles

2 teaspoons kosher salt, or to taste

Juice of 2 limes

In a large, heavy skillet, heat the lard over medium-high heat until almost rippling. Add the peanuts, garlic, and chiles. Cook, stirring constantly, for 10 to 12 minutes or until the peanut skins have darkened. Add the salt and lime juice to the pan and give another good stir. Serve at once.

Chileajo
Vegetable Medley in Garlic-Chile Sauce

1 pound medium-small waxy potatoes such as Red Bliss, unpeeled

8 ounces young green beans

1 cup fresh shelled peas (optional)

2 medium carrots

1/2 small cauliflower

3 ounces guajillo chiles (about 20 chiles; page 47) or 2 ounces guajillos (about 14 chiles) and 1 ounce amarillo chiles (about 10 small chiles; page 45)

One 1-inch piece *canela* (page 30)

10 garlic cloves, coarsely chopped

1 teaspoon dried thyme, crumbled

6 teaspoons cider vinegar

1 1/2 to 2 teaspoons salt, or to taste

8 ounces *queso fresco*, crumbled, or 4 ounces *queso añejo*, grated (page 31); or substitute equal amounts of crumbled young or grated aged ricotta salata

1 medium onion, cut into paper-thin half-moons

1 1/2 teaspoons dried Mexican oregano, crumbled (page 38)

Vegetable oil for frying

24 small (3-inch) corn tortillas

*D*espite the name, this is unrelated to Chileajo con Puerco (page 152) except for the presence of the chile and garlic that give it its name. It is one of the classic Oaxacan street snacks, especially at fiesta time when food stands are crowded all around the beautiful Oaxaca City *Zócalo* (town square). Here you find women selling this wonderful specialty—a garlicky, spicy vegetable melange on a crisp fried corn tortilla, topped with a delicious combination of crumbled cheese, thinly sliced onion, and oregano. It's inspired.

If you can find amarillo chiles, use a combination of them and the less characteristic, more available guajillos. Do not griddle-dry the amarillos, as they scorch easily. The tortillas used for chileajo are very small, about 3 inches in diameter. If you cannot find such a thing, cut out 3-inch rounds from larger commercial corn tortillas.

About 4 cups (enough for 6 to 8 servings)

First prepare the vegetables: Bring a large pot of salted water to a boil. Also, have ready a large bowl of ice water, with more ice in reserve. Add the potatoes and cook until barely tender, about 15 minutes (depending on their size). Lift out, drain, peel, and cut into 1/2-inch dice. Remove the strings from the green beans if necessary. Cut into short pieces (about 1/4 inch) and cook with the peas until barely tender, about 5 to 7 minutes. Scoop out the beans and peas with a strainer or slotted spoon and at once plunge them into the ice bath to stop the cooking. Scoop out and drain. Peel the carrots, cut into 1/4-inch dice, and cook until barely tender, about 3 to 5 minutes, chilling and draining in the same way. Separate the cauliflower into small florets; cook until barely tender, about 4 to 6 minutes, chilling and draining in the same way. Set the vegetables aside.

Wash and griddle-dry the guajillo chiles by the directions on page 45. Place the guajillo and amarillo chiles in a deep bowl, cover generously with boiling water, and let soak for 20 minutes. Meanwhile, grind the *canela* in an electric coffee or spice grinder.

Drain the chiles and place in a blender with the ground *canela*, garlic, thyme, vinegar, and enough water to facilitate blending (about 1 cup). Process to a smooth purée, about 3 minutes on high. With a wooden spoon or pusher, force the purée through a medium-mesh sieve into a bowl.

In a large non-reactive bowl, toss the cooked vegetables with the puréed chile mixture and salt. Cover with plastic wrap and refrigerate for at least 4 hours, preferably longer. It will be better if left overnight—or even better after two days.

When ready to serve, combine the cheese, sliced onion, and oregano in a small bowl and toss to distribute evenly. Pour vegetable oil into a large, deep skillet to a depth of 1 inch and heat to 375°F. Fry the tortillas, 2 at a time, just until crisp (20 to 30 seconds on each side). Lift out to drain on paper towels as they are done. Top each with a few spoonfuls of the marinated vegetables and scatter some of the cheese-onion mixture over the vegetables. You may omit the fried tortillas and serve with fresh corn tortillas or fried tortilla chips.

Variation: *The chileajo mixture also makes a good side dish. Omit the fried tortillas and heap the marinated vegetables on a serving platter, topping with the cheese-onion mixture.*

Verduras en Vinagre
Vinegar-Marinated Vegetables

For the piedrazos (optional)

One 1-pound round loaf coarse-
textured Italian whole-wheat
bread or other very coarse,
hearty peasant-style loaf

For the vegetables

1 pound small new red potatoes,
unpeeled

3 medium carrots

2 medium zucchini

1/2 small cauliflower, separated into
florets

One 10-ounce basket pearl onions,
peeled

For the marinade

1 large onion

2 whole heads of garlic, unpeeled

2 cups cider vinegar

2 teaspoons dried Oaxacan oregano
or 1 teaspoon dried Mexican
oregano, crumbled (page 38)

2 to 4 Oaxacan pasilla chiles (page 47)
or dried chipotle chiles (page 46)

1 teaspoon whole black peppercorns

Oaxacans love everything in vinegar, particularly if it is flavored with the smoky Oaxacan pasilla chile. One frequent sight on street corners is carts selling this unique snack with or without *piedrazos*—hard dried wedges of rough-textured whole-wheat bread that you dip into the vinegar marinade to make them soft enough to eat. *Piedrazos* literally means "rocks," which gives you an idea what they are like before dipping.

The vinegar used in Oaxaca would most often be homemade pineapple vinegar. In this country I usually substitute cider vinegar. Feel free to vary the selection of vegetables to your liking, but remember that they should be firm-textured. Popular choices include new potatoes, carrots, cauliflower, zucchini, and pearl onions.

About 6 servings

Cut the bread for the piedrazos into about 10 wedges and let stand until thoroughly dried out, 2 or 3 days.

Preheat the oven to 200°F and bake for 4 hours, until rock-hard but not browned. Set aside.

Prepare the vegetables: Bring a large pot of salted water to a boil; have ready a large bowl of ice water with additional ice in reserve. Add the potatoes to the boiling water and cook until just tender, about 15 minutes. Lift out, drain, and cut in half crosswise. Peel the carrots and cut into 1/2-inch slices. Cook 3 to 4 minutes or until just crisp-tender; scoop out with a strainer or slotted spoon and at once plunge into the ice batch to stop the cooking. Scoop out and drain. Cut the zucchini into 1/2-inch slices; cook until just crisp-tender, about 3 minutes. Chill and drain in the same way. Add the cauliflower; cook for 3 to 4 minutes, chill and drain in the same way. Finish by cooking the pearl onions for 5 minutes, chilling, and draining. Set the drained vegetables aside while you prepare the marinade.

Cut the onion into quarters. Leave the heads of garlic whole but with a sharp knife, score the tips of the outer cloves to expose some of the flesh.

In a medium-size non-reactive saucepan, combine the vinegar with 3 cups of water and bring to a boil over high heat. Add the onion, garlic, oregano, chiles and peppercorns. Let the mixture return to a boil and cook for 5 minutes. Transfer to a heatproof glass container and let cool to room temperature; add the prepared vegetables. When thoroughly cooled, cover tightly and let stand at room temperature for at least 1 week. (It will get better and better as time goes on—I've kept it successfully up to 4 weeks. Refrigerate if desired, but no harm will come to it at room temperature.) Serve with the optional *piedrazos*, which each person dunks into the marinade to soften.

VARIATION

Frutas en Vinagre
Fruits in Vinegar

Combine all the ingredients for the marinade and prepare as for Verduras en Vinagre. Add the fruit to the hot marinade and let cool to room temperature. Store as for Verduras en Vinagre.

For the fruits

2 large quinces (about 1 1/2 pounds), with tough part near the stem end removed, cored, and cut in eighths

or

8 small crabapples, stems removed, pricked all over with a fork

For the marinade

2 cups cider vinegar

2 Oaxacan pasilla chiles or 2 dried chipotle chiles

1/3 cup (about 2 ounces) grated Mexican brown loaf sugar (*panela* or *piloncillo*; page 40)

1 teaspoon Oaxacan oregano or 1/4 teaspoon Mexican oregano

1 teaspoon whole black peppercorns

1 head of garlic, unpeeled

Chiles Verdes Rellenos
Stuffed Green Chiles

8 fresh Anaheim chiles (page 43)

4 tablespoons (approximately) *asiento* (page 36) or lard (preferably home-rendered; pages 36 to 38)

Salt (a few pinches)

6 to 8 ounces *queso fresco*, crumbled (page 31)

16 to 20 (approximately) epazote leaves stripped from stems or 2 teaspoons dried epazote, crumbled (page 35)

*T*he secret of flavor in this appealing appetizer is *asiento*, the delicious residue of home-rendered lard. The next choice would be the lard itself, which won't have as good texture but will match the right taste. Bacon grease is inauthentic but flavorful. Don't try it with oil or shortening, which are totally tasteless.

Green Anaheim chiles are the best U.S. substitute for the Oaxacan chile de agua. In this case you do not peel them before cooking. They hold together better when roasted with the skin on; each diner can peel his own before eating.

8 servings

With a small sharp knife, cut a shallow 1 1/2-inch lengthwise incision in the side of each chile. Carefully scrape out the seeds without tearing the chile open any further. Dip your index finger into the *asiento* or lard, to scoop out a dollop of the fat and smear it generously over the interior of each chile. Rub a little salt over the interior. Gently fill some of the crumbled cheese into each and add two or three epazote leaves or some of the crumbled dried epazote, making sure that the incision will close neatly over the filling.

Heat a griddle or cast-iron skillet over high heat.

Griddle-roast the chiles until blackened on all sides, using tongs to turn and hold them shut as necessary to keep the filling from oozing out. Serve warm with Caldillo de Tomate (page 259).

Bocaditos de Papa
Potato-Cheese Fritters

*B*ocadito or *bocadillo* means a tidbit, literally a "little mouthful." These delicious examples were showing up all over the Isthmian city of Juchitán when I went there one spring to attend the saints'-day observations called *velas*. The potato bocaditos are very popular on plates of cocktail appetizers at the parties accompanying the *velas*. This typical version is from the restaurant Bar Jardín.

The cheese adds some salt, so taste before seasoning.

12 fritters

Bring a saucepan of salted water to a boil and drop in the potatoes. Cook, testing occasionally with a fork, until just done but not soggy, 12 to 15 minutes. Drain thoroughly. Transfer the potatoes to a large mixing bowl and mash thoroughly with a fork or potato masher. With a wooden spoon, beat in the eggs and cheese. Season well with pepper and optional salt. Shape the mixture between your palms to form 12 compact round cakes about 2 1/2 inches across.

Pour vegetable oil into a medium-size saucepan or deep skillet to a depth of 1 inch and heat to 375°F over medium-high heat. Adjusting the heat as necessary to maintain a steady temperature, fry the potato cakes 3 or 4 at a time until golden, about 1 to 2 minutes. As they are done lift out onto paper towels to drain. Serve immediately.

1 pound mealy-type potatoes such as russets (2 large potatoes), peeled and cut into thick chunks (about 1 1/2 inches)

3 large eggs, lightly beaten

1 cup finely crumbled *queso cotija* (page 31) or grated aged ricotta salata

Freshly ground black pepper

1/4 to 1/2 teaspoon salt (optional)

Vegetable oil for frying

Gorditas Infladas
Puffed Masa and Bean Tortillas

2 cups (1 pound) *masa* (page 93), fresh or reconstituted by mixing 1 1/2 cups *masa harina* (page 94) to a paste with 1 1/4 cups warm water

1 cup Frijoles Negros Colados (page 235)

Vegetable oil for frying

"Gorditas," or "little fat ones," are a kind of thickish tortilla popular all over Mexico that is often fried rather than griddle-baked. The usual *gorditas* puff up enough in cooking to be completely or partly split and filled with anything from fish hash to shredded cheese. This interesting variation is from Tuxtepec, near the northernmost tip of Oaxaca State, and probably migrated there from the neighboring state of Veracruz. The basic *masa* (tortilla dough) is combined with a rich bean purée and the resulting *gorditas* are rolled out thinner than usual, so that they puff up some but not enough to be split and filled. The lightly puffed *gorditas* are eaten hot, with a freshly made table sauce.

10 to 12 gorditas

Place the *masa* and beans in a food processor and process until smoothly combined. Divide the mixture into 10 to 12 equal-size pieces and roll them between your palms to form ping-pong-size balls.

Prepare a tortilla press by the directions on page 100. Press each ball of dough into a 4- to 5-inch round. As they are pressed, place side by side on 1 or 2 baking sheets or a flat surface lined with parchment or wax paper; cover with a damp tea towel.

Pour vegetable oil into a heavy medium-size skillet to a depth of 1/2 inch. Heat over medium-high heat to 375°F. Fry the *gorditas*, one at a time, until puffed and golden, about 15 seconds on each side. As they are done, lift out onto paper towels to drain. Serve at once with Salsa de Chile Pasilla (page 254) or another chosen table sauce; I especially like them with Salsa de Gusanitos (page 261) when I have the ingredients on hand.

Queso en Salsa de Epazote
Melted Cheese in Epazote Sauce

*T*he flavor of this dish has stuck in my memory since I first had it at a simple little restaurant in Mitla in the Valley of Oaxaca. The ingredients are crucial: fresh epazote, the Oaxacan string cheese that melts so beautifully in cooking, and long, fleshy green chiles as close as you can get to Oaxacan *chiles de agua* (page 43). I have found that Anaheim chiles are a good match.

If you cannot find fresh epazote, the dried will be a distant but just acceptable substitute. Versions of Oaxacan cheese are now available in this country, but not everywhere. It can be replaced with mozzarella or crumbly white *queso fresco*, which gives a different effect because it never melts into luscious strings but is good in its own right. Eat the dish piping hot, before the cheese cools.

6 servings

4 large green Anaheim chiles (page 43)

1 cup fresh epazote leaves stripped from the stems (from about 4 to 5 large sprigs; page 35) or 3 tablespoons dried epazote reconstituted in 2 tablespoons boiling water

2 tablespoons vegetable oil

Salt (optional)

1 pound Oaxacan string cheese, mozzarella, or *queso fresco* (page 31), cut into 1/2-inch chunks

Griddle-roast the chiles by the directions on page 42 and place in a paper or plastic bag for about 10 minutes to loosen the skins. Remove the tops; peel and seed the chiles. Place the chiles and epazote in a food processor and process to a purée.

In a medium-size saucepan, heat the oil over medium-high heat until rippling and add the chile mixture. Cook, stirring constantly, for 2 to 3 minutes. Add 1 cup water and boil for 2 minutes. It should be the consistency of a thin unbound sauce. Add a pinch or two of salt if you wish, but the cheese will contribute some.

Stir in the diced cheese and cook for 5 minutes. Serve immediately with freshly made corn tortillas.

Chiles Rellenos de Carne
Meat-Filled Poblano Chiles

6 poblano chiles (page 45)

Vegetable oil for frying chiles, plus more for later sautéing and batter-frying

1/2 cup coarsely chopped blanched almonds

2 medium tomatoes

One 1 1/2-inch piece *canela* (page 30)

1 medium onion, finely chopped

1 large garlic clove, minced

1/4 teaspoon ground cloves

2 teaspoons fresh thyme leaves, minced, or 1 teaspoon dried, crumbled

1/2 cup dark raisins, chopped

2 to 2 1/2 cups shredded cooked pork (page 73)

Freshly ground black pepper

1 1/2 teaspoons salt, or to taste

1 cup unbleached all-purpose flour

2 large eggs, separated

Venancia Toledo Hernández introduced me to this savory, slightly sweet dish at her home in Ixtepec, one of the notable culinary centers of the Isthmus of Tehuantepec. The dish is equally good made with beef—it's a perfect way of using up leftover roast beef or pot roast. Shred the cooked meat as finely as you can; the texture of the filling should be almost paste-like.

6 servings

Prepare the chiles for stuffing by the frying method given on page 43. Set aside.

Preheat the oven to 350°F.

Spread the almonds on a baking sheet and bake until golden brown, about 10 minutes. Set aside.

While the almonds are toasting, roast the tomatoes by the directions on page 26. When they are cool enough to handle, peel and seed them. Chop the flesh fine and set aside.

Grind the *canela* in an electric coffee or spice grinder. In a medium-size skillet, heat 3 tablespoons of the oil over medium-high heat until rippling. Add the onion and garlic and cook for 2 minutes, stirring often. Stir in the *canela*, cloves and thyme. Add the chopped tomatoes and raisins and cook, stirring, for 5 minutes. Add the shredded meat and cook for another 5 minutes. Season with pepper and 1 teaspoon salt, or to taste. Stir in the toasted almonds, remove from the heat, and let cool to near room temperature. Carefully stuff the mixture into the chiles through the slit on the side, taking care not to rip the chile.

Mix the flour with the remaining 1/2 teaspoon salt and spread on a plate. In a mixing bowl, beat the egg whites to stiff peaks. Add the yolks one at a time, beating well after each addition.

Pour vegetable oil (including any left from frying the chiles) to a depth of 1 inch into a large, heavy skillet or saucepan about 3 to 4 inches deep. Heat over medium-high heat to 375°F.

Roll the chiles in the flour to coat lightly on all sides. Working with 1 or 2 chiles at a time, shake off excess flour, dip the chiles into the egg batter (holding them by the stem and tip, letting any excess batter drip back), and carefully slip them into the hot oil. Spoon a little of the oil over each to help set the exposed egg batter so that it will not disintegrate when you turn the chiles. Cook for 1 minute. Carefully turn the chiles over with a spatula. The cooked side should be just light golden. Cook for 1 minute more. Lift out onto paper towels to drain while you fry the remaining chiles. Serve at once with Caldillo de Tomate (page 259) or Salsa Roja (page 258).

Variation: In Oaxaca the batter-frying method is standard for chiles rellenos. But they are equally good briefly baked in a very hot oven, as I usually like to prepare chiles rellenos at my restaurant. For this method, omit the flour and eggs. Raise the oven temperature to 500°F after toasting the almonds. Make the filling and stuff the chiles as directed above. Place them on a baking sheet and bake for 5 to 7 minutes.

Chiles Rellenos de Pollo
Chicken-Filled Poblano Chiles

6 poblano chiles (page 45)

Vegetable oil for frying chiles, plus more for later sautéing and batter-frying

One 1/2-inch to 1-inch piece *canela* (page 30)

1 small onion, finely chopped

1 large ripe tomato, peeled, seeded, and finely chopped

2 garlic cloves, coarsely chopped

1/2 teaspoon dried thyme, crumbled

1 teaspoon dried Oaxacan oregano or 1/2 teaspoon dried Mexican oregano, crumbled (page 38)

2 to 2 1/2 cups cooked shredded chicken (page 75)

1 1/2 teaspoons salt, or to taste

1 cup all-purpose flour

2 large eggs, separated

*A*s with Chiles Rellenos de Carne, the chicken-filled version can be baked rather than batter-fried. The recipe is based on the chiles rellenos I had at El Topíl in Oaxaca City.

6 *servings*

Prepare the chiles for stuffing by the frying method given on page 43. Set aside.

Grind the *canela* in an electric coffee or spice grinder. In a medium-size skillet, heat 2 tablespoons of the oil over medium-high heat until rippling. Add the onion and cook, stirring, for 2 minutes. Stir in the chopped tomato and reduce the heat to medium. Cook, uncovered, stirring frequently, for 10 minutes, until somewhat thickened.

Using a mortar and pestle or the flat of a heavy knife blade, mash the garlic to a paste with the thyme and oregano. Add to the tomato mixture. Stir in the shredded chicken, ground *canela*, and 1 teaspoon salt, or to taste. Cook, uncovered, over medium heat for 10 minutes, stirring occasionally. Remove from the heat and let cool to near room temperature. Carefully stuff the mixture into the chiles through the slit on the side, taking care not to tear the chile.

Mix the flour with the remaining 1/2 teaspoon salt and spread on a plate. In a mixing bowl, beat the egg whites to stiff peaks and add the yolks one at a time, beating well after each addition.

Pour vegetable oil (including any left from frying the chiles) to a depth of 1 inch into a large, heavy skillet or saucepan about 3 to 4 inches deep. Heat over medium-high heat to 375°F.

Roll the chiles in the flour to coat lightly on all sides. Working with 1 or 2 chiles at a time, shake off excess flour, dip the chiles into the egg batter (holding them by the stem and tip, letting any excess batter drip back), and carefully slip them into the hot oil. Spoon a little of the oil over each to help set the exposed egg batter so that it will not disintegrate when you turn the chiles. Cook for 1 minute. Carefully turn the chiles over with a spatula. The cooked side should be just light golden. Cook for 1 minute more. Lift out onto paper towels to drain while you fry the remaining chiles. Serve at once with Caldillo de Tomate (page 259) or Salsa Roja (page 258).

Variation: For the simpler baked version, omit the flour and eggs. Proceed as directed above, but preheat the oven to 500°F before you begin stuffing the chiles. Place the chiles on a baking sheet and bake 5 to 7 minutes.

Chintextle
Dried Shrimp and Chile Spread

1 cup hulled pumpkin seeds

2 guajillo chiles, 1 Oaxacan pasilla chile, or 2 morita chiles (see page 47), tops and seeds removed

1/2 cup cleaned dried shrimp (contents of one 3 1/2-ounce package; page 33)

1 cup cooked black beans

Chintextle is a very old dish harking back to times when people needed something both nutritious and portable to take on long foot journeys between isolated regions of Oaxaca. It is a powerfully seasoned paste that varies from cook to cook. The most constant factor in all versions is the dried shrimp, an ingredient that visitors from other cultures find to be an acquired taste.

In Oaxaca, chintextle is usually served with small corn tortillas or tostadas; I've developed an unorthodox fondness for it as a sandwich spread. With this fairly dry mixture, the food processor is my preferred grinding method.

About 2 cups

Heat a griddle or large, heavy skillet over medium heat. Scatter the pumpkin seeds, chiles, and shrimp on the griddle and cook, stirring and tossing constantly, for about 2 minutes, or until lightly and evenly toasted on all sides. Remove from the griddle and let cool slightly.

Place the toasted mixture in a food processor and process until uniformly ground. Add the beans and process to a smooth paste.

Serve with fresh corn tortillas or fried tortilla chips.

Gaspacho
Vegetables and Shredded Beef in Vinaigrette

Gaspacho or *gazpacho* hasn't always been just a blenderized cold soup. There have been many versions going back far into Spanish culinary history and featuring anything from a thick bread salad mixture like an Italian *panzanella* to marinated seafood. So this dish that I was surprised to find being called *gaspacho* in a little restaurant probably isn't as weird as it looks. It's a salad of shredded cooked beef with tomatoes, avocados, and other vegetables, all moistened with vinegar. My version is a free-form interpretation using an oil-based vinaigrette in place of plain vinegar and allowing a short marination period for the meat to absorb the dressing.

About 6 servings

Place the meat in a large saucepan or Dutch oven with the onion, 2 of the garlic cloves, 6 sprigs of mint, the peppercorns and 1 teaspoon salt (or to taste). Add enough cold water to cover by 1 inch. Bring to a boil over high heat; quickly reduce the heat to medium-low and cook, partly covered, until the meat is well cooked, about 1 1/2 to 2 hours. Remove the meat, saving the stock for another purpose.

When the meat is cool enough to handle, cut it across the grain into 3 large chunks and pull into fine shreds. Transfer the meat to a bowl large enough to hold all the remaining ingredients.

Make a vinaigrette: Peel the remaining garlic clove and using a mortar and pestle or the flat of a heavy knife blade, crush it to a paste with the remaining 1 teaspoon salt. In a small bowl, whisk together the crushed garlic with the vinegar, olive oil, and freshly ground pepper to taste. Pour the dressing over the shredded meat and toss to combine. Let marinate, covered, for 1 hour at room temperature.

Prepare the other salad ingredients: Finely chop the tomatoes. Remove and discard the tops and seeds of the chiles; mince the flesh. Slice the radishes thinly and cut into fine julienne. Peel and pit the avocados; cut the flesh into 1/2-inch dice. Strip the leaves from the remaining mint sprigs and chop coarsely. Add all these ingredients to the marinated meat and toss to combine thoroughly. Taste for seasoning; add more salt and pepper if desired.

One 2-pound flank steak

1 medium onion, unpeeled

3 large garlic cloves, unpeeled

12 sprigs fresh mint

1/2 teaspoon whole black peppercorns, bruised

2 teaspoons salt, or to taste

3 tablespoons distilled white vinegar

1/2 cup olive oil

Freshly ground black pepper

2 large ripe tomatoes (about 1 1/2 pounds)

3 fresh green chiles such as serranos or jalapeños

1 bunch radishes (about 8 to 10), trimmed and scrubbed but unpeeled

2 ripe Hass avocados

Empanadas de Sardina

Sardine Turnovers

Masa para Empanadas (page 299)

Four 3 3/4-ounce cans sardines
packed in oil

2 canned chipotle chiles *en adobo*
(page 46), finely chopped

2 tablespoons vegetable oil

1 small onion, finely chopped

3 garlic cloves, minced

2 large eggs, lightly beaten, plus
another for optional egg glaze

Rosa Martha Toledo and Julio Bustillos serve these delicious little half-moons as a cocktail party appetizer at their garden restaurant, Bar Jardín in Juchitán. Odilia Román, the chef, shared her recipe with me. You can vary the amount of chiles to taste—this amount makes a fairly spicy filling.

If you are not a sardine lover, use two 6-ounce cans tuna packed in oil instead.

24 empanadas

Prepare the dough.

Preheat the oven to 400°F.

Drain the sardines well. Place them in a small bowl and mash with a fork, removing any coarse bits of bones that remain. Mix in the minced chipotles. Set aside.

In a small skillet, heat the vegetable oil over medium-high heat and add the onion and garlic. Cook, stirring frequently, for 2 to 3 minutes, or until translucent and lightly colored. Add the sardine mixture and cook for another 2 minutes. Remove from the heat and let cool to near room temperature. Stir in the eggs.

Roll out and cut the dough as described on page 299. You will have 24 four-inch rounds of dough. Place 1 tablespoon of the filling mixture on one side of each round and fold it over into a half-moon, firmly crimping the edges with your fingers or a fork. The empanadas are especially attractive if lightly brushed with an egg glaze made by briefly whisking 1 egg in a small bowl with 2 to 3 tablespoons of water.

Place the empanadas on 1 or 2 baking sheets and bake for about 12 minutes.

Molotes
Corn Masa Turnovers

"Turnovers" is really not an exact translation. Molotes, a popular filled *masa* specialty of Oaxaca, are most often formed into a shape between a "French twist" (as close as I can get to the literal meaning), a long Italian roll, and a big misshapen cigar with tapered ends. However, other shapes are also known, and I have opted for simple half-moons rather than the more characteristic shape.

About 20 to 24 molotes

Cut the potatoes into fine (1/4 inch or less) dice and drop into a saucepan of boiling salted water. Cook until barely tender, about 5 minutes; pour into a colander and rinse under cold running water to stop the cooking. Set aside to drain thoroughly.

If the chorizo is in sausage casings, pull off and discard the casings.

In a heavy medium-size skillet, heat the lard over medium heat until almost rippling. Add the chorizo and cook for 2 minutes, stirring constantly to break up the meat. Add the potatoes and stir well to combine; cook for 2 minutes longer. Set aside to cool while you make the dough.

Combine the *masa harina*, flour, baking powder, and salt in a medium-size bowl; mix with your fingers. Moisten the mixture with warm water, adding 3 to 4 tablespoons at a time until the mixture forms a firm but pliable dough.

Prepare a tortilla press as described on page 100. Break off walnut-size pieces of the dough and roll into balls between your palms. Press into 3-inch rounds. As they are pressed out, place side by side on a baking sheet or flat surface lined with parchment or wax paper and cover with a damp tea towel.

Place 2 to 3 teaspoons of the chorizo-potato filling on one side of each round and fold over into a half-moon, firmly crimping the edges to seal well.

Choose a heavy medium-size saucepan at least 3 inches deep. Pour in vegetable oil to a depth of 1 inch. Heat over medium-high heat to 375°F. Add the molotes, 4 or 5 at a time, and fry until golden on both sides, about 2 minutes in all. As they are done lift out onto paper towels to drain. Serve at once with Salsa de Chile Pasilla (page 254) or any preferred table sauce.

Note: *The filled molotes can be refrigerated for up to a day before frying, covered well with a barely damp tea towel and plastic wrap. Let stand uncovered at room temperature for a short while before frying.*

1/2 pound waxy boiling potatoes such as Red Bliss (2 medium potatoes), peeled

1/2 pound (1 cup) homemade chorizo mixture (page 208)

1 tablespoon lard (preferably home-rendered; page 36) or vegetable oil

2 cups *masa harina* (page 94)

2 tablespoons all-purpose flour

1 teaspoon baking powder

1/2 teaspoon salt

Vegetable oil for frying

Tortitas de Camarón
Tiny Omelette Soufflés with Dried Shrimp

2 large eggs, at room temperature

1/4 cup vegetable oil

32 dried shrimp (page 33), heads removed, soaked in several changes of water to remove excess salt and drained

Dried shrimp is one of the defining notes in the food of Oaxaca. People have been salting and sun-drying boiled shrimp in the Isthmus of Tehuantepec since time immemorial. It is a way of preserving it for transport to distant areas without refrigeration. Of course, fresh shrimp is also valued. But it arrives in a twice-yearly glut during February and September. (I saw pink mountains of new shrimp at the village market of San Mateo del Mar in the main fishing region of the Isthmus—clearly more than local families could consume in the fresh state.) The dried product is a necessity that Oaxacans also consider a great delicacy. The flavor is so beloved that even now, when freezing technology could bring "fresh" shrimp to the more affluent, everybody cooks with dried shrimp all over the state.

This way of using the deliciously briny little shrimp comes from my generous and flamboyant Isthmian friend Venancia Toledo Hernández, who opened up so much of the regional cuisine to me. I came to her house one morning for an all-day cooking session and she greeted me with a splendid breakfast of meat-filled poblano chiles (page 60), some exquisite bean tamales, and these tortitas. The word is not exactly translatable, but the dish is a little like an old-fashioned fluffy omelet except that the eggs are not separated—you whip them whole as if starting to make a génoise batter for a cake. This is the most difficult stage. Have the eggs at room temperature and if possible use a good hand-held electric mixer to beat them in a small deep bowl.

Venancia serves the tortitas with a spicy tomato sauce that you may also find useful for other purposes.

4 tortitas

In a small, slightly warmed deep bowl, beat the eggs until very thick, fluffy, and lemon-colored. This requires patience and is best done with a hand-held electric mixer at high speed.

In a large skillet, heat the oil to rippling over medium-high heat. Spoon 2 small portions (about 1/4 to 1/3 cup each) of the egg mixture into the pan. With the back of a spoon, immediately spread each portion out to a circle about

4 inches across. Working rapidly, scatter 8 shrimp over each and spoon a little more egg over the shrimp, smoothing with a spoon. Spoon a little of the hot oil over each of the little "omelets" to help set the beaten egg. Turn and cook the other side lightly. Remove from the pan to a paper towel to drain. Repeat with the remaining egg and shrimp. Serve immediately with Salsa de Tomate para Tortitas (recipe follows).

Salsa de Tomate para Tortitas
Tomato Sauce for Tortitas

About 1 cup

1 large ripe tomato
3 árbol chiles (page 46)
1/2 teaspoon dried Mediterranean oregano or dried thyme, crumbled (optional)
1/2 teaspoon salt, or to taste

Bring a small saucepan of water to a boil and drop in the tomato and chiles. Adjust the heat to medium and cook for 10 minutes. Drain. When cool enough to handle, peel the tomato and remove the tops of the chiles. Purée in a blender or food processor with the oregano or thyme and salt.

Totopos baking in sunken clay oven

Soups

Soups play a very important role in Oaxacan meals, though not the same role as the dainty consommés and creamy puréed soups we in this country often serve in small amounts as first courses.

Small portions are definitely not appropriate when it comes to serving Oaxacan soups! Usually the authentic way to serve them is as meals in themselves. Also, people in Oaxaca don't necessarily draw distinctions between soups and stews, or even soups and sauces. Many of the important sauce-based dishes can acquire the nature of soups by simply adding liquid. In fact, some dishes we'd call soups are known as *molitos* ("little *moles*").

More often than not, the cooking liquid of choice for soups is water. Stocks are important in many sauces, but Oaxacans are too thrifty to make French-type stocks where the cooked meats get thrown away. In soup-making they generally expect the ingredients to create their own stock or plan to reap a good stock as a by-product of cooking something else. Here I tend to make a judgment call depending on the ingredients I am working with. Unfortunately, a lot of our U.S. produce just seems to contribute less "presence" and body to the soup than the Oaxacan counterparts—I'm thinking especially of our dull, oversweet corn. For this reason, I usually compensate by substituting homemade chicken stock for the water that my Oaxacan friends probably would use. I leave the matter to your preference—but I have to say that water is more authentic than bouillon cubes or canned broth.

Caldo de Puerco/
Carne de Puerco Cocida
Pork Stock/Shredded Pork

This is a pork-based equivalent of the following recipe, but the stock is richer and more concentrated. You can easily double the recipe and freeze any stock not needed at the moment.

My favorite cut of meat for cooked shredded pork is a nice piece of Boston shoulder butt with a thin layer of fat (to keep the meat moist) and the bone in (to give body and flavor). When I need stock but not the cooked meat, I often replace the pork butt with a combination of 2 pounds pork neck bones and 1 pound spareribs.

About 3 to 4 cups

3 pounds pork butt, bone in, trimmed of most but not all fat

1 head of garlic, unpeeled, halved crosswise

1 teaspoon whole black peppercorns, bruised

3 bay leaves

1 teaspoon salt, or to taste

For Caldo de Puerco (Pork Stock)

Place the meat with all other ingredients in a small stockpot or deep 5- to 6-quart saucepan. Add enough cold water to cover well (10 to 12 cups). Bring to a boil over high heat and immediately reduce the heat to low. Remove any foam that collects on top. Simmer, partly covered, until the meat is tender, about 2 to 2 1/2 hours. Lift out the pork, letting it drain well, and set aside. Raise the heat to high and boil the stock until reduced to about 3 to 4 cups. Strain the stock through a fine-mesh sieve, discarding the solids; let sit until the fat can be skimmed off (or refrigerate several hours and lift off the solidified fat).

The stock will keep, tightly covered, 4 to 5 days in the refrigerator or up to 6 months in the freezer.

For Carne de Puerco (Cooked Shredded Pork)

Prepare Caldo de Puerco. When you have removed the meat from the stock, let it cool to room temperature. Remove and discard any visible fat. Pull the meat from the bones, carefully tear it into long shreds, and refrigerate if not using at once. You should have about 3 to 4 cups. Use within 2 or 3 days.

Caldo de Pollo/Pollo Cocido
Chicken Stock/Cooked Shredded Chicken

One 3 1/2 to 4-pound chicken

1 medium onion, unpeeled

3 garlic cloves, unpeeled

1 whole carrot, scrubbed but
    unpeeled

2 bay leaves

1 teaspoon whole black peppercorns

1 teaspoon salt, or to taste

Homemade stock is a crucial part of many Oaxacan sauce-based dishes. So is simply boiled meat. The two are a logical pairing. When you cook chicken or pork in water you end up with the makings for some soups or the liquid to use to purée *mole* pastes, while at the same time you will have the cooked shredded chicken or pork for which so many of my recipes call. And as noted above, I often use stock for soups when cooking in the U.S., to deepen the flavor of things.

There are no special refinements to Oaxacan chicken stock. It's identical to the simple, delicate stock made all over Mexico and given in my first book. Do not try to intensify the taste with extra herbs and other ingredients. This is not a powerful consommé but a light background stock that can be made equally well with the chicken cut in pieces or left whole. When you want a richer flavor, you achieve it not by overseasoning but by sautéing a few aromatic vegetables and adding them to the stock as described on page 75, then straining them out after they have contributed their essence. This is an especially good idea considering the difference between the full-flavored Oaxacan chicken and our anemic specimens.

If you don't need the cooked meat, you can always make the stock with 4 to 5 pounds chicken backs, wings, and necks instead of the whole bird. I think the flavor is finer with a whole chicken. If desired, double the recipe—the stock freezes well and I always like having some on hand. Canned chicken broth is no equivalent.

About 8 to 9 cups (will vary with shape of pot)

For Caldo de Pollo (Basic Chicken Stock)

    Put the chicken and all other ingredients into a small stockpot or a 5- to 6-quart Dutch oven. Add enough cold water to cover well (10 to 12 cups, depending on the shape of the pot). Bring to a boil over high heat and immediately reduce the heat to low. Remove any foam that has collected on top. Simmer, partly covered, until the meat is just cooked, about 30 minutes. Lift out the chicken, letting it drain, and set aside. Strain the stock through a fine-mesh sieve, discarding the solids; let sit until the fat can be skimmed off. (This is easier if the stock is refrigerated for several hours.) The stock will keep, tightly covered, 4 to 5 days in the refrigerator or up to 6 months in the freezer.

For Caldo de Pollo Concentrado (Enriched Chicken Stock)

Prepare Caldo de Pollo as described above and return the strained, degreased stock to a medium-size saucepan over medium heat. In a medium-size skillet, heat 2 tablespoons lard or vegetable oil over medium-high heat until rippling. Add 1 cup chopped onion and 1 minced garlic clove. Cook, stirring occasionally, for about 3 minutes. Add 1 chopped ripe medium-size tomato and cook another 3 minutes. As your Caldo de Pollo reaches a boil, add the sautéed vegetables and reduce the heat to low. Cook, uncovered, for 10 minutes. Strain through a fine-mesh sieve, discarding the solids.

Variation: For a delicious light soup, heat 6 cups Enriched Chicken Stock with 1 cup Caldillo de Tomate (page 259).

For Pollo Cocido (Cooked Shredded Chicken)

Prepare Caldo de Pollo. When you have lifted the chicken out of the stock, let it cool enough to handle. Remove and discard the skin. Carefully pull the meat from the bones, discarding any remaining fat or gristly bits. Tear the meat into fine shreds and refrigerate if not using at once. You should have about 3 cups. Use within 1 or 2 days.

Caldo de Verduras
Vegetable Soup

1 medium tomato

1 small onion, coarsely chopped

2 garlic cloves

1 Oaxacan pasilla chile (page 47) or 2 morita chiles, seeds removed if desired, or 1 canned chipotle chile en adobo (pages 46 and 47)

6 cups homemade chicken stock (page 74) or water

3 cactus paddles (nopalitos), cleaned and cut into 1/2-inch dice (page 29)

2 tablespoons vegetable oil

8 ounces young green beans, strings removed if necessary, cut into 1/2-inch pieces

1 zucchini, sliced into 1/2-inch rounds

1 chayote, peeled, seeded, and cut into 1/2-inch dice

1 cup corn kernels, preferably white (cut from fresh corn or frozen and thawed)

5 to 6 squash blossoms, cut into several pieces each (optional)

5 sprigs cilantro, leaves only

Lime wedges

Fresh corn tortillas

*T*his is a wonderful soup to make in the summer when you can get squash blossoms, but the soup also works well without them.

There is one distortion of the original recipe that cannot be avoided: the tender, sugary kernels of U.S. fresh corn are all wrong. Perhaps with more Mexican people living here, the authentic starchy corn will start showing up in farmers' markets. I know that some home gardeners interested in heirloom seeds are raising these varieties.

6 to 8 servings

Griddle-roast the tomato by the directions on page 26. When it is cool enough to handle, peel, saving the juices. Place in a blender with the onion, garlic, chile, and 1 cup of the chicken stock. Process to a purée. With a wooden spoon or pusher, force the mixture through a medium-mesh sieve into a bowl and set aside.

Bring a small saucepan of water to a boil and add the diced cactus paddles. Cook, uncovered, over medium heat for 3 to 5 minutes or until crisp-tender (see page 29). Pour into a colander and rinse under hot and then cold running water to remove some of their sticky juices. Drain well.

In a large saucepan, heat the oil over medium-high heat until rippling. Add the drained nopalitos along with the beans, zucchini, chayote, corn, and squash blossoms. Cook, stirring frequently, for about 5 minutes. Stir in the reserved tomato-chile mixture. Cook for 2 minutes; add the remaining chicken stock and cilantro. Bring back to a boil and serve at once with lime wedges and freshly made corn tortillas.

Cocina de Coles
Cabbage Soup

I have had this robust soup at market stalls in Oaxaca City. Some people do a thrifty trick with the leftovers—they drain off the stock and mix the cooked cabbage and chickpeas (either plain or sautéed in a little lard with Mole Coloradito, page 158) to make a filling for small, freshly made corn tortillas folded in half like soft tacos. They eat these as an *antojito* (snack) under the name *tesupos*. Try it when you have a supply of Coloradito on hand.

In Mexico, chickpeas are almost never eaten without the skins removed. This makes them much more pleasant to eat and more digestible. Just let the cooked chickpeas sit until you can handle them and rub between your palms, a handful at a time, until the skins come off.

6 servings

1 medium-size ripe tomato

1 small onion

1 large garlic clove

1/2 pound (about 1 cup) homemade chorizo mixture (page 208)

1 tablespoon vegetable oil

5 slices bacon, coarsely chopped

1/2 small white cabbage (1/2 to 3/4 pound), core removed, thinly sliced

1 cup cooked chickpeas, skins removed

6 cups homemade chicken stock (page 74) or water

1 tablespoon Italian parsley leaves

1 1/2 teaspoons salt, or to taste

Freshly ground black pepper

Griddle-roast the tomato by the directions on page 26. When it is cool enough to handle, peel, saving the juices. Place in a blender with the onion and garlic and process to a purée. With a wooden spoon or pusher, force the mixture through a medium-mesh sieve into a bowl and set aside.

If the chorizo is in sausage casings, remove and discard them.

In a small stockpot or large saucepan, heat the oil over medium-high heat until rippling. Reduce the heat to medium-low; add the chorizo and bacon and cook, stirring frequently, until the meat is starting to cook in its own rendered fat, about 5 minutes. Add the cabbage and toss to coat with the fat; raise the heat to medium-high and cook, stirring occasionally, for 3 to 4 minutes. Stir in the reserved tomato mixture and cook for 5 minutes. Add the chickpeas, stock, and parsley. Bring back to a boil; season with salt and pepper. Reduce the heat to low and cook, partly covered, for 20 minutes. Serve immediately.

Caldo de Guajolote
Turkey Soup

5 guajillo chiles (page 47), tops and
    seeds removed

3 árbol chiles (page 46), tops and
    seeds removed

Salt for seasoning

One 6-pound turkey, cut into
    8 pieces

2 garlic cloves, coarsely chopped

1 medium onion, coarsely chopped

4 *hoja santa* leaves, preferably fresh
    (page 36)

5 sprigs cilantro

2 tablespoons vegetable oil

*I*n Oaxaca, turkey is a lot closer to the native pre-Hispanic bird than the big overbred creatures sold in the U.S. Oaxacan turkeys are small and not so cardboard-like. Almost never would they be roasted as is done in the U.S. People in Oaxaca usually braise turkey (as in *moles*), pit-barbecue it, or cook it in soups.

In ancient times turkey was sacrificed on all important days of the intricate pre-Hispanic calendar, and the custom has not disappeared in the remote villages. The following soup is very close to one that is still made with turkeys sacrificed as offerings at hillside shrines in the land of the Mixe Indians around Mount Zempoaltépetl, Oaxaca State's highest mountain.

The turkey is grilled over wood or charcoal before being cooked in the soup, and this is the secret of the dish's distinctive, un-soupy flavor. You can also oven-broil it if necessary, but it will not be as good. If you cannot purchase a turkey of the right size (6 pounds, or 7 at most), use 3 turkey legs (drumstick and thighs). I like to serve this main-dish soup with large, bone-in pieces of turkey in each bowl; if you think this is too awkward, remove the meat from the bones before serving and distribute some in each portion.

About 8 servings

Prepare a charcoal grill. While the coals are heating, rinse and griddle-dry the chiles by the directions on page 45. Place in a deep bowl, cover generously with boiling water, and let soak for at least 20 minutes.

Salt the turkey pieces generously on all sides. Place on the rack and grill over moderate heat for 10 minutes on each side. Set aside in a bowl to catch the juices while you prepare the seasoning paste.

Drain the soaked chiles and place in a blender with the garlic, onion, *hoja santa*, cilantro, and 1/4 cup water. Process to a purée, stopping occasionally to scrape down the sides with a rubber spatula. With a wooden spoon or pusher, force the mixture through a medium-mesh sieve into a bowl.

In a stockpot or Dutch oven large enough to hold the turkey pieces, heat the oil over medium-high heat until rippling. Add the chile purée and cook, stirring frequently, for 5 minutes. Add the turkey pieces and 3 1/2 quarts water. Bring to a boil over high heat, then reduce the heat to low. Cook, covered, until the thigh and drumstick meat is tender, 40 minutes to 1 hour (less for a 6-pound turkey, more for parts from a larger turkey).

Serve in very large soup bowls. Either distribute a sizable bone-in chunk of turkey to each bowl, or set the meat aside to cool slightly and remove it from the bones prior to putting some of the meat into each bowl and briefly rewarm the soup before serving.

Caldo de Camarones Secos
Dried Shrimp Soup

1 1/2 to 2 cups (7 ounces) dried
  shrimp (page 33)

2 large tomatoes, chopped

1 medium onion, quartered

2 garlic cloves

Two 6-inch sprigs fresh epazote or
  1 tablespoon dried, crumbled
  (page 35)

3 tablespoons chopped *chepil* leaves
  stripped from stems (from a
  defrosted packet of frozen *chepil*;
  see page 32)

1 cup (8 ounces) fresh *masa* (page
  93), or 6 tablespoons *masa harina*
  (page 94) mixed with 6 tablespoons water

2 tablespoons vegetable oil

1/8 to 1/4 teaspoon salt (optional)

Lime wedges

2 cups Salsa de Chile Pasilla
  (page 254)

*D*ried shrimp from the Isthmus of Tehuantepec is an integral part of Oaxacan cuisine. To me the bold, briny flavor is addictive—like a whole ocean concentrated into a teaspoon. This soup from Venancia Toledo Hernández is a great vehicle for the special effect of dried shrimp.

6 to 8 servings

Carefully pick over the dried shrimp by the directions on page 33 and rinse them well under cold running water. Place in a large saucepan with the toma-toes, onion, garlic, epazote, *chepil*, and 3 quarts cold water. Bring to a boil over high heat; reduce the heat to low and cook, partly covered, until the shrimp are softened, about 30 minutes.

Remove the soup from the heat and strain through a fine-mesh sieve, reserving the shrimp stock and solids separately. Rinse out the saucepan and set aside.

Let the shrimp and vegetables cool almost to room temperature, then process to a purée in a food processor or blender. Set aside.

In a small bowl, combine the *masa* with 1 cup cold water. Mix to make as smooth a paste as possible (it may tend to form lumps) and set aside.

Return the saucepan to the stove over medium-high heat. Add the veg-etable oil and heat until almost smoking. Add the puréed shrimp and vegetables (watch out for splatters). Cook, covered, stirring occasionally, for 3 minutes. Add the reserved stock and bring to a boil; reduce the heat to medium-low and cook, covered, stirring occasionally, for 15 minutes.

With a wooden spoon or pusher, force the reserved *masa* mixture through the sieve into the simmering soup. Taste for seasoning and whisk in the salt if desired (the shrimp themselves may provide enough). Cook, uncovered, whisk-ing frequently, until somewhat thickened, 7 to 10 minutes. It should be the con-sistency of a bisque or cream soup.

Serve the soup with lime wedges and pass a bowl of Salsa de Chile Pasilla (page 254) for guests to help themselves.

Caldo Guisado
Short Ribs in Rich Soup

*T*his is definitely a one-dish meal—it assaults your senses with so many flavors you'd never be able to taste anything else afterward! I found it in the Isthmus of Tehuantepec, where they love the sweet-sour combination of raisins with pickled ingredients. If possible, make the soup a day ahead and refrigerate it. Not only can you degrease it more easily when it is cold, but it has more flavor when reheated the next day.

6 to 8 servings

Place the ribs and marrow bones in a large stockpot and cover with water. Bring to a boil over high heat, then reduce the heat to medium-low. Remove any foam that collects on the surface.

While the soup is coming to a boil, grind the achiote seeds as fine as possible in an electric coffee or spice grinder and transfer to a small bowl. (They are very hard, so be patient.) Grind the peppercorns, oregano, *canela*, and cumin together and combine with the achiote. Add the ground spices to the soup once you have removed the foam.

In a medium-size skillet, heat the oil over medium-high heat. Add the onion and garlic and cook, stirring frequently, for 3 minutes. Reduce the heat slightly and add the scallions and tomatoes. Cook, uncovered, stirring occasionally, for 10 minutes more. Add the sautéed vegetables to the soup and cook, partly covered, for 2 hours.

Add the plantain, raisins, olives, capers, and pickled jalapeños. Let the soup return to a boil; reduce the heat to medium-low and simmer for another 30 minutes.

Remove and discard the marrow bones. Serve immediately if desired; or cool and refrigerate overnight, reheating just before serving. I serve the soup with the meat on the ribs, but if you prefer you can remove the meat and distribute some in each serving.

5 pounds beef short ribs

1 1/2 pounds beef marrow bones

1 tablespoon achiote seeds (page 28)

1 teaspoon whole black peppercorns, bruised

1 1/2 teaspoons dried Mexican oregano (page 38), crumbled

One 2-inch piece *canela* (page 30)

1/4 teaspoon cumin seeds

2 tablespoons vegetable oil

1 large onion, chopped

4 garlic cloves, minced

4 scallions, white and part of the green tops, chopped

2 large ripe tomatoes (about 1 1/2 pounds), chopped

1 large ripe plantain (page 39), peeled and sliced into 1/2-inch rounds

1/3 cup dark raisins

One 6 1/2-ounce jar pimiento-stuffed green olives, drained

One 3 1/2-ounce jar capers, drained

4 pickled jalapeño chiles (page 45), thinly sliced

Che Guiña
Masa-Thickened Beef Soup with Chiles

2 pounds beef short ribs, cut into 2-inch lengths

1 teaspoon salt, or to taste

7 garlic cloves, unpeeled

15-18 whole black peppercorns, bruised

5 guajillo chiles (page 47), tops and seeds removed

2 whole cloves

3 medium ripe tomatoes, coarsely chopped

1 small onion, coarsely chopped

1 cup (8 ounces) fresh *masa* (page 93), or 6 tablespoons *masa harina* (page 94) mixed with 6 tablespoons water

2 tablespoons vegetable oil

Four 6-inch sprigs epazote or 2 tablespoons dried epazote, crumbled (page 35)

Lime wedges

$\mathcal{B}$eef is butchered differently in southern Mexico than in the U.S. or even the north of Mexico, where I grew up. In Oaxaca, when all the important cuts have been taken from the carcass, various hunks of bone with meat attached remain for sale—very daunting-looking as they hang over the flyspecked butcher stalls that are a village's usual source of meat. These pieces of bone with irregular leavings of meat are appropriately called *retazo*, which means odds and ends of something (like fabric remnants). Lacking the kind of *retazo* that is sold in Oaxaca, I make this comforting soup with meaty beef bones. If the only bones you can find are meatless, you can use 1 pound of bones to 1 pound of boneless stewing meat. But the approach I like best is to use short ribs as suggested below, asking the butcher to cut them into 2-inch lengths.

The recipe is from the Isthmus and was given to me by Odilia Román of Bar Jardín in Juchitán. The name refers to the chiles (*guiña* in Zapotec).

4 servings

Place the meat, salt, 5 unpeeled garlic cloves, and 10 to 12 peppercorns in a large saucepan or small stockpot. Add 2 quarts water and bring to a boil over medium-high heat. Reduce the heat to low. Remove any foam that has collected on the surface; cook, partly covered, until the meat is tender, about 1 1/2 hours. Remove and set aside the chunks of rib. Strain the stock through a fine-mesh sieve and set aside, discarding the solids. Rinse out and dry the soup pot.

While the meat is cooking, make the seasoning paste. Wash and griddle-dry the chiles by the directions on page 45. Place in a bowl, covering generously with boiling water, and let soak for at least 20 minutes. Drain.

Grind the cloves and the remaining peppercorns together in an electric coffee or spice grinder. Peel the remaining garlic and place in a blender with the chiles, ground spices, tomatoes, and onion. Process to a smooth purée. With a wooden spoon or pusher, force the mixture through a medium-mesh sieve into a bowl. Set aside.

In a small bowl, mix the *masa* smoothly with 1 cup of the beef stock.

Return the soup pot to the stove over medium heat; add the oil and heat until rippling. Pour in the purée and cook, partly covered, stirring occasionally, for 15 minutes. With a wooden spoon, rub the thinned *masa* through a medium-mesh sieve into the hot mixture. Cook for 1 minute, whisking rapidly to prevent lumping. Add the rest of the beef stock, whisking to combine thoroughly. Cook, uncovered, whisking frequently until lightly thickened, about 10 minutes. Return the ribs to the pot. Add the epazote and cook, stirring occasionally, until the meat is heated through, about 5 minutes. Serve at once with lime wedges.

Magic objects for bultos (packages of ritual offerings) at the market in Huautla de Jiménez

Molito de Res

Beef Soup with Vegetables

*T*he Isthmus of Tehuantepec has many dishes known as *molitos* or "little *moles*." Some are sauces thickened with ground dried shrimp or other ingredients. Others, like this vegetable-beef medley that I ate at Adelina Santiago's market stall "Fonda Adelina" in Juchitán, are what most people call soups. It is a common one-dish lunch meal.

The flavor of the soup depends on reducing the broth a lot in cooking, so it cooks over fairly lively heat.

About 6 servings

Place the meat and bones in a stockpot or large Dutch oven with 3 1/2 quarts cold water. Add the onion, garlic, and peppercorns. Bring to a boil over high heat. Reduce the heat to medium; the stock should continue to simmer fairly briskly. Remove any foam that collects on the surface. Cook, partly covered, until the meat is tender, about 1 1/4 to 1 1/2 hours.

Remove from the heat. Lift out the ribs and set aside. Strain the stock through a fine-mesh sieve and discard the solids. Rinse out the stockpot; return the stock to the pot. You should have about 6 cups; boil rapidly to reduce if necessary. Taste the broth and add 1 1/2 teaspoons salt or to taste. Adjust the heat to medium-low.

Return the ribs to the pot. Add the carrots, cabbage, plantain, potatoes, tomato, and herbs to the remaining broth and cook, partly covered, for 15 minutes. Add the corn, zucchini, green beans, and chickpeas. Cook, partly covered, just until the zucchini and green beans are crisp-tender, about 5 to 7 minutes. Serve at once in large soup bowls with a plate of lime wedges; accompany with Salsa de Chile Serrano con Limón (page 255) or Salsa de Chile Pasilla (page 254) and freshly made corn tortillas.

2 pounds meaty beef short ribs

2 pounds beef marrow bones

1 medium onion, unpeeled

1 whole head of garlic, unpeeled

1 teaspoon whole black peppercorns, bruised

1 1/2 teaspoons salt, or to taste

3 large carrots, cut into large chunks

1 small white cabbage (about 1 pound), cored and quartered

1 large semi-ripe plantain (page 39), peeled and cut into 2-inch chunks

6 small Red Bliss potatoes, scrubbed but not peeled

1 large tomato, chopped

6 large sprigs Italian parsley

6 sprigs fresh mint

2 large fresh or frozen ears of corn, chopped crosswise into 3 pieces each

4 medium zucchini, stem ends trimmed, cut into large chunks

1/2 pound young green beans, strings removed if necessary, cut in half

1 cup cooked chickpeas, skins removed (page 32), or one 15-ounce can chickpeas, drained and rinsed, skins removed

Lime wedges

Molito de Garbanzo

Toasted Chickpea Soup

1 1/4 cups (8 ounces) dried
  chickpeas

1 jalapeño chile, or more to taste

2 tablespoons lard (preferably
  home-rendered; page 36)
  or vegetable oil

1 small onion, chopped

1 large garlic clove, minced

1 large ripe tomato, chopped

6 cups homemade chicken stock
  (page 74) or water

4 sprigs fresh mint, or 1 teaspoon
  dried mint

1 teaspoon salt, or to taste

Oaxacan cooks use a range of flours ground from roasted dried legumes. In the markets you see plastic kilo bags of the different flour varieties with their different characteristic hues—bluish gray (black beans), pale pea-green (dried peas or lima beans), off-white (white beans), and the ones called for here, chickpeas, which turn out a sort of mustard color. They are used as thickeners and to some extent the different kinds are interchangeable. Roasted legume flours often form the basis of soups like this one from Luis Armando Hernández, who with his mother, Venancia Toledo Hernández, took the time to teach me many exciting dishes from the Isthmus of Tehuantepec.

The process is much easier in Oaxaca than in the version I give you here, because it will be necessary for most U.S. cooks to grind the chickpeas themselves. You may be able to find the right flour sold in large bags in Indian and Pakistani markets under the name of *besan*. However, be sure that it is made from *toasted* (not raw) dried chickpeas and has not been pre-seasoned with spices. Use 1 cup of *besan* in place of 1 1/4 cups whole dried chickpeas.

4 servings

Preheat the oven to 350°F.

Spread the chickpeas on a baking sheet. Bake for 30 to 35 minutes. They will probably still be pale on the outside, but the inside will be golden. Let cool to room temperature. Place in a food processor or (working in batches as necessary) in a coffee or spice grinder and process until ground to a fine flour. You should have about 1 cup.

Roast the jalapeño by the directions on page 42; peel it and mince.

In a medium-size saucepan, heat the lard over medium-high heat until rippling. Add the onion and garlic and cook, stirring occasionally, for about 3 minutes. Add the chile and the tomato; cook, stirring occasionally, for 5 minutes longer. Let cool slightly. Place in a blender and process to a purée. Set aside.

In a small stockpot or large saucepan, combine the ground chickpeas and 2 cups of the chicken stock and mix to dissolve smoothly. Set over medium-high heat and stir in the remaining stock, a little at a time.

Add the puréed tomato mixture, mint, and salt. Reduce the heat to low and cook until slightly thickened, about 10 minutes. Serve immediately.

Guiñado Xuba
Roast Corn and Pork Soup

*T*he Zapotec name is pronounced roughly "gheenyádo shooba" and refers to two of the main ingredients, *guiña* (chile) and *xuba* (corn). The always helpful Venancia Toledo Hernández taught me this characteristic dish from the Isthmus of Tehuantepec. You must search for the right white field corn, a floury or "dent" type. Do not try to make it with flint corn or parched sweet corn, which don't have enough starch.

About 6 servings

Preheat the oven to 400°F.

Spread the corn kernels on a baking sheet and bake for about 20 minutes. It should be a rich sunflower yellow—watch to be sure that it does not brown. Remove and let cool to room temperature. Place in a food processor and pulse to break up the kernels to the size of small barley grains. Shake in a fine-mesh sieve to winnow out the powdery chaff produced in processing. Place the crushed kernels in a small bowl and cover with water. Let soak for 1 hour; skim off and discard any particles of chaff that collect on the surface.

While the corn soaks, wash and griddle-dry the guajillo chiles by the directions on page 45. Place in a bowl, cover generously with boiling water, and let soak for 20 minutes.

Drain the soaked guajillos and place in a blender with the tomatoes, onion, garlic, and fresh chiles. Process to a smooth purée. With a wooden spoon or pusher, force the mixture through a medium-mesh sieve into a bowl.

In a medium-size stockpot or large saucepan, heat the oil over medium-high heat until rippling. Pour in the puréed mixture and cook, stirring occasionally, for 5 minutes.

Add the pork bones, meat, and epazote. Add 3 quarts water and bring back to a boil over high heat. Reduce the heat to low and cook, partly covered, for 40 minutes. Drain the soaked corn and add it to the pot. Add the salt; cook for another 40 minutes or until the meat is tender, stirring often to keep the corn from sticking. The corn will be softened but still a little chewy.

1 cup dried dent corn kernels (page 91)

2 guajillo chiles (page 47), tops and seeds removed

2 large tomatoes (about 1 1/2 pounds), coarsely chopped

1 medium onion, coarsely chopped

4 garlic cloves, coarsely chopped

3 small fresh chiles such as serranos or jalapeños, stems and tops removed, coarsely chopped (amount can be varied to taste)

2 tablespoons vegetable oil

1 pound meaty pork neck bones or spareribs

2 pounds boneless pork shoulder, cut into large (2-inch) cubes

Eight 6-inch epazote sprigs or 3 tablespoons dried epazote, crumbled (page 35)

1 1/2 teaspoons salt, or to taste

Husking corn to be ground for atole

Corn

Of all the ingredients in Oaxacan cooking, none has presented so many problems for me as the most basic—corn. And I assure you that nothing about U.S. cooking bothers Oaxacans, or actually all Mexicans, more than the corn. It's as if the grain and what's made from it were aimed at juvenile palates, like factory-farm table grapes and grape juice compared with the world of different wine grapes and wines. The range of Mexican corn varieties is rich and fascinating, and Oaxaca State is one of the greatest centers of corn-based cuisine. Unfortunately, U.S. sweet corn is a disaster when applied to dishes that use Oaxacan fresh corn, and even the main types of field corn that are ground into cornmeal here don't really have the right taste or texture for the different Oaxacan ground-corn dishes.

My hope is that with the number of Mexicans now living in and around the major U.S. cities, growers here will start raising some types of real Mexican corn. Meanwhile, cooks have to compromise.

The key ingredient of Mexican corn is starch. Most of the starch has been deliberately bred out of U.S. sweet corn to make it sweeter and more tender—just what Mexicans don't like about it! The mature corn varieties bred here for cornmeal do contain more starch, but it's usually a type technically called "hard" starch that doesn't soften and become absorbent in cooking. Oaxacan corn contains "soft" or the even more absorbent "floury" starch (no relation to commercial U.S. cornstarch) that can't be replaced with anything else. For this reason, I had to leave out an incredible number of corn dishes.

One famous specialty that I experimented with endlessly and had to give up on is *nicuatole*, a dessert that is made by extracting the starch from corn kernels and using it to set brilliantly colored jelled mixtures like the old-fashioned English "flummeries." The *totopos* of the Isthmus of Tehuantepec, a sort of corn-flour cracker baked on the walls of tandoor-like sunken ovens, are equally impossible to duplicate here. So are many of the soups and sauces thickened with flavorful ground corn.

However, I worked long and hard with other dishes where there was a chance of achieving good if not ideal facsimiles. As they say in Mexico, *A falta de pan, tortilla*—"If you don't have bread, eat a tortilla!" In most U.S. communities, you can buy dried field corn from seed suppliers or livestock feed stores, and this can work well. Unfortunately, "field corn" is an elastic term. Try to learn just what type of corn you are buying. In most of the recipes where dried corn is called for, I used a variety of "dent" corn, the starchiest type commonly sold here. (The mature kernels have an indented shape, hence the name.) "Flint" corn, as hard as the name implies, is usually less suitable. I found one kind of blue corn (available by mail order) that is fairly close to a type called *cónico* in Oaxaca, but I would beware of assuming that all blue corn is the same. The color doesn't necessarily indicate the cooking qualities.

In this chapter you will learn the basics of Oaxacan tortillas and tamales, but there are many other dishes using corn scattered throughout other chapters. I think your eyes will be opened to the rich possibilities of an ingredient that is treated so differently in this country.

About *Nixtamal* and *Masa*

2 pounds dried dent corn or starchy
blue corn kernels (page 91)

3 quarts water

1/4 cup *cal* (slaked lime; page 30)

*M*any centuries ago, Mexican cooks discovered that as good as corn is when eaten fresh or dried, it takes on an exciting new identity when treated with a solution of wood ashes, burnt seashells, or some other natural alkali. The process is called *nixtamalización*. *Nixtamal*, the resulting hominy-like product, is valuable both for nutritional reasons (some important nutrients are more available than in plain untreated corn) and for the unique flavor that the kernels develop. If you taste Mexican tortillas or tamales side by side with some of the similar corn dishes from other Latin American countries where the *nixtamal* process is not used, you'll recognize the difference. Compared with the haunting, penetrating, but subtle flavor and aroma of nixtamalized corn, something seems to be missing.

Making *nixtamal* at home at least once is worthwhile if only to see how simple corn is magically transformed into the foundation of the Mexican corn kitchen. Use the treated kernels for the *masita* in Barbacoa de Carnero con Masita (page 210), or read on to learn how to grind them into full-fledged *masa* (corn dough). The usual alkali today is *cal*, or calcium hydroxide. It can be ordered from drugstores by the ounce as "slaked lime." María and Ricardo's Tortilla Factory in Massachusetts will supply it by mail (page 320).

3 to 3 1/2 pounds (7 to 8 cups)

Place the corn in a colander and rinse under cold running water to wash off the dusty chaff. Combine the water and *cal* in a large non-reactive saucepan. Stir well to dissolve and add the corn, discarding any kernels that float.

Bring to a boil over high heat, then reduce the heat to low. The corn will be noticeably yellow (even blue corn will turn somewhat yellowish). Cook for 15 minutes, remove from heat, and let cool to room temperature. Let the corn soak, covered, for 4 hours at room temperature or overnight in the refrigerator. The kernels will now be visibly softened and swelled.

The last step is to remove the outer skins, now soft and gelatinous. Pour the contents of the saucepan into a large colander and rinse thoroughly under cold water. With the cold tap running, rub the kernels between the palms of your hands until the last of the gelatinous coating rinses off to reveal the kernel and corn germ (the inset pointed tip, which Mexicans often remove but I usually leave intact). When the coating is completely gone, thoroughly drain the *nixtamal*. It is now ready to use.

Nixtamal does not store well. It will keep, tightly covered, in the refrigerator for 2 or at the outside 3 days. If not using the full amount at once, freeze the surplus. It will keep for up to 3 months.

(I like to cook the *nixtamal* kernels in chicken stock until they pop open like flowers and eat the soup on a cold winter night.)

Masa (Treated Corn Dough)

In the Mexican kitchen, *masa* (Spanish for "dough") is what you get by grinding fresh *nixtamal* into a mass. When I say that Oaxacan corn dishes are incomparable, the *masa* that they're usually based on is the most crucial factor I have in mind. With no added fancy ingredients, the nixtamalized corn has such pure and good flavor that you can find yourself relishing the dough for its own sake.

The number of things you can do with *masa* is infinite. It can be thinned to make a drink (Atole Dulce, page 275). As a thickener, it lends wonderful flavor while binding soups or sauces. It makes delicious dumplings—the *chochoyotes* in Chichilo (page 162) should be tried by any dumpling fan. *Masa*-based tortillas are a fascinating family ranging from the small, thick *gordas* (when toasted, the chewy interior separates from the crusty outside) to the two branches of giant tortillas known as *blandas* (thin and soft; page 100) and *clayudas* (dense and sturdy; page 102). *Masa* can serve as a wrapping, shell, or base for any sort of filling and topping. This is how you encounter it in innumerable street snacks— hefty boat-shaped *tlacoyos*, the smaller fried shells called *garnachas*, or the simple empanadas made by folding a tortilla in half to wrap a *mole* filling (Empanadas de Amarillo, page 104).

Good *masa* is an indispensable ingredient for exploring Oaxacan cuisine. How do you obtain it in this country? I think most people would be wise to look for a tortilla factory—it's surprising how many turn up in local phone books across the country—and try to order it fresh-ground. If no tortilla factory exists anywhere near your home, you can order fresh *masa* by overnight express from María and Ricardo's Tortilla Factory in Massachusetts (see Mail Order Sources, page 320), who will also ship *masa* frozen. Fresh *masa* sours within about 2 days, so try to gauge the quantity you need and freeze any remainder.

I have tried *masa* from many different U.S. suppliers and usually find it good rather than superlative. The true, deep corn taste of Oaxacan *masa* isn't quite there. When the *masa* has to be thinned, I almost always use homemade chicken stock (page 74) instead of the more authentic water to try to boost the flavor, but it's not a perfect solution.

There are two alternatives to U. S. tortilla-factory *masa*. One is dehydrated powdered *masa*, often sold as *masa harina*. (Never confuse it with U.S. cornmeal, which is absolutely unacceptable!) It comes in 2- and 5-pound bags and has to be reconstituted by being mixed to a paste with liquid—again, I prefer chicken stock for extra body and flavor. Rehydrated *masa harina* is not as good as real *masa*, but I find it acceptable in all but a few cases. The two brands most widely available in this country are Maseca and Quaker; the latter can be ordered through any supermarket that carries Quaker cereals.

The basic technique of reconstituting *masa harina* is always the same, though the proportion of liquid may vary from recipe to recipe. Place the *masa harina* in a large mixing bowl and work in slightly warm water or stock with a wooden spoon or your bare hands until you have a fairly stiff dough—a little softer for tamales and firmer for tortillas. The exact amount of liquid needed tends to fluctuate from batch to batch.

The other possibility is to grind your own *masa* from homemade *nixtamal*. For centuries this was the only way of making *masa* in Mexico. People did it at home kneeling on the floor in front of the immemorial volcanic rock *metate*—a real Stone Age process that some people still use for small quantities when they want a particular consistency. But most cooks in Oaxaca now take their *nixtamal* to a local mill to be custom-ground (unless they buy fresh *masa* already ground to order). I have experimented with different home methods, and to my dismay they either didn't work or were nearly as grueling as bending over the *metate*! The problem is that the nixtamalized corn has enough starch to gum up most devices.

The food processor gave a very poor consistency. I tried the grain-grinding attachment of my KitchenAid electric mixer and can't recommend it—the attachment, actually intended for dry grains, works after a fashion, but it is very slow going. The solution I suggest if you passionately desire to grind your own *masa* is a hand-cranked, tinned cast-iron corn mill from South America—one Colombian machine is widely sold in Latin American stores under the brand names Corona and Universal—that clamps onto a table and can be adjusted to coarser or finer grinds. (As a general rule of thumb, coarsely ground *masa* is best for tamales, finely ground for tortillas and most other purposes such as thickening sauces. Keep the distinction in mind if ordering dough from a tortilla factory.)

Grinding with the mill is also difficult and time-consuming, but it is more efficient than the KitchenAid. I am giving directions for this method for the benefit of those who absolutely have to try everything by hand at least once, but I have to say that its practical uses are limited. To grind even 1 pound of *nixtamal* into *masa* can take close to 1 hour. It would have a definite advantage over buying factory *masa* only if you had access to some unusually good strain of corn.

Masa Molida a Mano

(Hand-ground Masa)

1 pound (about 2 cups) well-drained
  Nixtamal (page 92)

Water as necessary

***Slightly more than 1 pound (about 2 1/2 cups)* masa**

Clamp a cast-iron hand-operated corn mill firmly to a tabletop or counter with a plate or bowl under the grinding plates. Adjust the distance of the plates (by the calibration on my Universal mill, set at 3 for a fine and 5 for a coarse grind). Begin feeding handfuls of *nixtamal* into the hopper of the machine while turning the handle. Push down firmly with a wooden spoon or pusher to keep the kernels going in.

When all the corn is ground, gather up a handful between your fingers to judge the consistency. The ground *nixtamal* usually requires some water to form a proper dough. Add 2 to 3 tablespoons of water at a time, working the *masa* with your hands or a wooden spoon, until the mixture holds together well and is the consistency of a stiff cookie dough. The amount of water needed may be up to 1/2 to 2/3 cup.

Note: *Whether homemade or bought from a factory, fresh* masa *should be used quickly. Store in the refrigerator, tightly wrapped, for up to 2 days; freeze any unused portion. I find that* masa *for tortillas freezes less successfully than that for tamales, dumplings, and other purposes.*

About Tortillas

Tortillas in Oaxaca are virtually always corn tortillas from *masa*, not from wheat flour. Once you have tasted them, it's hard to be satisfied with most of the commercial U.S. tortillas. Commercial tortillas can be all right for some purposes, but for others they're no good at all. Think of trying to make one of those rustic Italian bread soups or salads out of pre-packaged supermarket white bread.

Even when U.S. cooks take the time to make their own tortillas, the same problem exists because—as I've already explained—we don't have some of the important corn varieties grown in Oaxaca. "Tortillas" there aren't just one standardized product. You can produce dramatically varied kinds for different purposes. The common accompaniment to meals are the huge, soft-textured, beautifully white *blandas*. On the other hand, the famous *clayudas* or *tlayudas* can be a meal in themselves (though they, too, occasionally serve as an accompaniment). They are large, chewy tortillas formed into a slightly thicker shape than *blandas*. *Clayudas* are griddle-baked until very dense and robust and usually eaten with toppings, like thin pizzas.

There are as many culinary uses for leftover as for fresh tortillas. They are wonderful heated in sauces or turned into casserole-like dishes. Unfortunately, this is where the problems presented by the wrong corn tend to rear their heads. Tortillas made with the fabulous starchy Oaxacan varieties never dissolve into a soggy mess when combined with sauces or other liquid ingredients. U.S. tortillas always turn soggy unless you go through the extra step of frying them before adding to sauces or casseroles. This is what I recommend in dishes like Chilaquiles con Salsa de Hoja Santa (page 132). It does add more fat, but also helps give the finished dish some texture.

Basic Corn Tortillas

1 1/2 pounds (about 3 cups) finely ground fresh *masa* (page 93) or reconstituted *masa* made by mixing 2 cups *masa harina* (page 94) with about 1 cup warm water to form a smooth, stiffish dough

2 teaspoons to 1 tablespoon vegetable oil, or as needed

*T*here is nothing specifically Oaxacan about these tortillas. They are nearly identical to the recipe I gave in my first book, *Food From My Heart*, for the kind of simple corn tortillas that are eaten all over Mexico.

Before beginning the recipe, please read my description of *nixtamal* and *masa* (pages 92 to 95). I recommend buying an inexpensive cast-aluminum tortilla press (or—if you can find one in a Mexican market—a large rectangular wooden one like those used in Oaxaca).

About 10 to 12 small (5- to 6-inch) tortillas

Before you begin, have ready a tortilla press (see Note, page 99, for alternative suggestion) and prepare a non-stick liner by cutting open two sides of a medium-size (about 6 inches square) heavy-duty plastic bag (such as a 1-quart zip-closing storage bag), to make a rectangle at least 12×6 inches. Open the press and place the liner in it with the creased edge next to the hinge.

Check the consistency of the *masa* by working it with your bare hand. It should be like a somewhat stiff but pliable cookie dough. Work in 2 to 4 tablespoons water if necessary.

Dampen your hands with cool water and shake off the excess. Shape the mixture into 10 to 12 ping-pong-size balls, remoistening your hands as necessary. Keep the balls of *masa* covered with a damp cloth to prevent them from drying out.

Heat a griddle or medium-size cast-iron skillet over high heat until a drop of water sizzles on contact. Quickly grease the griddle by moistening a bunched-up paper towel with a little vegetable oil and rubbing it over the surface. Adjust the heat as necessary to maintain a constant temperature on the griddle surface while you work.

Place a ball of dough in the center of the tortilla press between the two flaps of plastic. Lower the top of the press and push down on the handle to press out a tortilla between 5 and 6 inches in diameter and about 1/16 inch thick. Open the press. Peel off the top flap of plastic. Dampening your hands again if necessary, lift out the tortilla and peel away the bottom flap.

Place the tortilla on the hot griddle and cook about 1 1/2 minutes, until lightly flecked with brown on the underside. Turn with a spatula (I use my fingers) and cook for about 1 to 1 1/2 minutes on the other side. It may puff up slightly; if not, help the process by quickly pressing down on the tortilla with a bunched-up tea towel or a weight such as a heavy can. (If using a skillet, avoid brushing the hot sides!) Flip it over quickly and press on the other side. At once lift out onto a plate and wrap snugly in a cloth napkin or tea towel. Repeat with the remaining balls of dough, stacking and covering the tortillas as they are done.

Note: *If you have no tortilla press, there is one trick that I have found will work. It requires a small, round heavy object with a perfectly flat bottom such as a very small cast-iron skillet. Prepare the plastic liner as directed above, but place it directly on the counter with a ball of dough between the two flaps. Being super-careful not to tilt the weight unevenly, press straight down with the bottom of the skillet to form a flat, round 5- to 6-inch tortilla. Peel off the plastic as directed above and proceed with the recipe.*

Blandas
Large Soft Tortillas

1 1/2 pounds (about 3 cups) finely ground best-quality fresh *masa* (page 93)

2 teaspoons to 1 tablespoon vegetable oil

Oaxaca is known for outsize tortillas—big enough to be knights' shields. There is a very fine, soft kind and a hardy, dense kind. The former are called *blandas* and, though they can be made from different-colored strains of corn, are especially famous in a white version. In Oaxaca they are commonly 12 or even 15 inches in diameter, a size impractical for home cooks here to duplicate. The beautiful quality of the local corn *masa* is also impossible to recapture here. However, I am giving a rough equivalent based on the previous Basic Corn Tortillas. Mine are smaller than the originals, but even so they are too large to be made with an ordinary cast-aluminum tortilla press. If you cannot find one of the outsize wooden presses sometimes sold in Mexican neighborhood markets, you will have to use your hands, a rolling pin, or a heavy round object with a roughly 9-inch diameter and a perfectly flat bottom, such as a heavy casserole or cast-iron skillet. You will also need a larger plastic liner than that for a usual tortilla press.

Be very careful in pressing the tortillas and peeling them from the liner. Because of their thinness, they are more difficult to peel off in one piece. However, I find that a light dusting of *masa harina* makes the tortillas easier to peel off.

Use only fresh *masa* of the highest quality. Reconstituted *masa harina* does not have good enough flavor and texture for *blandas*.

6 to 8 blandas

Decide on a pressing method before beginning the recipe. Prepare a non-stick liner by cutting open two sides of a large heavy-duty plastic bag (such as a 1-gallon freezer storage bag) to make a rectangle at least 9 × 18 inches. If using a large tortilla press, open it and place the liner in it with the creased edge next to the hinge. Otherwise, simply place the liner on the counter and lightly dust it with dry *masa harina*.

Proceed as for Basic Corn Tortillas (page 98) up to the point of checking the consistency of the *masa* and moistening if necessary with a small amount of water. Form the dough into 6 to 8 equal-sized balls, keeping them covered with a damp cloth as you work.

Preheat a griddle or large cast-iron skillet over medium-high heat and lightly grease with the oil. Adjust the heat as necessary to maintain a constant temperature on the griddle surface.

Form the tortillas one at a time by placing each ball of dough between the plastic flaps (which should be lightly dusted with *masa harina* each time) and pressing into a circle about 8 inches in diameter. If using a rolling pin or your fingertips, try to keep the shape as round and even as possible. If pressing with the bottom of a heavy object, be super-careful to press straight down without tilting. (I use a combination method, first pressing and then rolling.) The tortilla must be of uniform thickness from edge to edge.

Peel off the plastic liner (they might tear but don't despair—glue them back together with your fingers when you put them on the cooking surface) and griddle-bake, regreasing the pan as necessary. Allow 1 1/2 minutes on the first side, then turn and cook 1 1/2 minutes on the second side while pushing down lightly with a bunched-up tea towel all over to help the tortillas puff slightly, and lastly, turn to cook about 1 minute on the first side, again pushing down. As they are done, wrap snugly in a napkin or tea towel.

Clayudas

Large, Dense Tortillas with Toppings

1 1/2 pounds (about 3 cups) finely
   ground best-quality *masa* (page 93)

2 teaspoons to 1 tablespoon
   vegetable oil

1/4 cup *Asiento* (page 36)

2 cups Frijoles Negros Colados
   (page 235), cooled

1 cup Salsa de Chile Pasilla
   (page 254), Salsa de Gusanitos
   (page 261), or other preferred
   homemade Oaxacan salsa

1 pound Oaxacan string cheese
   (page 31) or medium-sharp white
   cheddar, shredded

*T*o be perfectly honest, this recipe is only an approximation of something I can't bear to leave out. I have such wonderful memories of mild, heavenly evenings in Oaxaca City when people flock to the food stalls around the Benito Juárez market and sit eating clayudas as we would eat pizza. They are lustier, chewier cousins of *blandas*—huge tortillas cooked to a dense consistency and served with an array of toppings. In the classic version, the tortillas are first spread with a layer of *asiento* (the settled-out bottom layer that forms as rendered lard cools) and then topped with a layer of beans, a salsa, and shredded cheese.

When I came home I spent much time and effort trying to duplicate the pleasures of *clayudas*. As usual, I had to admit that the effect is different without starchy Oaxacan corn. The closest I came to the original was with homemade *masa* ground from a particular kind of blue corn supplied by María and Ricardo's Tortilla Factory (see Mail Order Sources, page 320). *Masa* made with dent corn also gives a satisfactory result. Don't try to make *clayudas* with packaged *masa harina*—it just doesn't have enough character. And don't try to find a low-calorie substitute for *asiento*. I suppose you could leave it out entirely (and miss half the flavor of the dish), or use bacon drippings (which have a very different taste), but *asiento* is so important that I really recommend the extra effort.

See the preceding recipe for Blandas for suggestions on pressing out the large tortillas.

6 *servings*

Decide on a pressing method from those mentioned for Blandas (page 100). Make a non-stick liner by cutting open two sides of a large heavy-duty plastic bag (such as a 1-gallon freezer storage bag) to make a rectangle at least 9×18 inches. If using a large tortilla press, open it and place the liner in it with the creased edge next to the hinge. Otherwise, place the liner directly on the counter and lightly dust it with 1 to 2 teaspoons dry *masa harina*.

Proceed as for Basic Corn Tortillas (page 98) up to the point of checking the consistency of the *masa*, moistening if necessary with a little water. Form the dough into 6 equal-sized balls, covering them with a damp cloth as you work.

Preheat a griddle or large cast-iron skillet over medium heat and lightly grease with the oil. Adjust the heat as necessary to maintain a constant temperature on the griddle surface.

Form the tortillas one at a time by placing each ball of dough between the plastic flaps (which should be dusted with *masa harina* each time) and pressing into a circle about 8 inches in diameter. If not using a wooden tortilla press, press down with the bottom of a heavy object, being super-careful to press straight down without tilting. Then use a rolling pin or your fingertips to press out the tortilla to the desired size. Try to keep the shape round and symmetrical. The tortilla must be of uniform thickness from edge to edge.

Peel off the plastic liner (the tortilla might tear but don't worry, you can glue it back together when you put it on the cooking surface) and griddle-bake as for Basic Corn Tortillas, but without the step of pushing down on the tortilla to make it puff up. Allow 1 1/2 minutes on the first side, 1 1/2 minutes on the second side, and another 1 1/2 minutes on the first side. Regrease the pan as necessary. As they are done, cover with a napkin or tea towel.

Uncover one clayuda at a time and spread with about 2 teaspoons of the *asiento*. Add about 1/3 cup of the puréed beans. Spoon 3 tablespoons of the salsa over the beans and top with about 3 tablespoons of the shredded cheese. Rewarm on the griddle, one at a time, to melt the cheese. Serve at once.

Empanadas de Amarillo
Folded Tortillas with Amarillo

For the filling

1 recipe (2 1/2 to 3 cups) Amarillo I
(page 142)

1 cup cooked shredded chicken
(page 75)

1 cup shredded Oaxacan string
cheese (page 31)

4 fresh *hoja santa* leaves (page 36),
torn into 2 to 3 pieces each,
or 10 to 12 cilantro sprigs

For the tortillas

1 pound (about 2 cups) *masa*
(page 93), fresh or reconstituted
by mixing 2 cups *masa harina*
(page 94) with approximately
1 cup water

2 tablespoons lard (preferably
home-rendered; page 36)

"Empanadas" in this case means not pastry turnovers but fresh corn tortillas (enriched with a little lard in the dough) folded in half around a filling of Mole Amarillo with shredded chicken and cheese. It is a universal Oaxacan street snack and makes a great party appetizer.

Before beginning the recipe, see the directions for preparing a tortilla press with a plastic liner (or shaping tortillas without a press) on pages 100 to 101.

10 to 12 empanadas (5 to 6 servings)

Heat the Amarillo and keep warm while making the tortillas.

In a large mixing bowl, combine the *masa* with the lard, working them together well with your hands. Form the mixture into 10 to 12 ping-pong-size balls. Have ready a tortilla press and plastic liner; press the balls of *masa*, one at a time, into 6-inch tortillas. Heat a griddle or heavy skillet over medium-high heat until a drop of water sizzles on contact. Place a tortilla on the griddle and cook on one side for 1 minute. Flip over and place about 3 tablespoons of the Amarillo in the center. Sprinkle with 2 tablespoons each of shredded chicken and cheese and a piece of *hoja santa* or cilantro sprig; fold the tortilla over into a turnover shape, pressing down the sides to seal. Cook the empanada on each side until slightly browned, about 1 minute per side. Repeat with the remaining tortillas. Serve at once.

About Tamales

Everywhere in Mexico tamales are fiesta food—the equivalent of "Let's celebrate!" On all occasions like weddings, baptisms, and village saint's days when only the best will do, some kind of tamales will be the most treasured item on the menu. The further south you go in the country, the more amazing and inventive the range of different tamales becomes. Chiapas, Oaxaca's next neighbor and the southernmost state of Mexico, is considered the premier tamal state. But Oaxacan tamales are nearly as famous. The more of them I discover, the more there still is to discover.

The usual concept of a tamal is that it's a *masa* mixture, with or without other ingredients, cooked in a steamer inside a folded packet of leaves or husks. But Oaxacan tamales aren't necessarily limited to that. There are tamales that are baked in ovens or on griddles, and ones made with no real wrapping. The regional variations are dizzying. In Teotitlán del Valle I have had tamales in the Valley Zapotec style that are made by forming thin corn tortillas, topping them with some Mole Amarillo and shredded chicken, and elegantly rolling them in cornstalk leaves to create a pure, virtually fatless dish probably very close to Oaxaca's pre-Hispanic roots. (See Tamales de Amarillo, page 122.) In the Isthmus of Tehuantepec they pile on the fat in proportions that amaze even other Mexicans, who usually like richness in tamales. I regularly found tamales containing equal proportions (by weight) of *masa* and lard, sometimes with ground pork cracklings added for good measure. (See Tamales de Camarón, page 128, for one slightly toned-down adaptation.)

They have other tricks with tamales in the Isthmus. Often they ignore the usual Mexican way of spreading a dollop of prepared *masa*-lard mixture in one layer over a corn husk before folding it; instead they shape the mixture into a ball and construct a clever little cradle of several husks around it. (I could not find corn husks in the U.S. that had the right thickness to duplicate the method, so my tamal recipes generally use the more orthodox wrapping technique.) Or they put a tamal-like mixture and a bit of special filling onto a bit of leaf used for an aromatic underpinning. The small, tender, glossy leaves of the almond trees that grow throughout the Isthmus are used this way for an "undressed" version of the seafood tamales called *gueta bi'ngui* (page 126).

Banana-leaf tamales are popular everywhere. (Bananas, like almonds, were brought to Oaxaca from the Old World by the Spanish.) The leaf releases oils in cooking that lend a delicate aroma to the food. I am very fond of this fragrant quality and often switch around traditional wrappers and contents, pairing up banana leaves with fillings that would traditionally be cooked in corn husks. Try it—banana leaves are widely available in Latin American and tropical Asian markets. Just remember that they are seldom formed into packets as small as corn-husk tamales. An average-size corn-husk tamal usually takes about 1/4 to 1/3 of *masa*-lard mixture plus a tablespoon of any flavored meat (or other) filling that you are adding. With a usual banana-leaf tamal you can expect to use about 1/2 to 3/4 cup of *masa* mixture and between 1/4 and 1/3 cup of the chosen filling.

Basic Tamal Procedures

For Corn-husk Tamales

Dried corn husks are sold in Latin American stores in different-size packages (4 ounces, 8 ounces, or 1 pound). They are always softened by soaking in hot water before being used to wrap tamales. I suggest buying one or more 1-pound packages at a time, since most of my recipes are for fairly large quantities and you cannot always count on getting the same number of usable husks per package. Sometimes it is easy to select the suggested number of husks as soon as you open the package; sometimes they can't be pulled apart and counted until they have been soaked. A package may contain a larger or smaller number of unusable crinkly bits. Another unpredictable factor is that some husks may prove to be torn, or that they may be smaller than expected so that you end up with slightly too much filling. For this reason I suggest always selecting 4 or 5 extra husks beyond the number mentioned in the recipe to have a bit of backup.

The procedure for soaking is simple: Place the corn husks in a deep bowl and cover generously with hot water. Let soak for 30 minutes or longer while you prepare the other ingredients. Drain the husks and pat dry before starting to add the filling or fillings. (Usually, though not always, you will be making a *masa*-lard filling and a smaller amount of a separate, more highly flavored filling.)

Working with a few at a time, fill the tamales by using a thin spatula to spread the designated amount (usually about 1/4 to 1/3 cup) of the *masa* mixture across the wider end of the husk, covering it from side to side and extending about halfway up to the narrow tip. (If you run out of proper-sized husks, paste together

106

Banana-leaf (foreground) and corn-husk tamales at the Mercado de Abasto in Oaxaca City

two smaller ones with a bit of *masa* before spreading.) Place the designated amount (usually about 1 to 2 tablespoons) of any separate filling in the center of the *masa*.

Now the tamal must be folded. Small tamales can be rolled up lengthwise like cigarettes. The usual method for average-sized tamales is to bring the right edge over to the center and fold the left side over it, then fold the narrow end of the packet even with the wide end. You will have a tamal folded in half crosswise that needs no further tying or sealing. As they are filled and folded, place the tamales on a baking sheet until ready to cook. If you plan to hold them longer than 1/2 hour before cooking, they must be refrigerated, as the *masa* sours quickly. (Uncooked tamales, covered with plastic wrap, can be refrigerated for up to a day or frozen for up to 1 month. You do not need to thaw them before cooking, but you should increase the cooking time by 10 minutes.)

Have ready a steamer with a basket or steaming insert, or improvise your own arrangement. It is not always necessary to have the tamales raised all the way above the level of the boiling water. Sometimes if they are well wrapped, you can simply put them on the bottom of a large Dutch oven or soup pot, *open ends facing up*, propped teepee-style against a central support like a large ball of wadded-up aluminum foil. Or if you prefer, place a wire rack on supports like sawed-off tin cans and arrange the tamales on the rack, again with open ends up. I like to place some extra corn husks over the tamales to help absorb steam. Pour boiling water into the pan to a depth of at least 1 inch, cover very tightly, and steam over medium-low heat to maintain a simmer (not a boil) until fully cooked, usually 45 minutes to 1 hour. Keep a kettle of water hot on another burner; from time to time check on the water level in the steamer and replenish with boiling water as necessary, always being careful to shield your face from the steam. When the tamales are done, uncover the pan. Let the tamales stand 10 minutes before serving. Each guest unwraps his own.

For Banana-Leaf Tamales

One-pound packages of frozen banana leaves are available in Latin and tropical Asian markets, but they are not totally problem-free. Often you find that the pieces have split so badly before you remove them from the package that they won't yield the proper number of trimmed rectangles to wrap the filling. It's a useful precaution to buy an extra package for backup.

In any case, thaw the frozen leaves, remove from the package, and gently unfold on the counter. Wipe the pieces with a clean damp cloth. Cut into squares or rectangles of the designated size. (14×11 inches is a good all-purpose size.) Try as much as possible to keep from splitting the leaves. But if you end up with unavoidable splits, cut some smaller pieces to serve as patches. Tear off long thin strips from the trimmings, to be used later as "string" ties, 1 long one or 2 tied together per tamal. (Kitchen twine is fine if you don't have enough suitable trimmings.)

Prepare the other ingredients as directed in the recipe. Soften the trimmed banana-leaf rectangles by holding each over an open flame for a few seconds or briefly heating on a hot griddle. (This brings out the flavor and helps keep brittle leaves from splitting when you fold them into packets.)

Working with 1 piece at a time, place the designated amount of *masa* mixture (usually about 1/2 to 2/3 cup) in the center and spread it out into an oval about 4×3 inches. Place the designated amount (anything from about 3 tablespoons to 1/3 cup) of any additional filling in the center of the *masa* oval. Fold over the right and left edges of the rectangle toward each other, overlapping slightly. Fold the top and bottom edges toward each other. You should have a neat flat packet (usually about 5×4 inches if you start with a 14×11-inch rectangle). Tie securely with leaf "string" ties.

Have a steamer arrangement ready. Banana-leaf tamales should lie on a flat platform such as a wire rack raised well above the level of the boiling water. Arrange them in layers as necessary, seam side up. Place some extra banana-leaf pieces on top to help absorb steam. Pour boiling water into the bottom of the pan to a depth of 1 to 2 inches, cover tightly, and steam over medium heat for the specified length of time (usually 45 minutes to 1 hour). Keep a kettle of water hot on another burner; occasionally check the water level in the steamer and replenish as necessary, always shielding your face from the steam. When they are done, remove the lid and let the tamales stand for 10 minutes before serving. Each guest unwraps his own.

Basic Tamal Dough

*P*erhaps this is a misnomer. There is no such thing as a basic tamal dough used by all Oaxacan cooks for all sorts of tamales. The proportion of fat—always lard, with no substitutes—to prepared corn dough varies so enormously that no one formula will do. However, the general procedure almost always follows the same routine.

Those of you who have used my first book, *Food From My Heart,* will notice that the following directions don't quite match the Basic Tamal Dough given there. The reason is that though the same three essential ingredients—lard, *masa*, and salt—are still the basis of the dish, one of them has different qualities in Oaxaca. The local lard has a very special character. For Oaxacan food generally but especially for tamales, I feel it is important to use the home-rendered lard for which I give directions on page 36 or the closest thing you can get to it, lard rendered at a small Latin American butcher shop and put up with no additives. (Hungarian and German butchers also sometimes have good lard.) It is too soft to develop the fluffiness of commercial hydrogenated lard, but it contributes fantastic flavor.

The quality of the corn *masa* (page 93) is also crucial. *Masa* for tamales is ground coarser than for tortillas and (in Oaxaca at least) has the full flavor and texture of the local corn varieties. *Masa* prepared from packaged *masa harina* is too fine for best results, though it is acceptable in a pinch. Do your best to find (or make) fresh *masa* ground for tamales.

The third component is salt. The amounts used in good tamal dough often seem excessive to U.S. cooks. However, I would remind you first that (like the fat) some of it dissolves out in steaming and, second, that undersalted tamales always seem insipid and somehow incomplete.

Please note that in my recipes the preferred way of measuring lard and *masa* is always by weight. All professional cooks know that this is the most accurate method. In other recipes I'm willing to go along with the convention of giving cup measurements first, but for tamal dough the scale tells more than the cup. For the record, 1 pound of *masa* equals slightly more or less than 2 cups, depending on the type of corn and the amount of water absorbed; 1 pound of home-rendered lard equals about 2 cups. Mass-produced hydrogenated lard will be closer to 2 1/2 or 2 1/3 cups because it has more air beaten into it.

The following general method can be applied to nearly any tamal recipe.

Yield varies according to the proportions used, but a general guideline is that 1/3 pound of lard and 1 pound of masa *will produce 1 1/3 pounds of* masa *filling, enough for 15 average-size to large corn-husk tamales or 8 average-size banana-leaf tamales.*

Place the specified amount of lard in a mixing bowl or the large bowl of an electric mixer set at medium speed. With a wooden spoon or the mixer blades, beat for 1 to 2 minutes, until somewhat aerated. Begin beating in the *masa* a handful at a time, stopping occasionally to scrape down the sides of the bowl with a rubber spatula. At this point you must make a judgment call—whether or not to add a little liquid. Unless otherwise specified, the consistency should be that of a very thick, pasty porridge. When working with *masa* made from *masa harina* I sometimes find that I need to add 5 to 6 tablespoons of water or chicken stock to achieve this consistency. With other batches, I don't need to add any liquid. When the desired consistency is reached, beat in the salt.

Lard (preferably home-rendered; page 36)

Masa, coarse-ground fresh if possible (page 93), or reconstituted *masa* made by mixing *masa harina* (page 94) with warm water or homemade chicken stock (page 74) to form a paste

Additional water or chicken stock (optional, depending on consistency of *masa*)

Salt

Tamales de Chepil

Chepil Tamales

20 to 24 small dried corn husks
  (page 106)

8 ounces (about 1 cup) lard
  (preferably home-rendered;
  page 36)

1 1/2 pounds (about 3 cups) coarsely
  ground fresh *masa* (page 93),
  homemade or bought from a
  supplier, or reconstituted *masa*
  made by mixing 2 3/4 cups
  masa harina (page 94) with
  about 1 3/4 cups chicken stock
  (preferably homemade; page 74)
  or water

2 teaspoons salt

One 6-ounce package frozen *chepil*
  (page 32), thawed and leaves
  stripped from stems

4 ounces *queso añejo* (page 31),
  crumbled (about 1 cup) or aged
  ricotta salata, grated

With one bite of these elegant tamales, the distinctive grassy flavor of the southern Mexican herb called *chepil* or *chipilín* transports me to Oaxaca. When I first encountered it, *chepil* was unknown in the U.S. In the last few years I've been amazed and delighted to find it here by the name *chipilín* in many Latin American grocery stores, in a good frozen version from Guatemala. There is no substitute, but if unable to find the crucial ingredient you can turn Tamales de Chepil into Tamales de Cilantro by using 1 cup cilantro leaves stripped from the stems. The flavor, though quite unlike, will be fresh and herbal.

These tamales make a delicious side dish with roasted or pit-barbecued meats, or with stews such as Chichilo con Chochoyotes (page 162). I also love them as a first course served with Salsa de Chile Pasilla (page 254). Sometimes I deliberately make more than I need in order to turn the leftovers into Sopa Seca de Tamales de Chepil (page 113).

20 to 24 tamales (10 to 12 servings as a first course or side dish or as part of buffet-party menu)

Have ready a steamer arrangement.

Place the corn husks in a deep bowl, cover with hot water, and let soak for about 30 minutes.

In a large mixing bowl or electric mixer bowl, combine the lard, *masa*, and salt by the directions for Basic Tamal Dough (page 110). Add the *chepil* and cheese and beat until well incorporated.

Drain the corn husks and pat dry. Using about 3 to 4 tablespoons of the *masa* mixture per husk, fill, fold, and steam the tamales by the directions on page 106.

Sopa Seca de Tamales de Chepil

Casseroled Chepil Tamales

María Concepción Portillo de Carballido, my first Oaxacan cooking teacher, introduced me to this satisfying dish. For those who don't know the term *sopa seca* ("dry soup"), it covers a lot of dishes where starchy ingredients like rice, pasta, or in this case tamales absorb liquid. Tamales have great possibilities as a *sopa seca*—it's worth making them just for this purpose if you don't have leftovers. Double the recipe for a great party buffet dish.

Other kinds of tamales are delicious served this way. If you don't feel like making the creamy poblano sauce given here, try baking these or other steamed tamales with 2 to 3 cups Caldillo de Tomate (page 259).

4 servings

8 Tamales de Chepil (page 112), cooled

3 poblano chiles (page 45)

1 large ripe tomato

1 tablespoon lard (preferably home-rendered; page 36) or vegetable oil

1 small onion, finely chopped

1 small garlic clove, minced

1/2 cup Mexican *crema* (page 33) or heavy cream

1/2 teaspoon salt, or to taste

Freshly ground black pepper

Remove the tamales from their wrappings and cut into 1/2-inch slices.

Griddle-roast the poblano chiles and tomato by the directions on page 26. Place the chiles in a plastic or paper bag for 10 to 12 minutes to soften the skins; peel, seed, and cut into strips about 1/4 inch wide. Peel the tomato, briefly process in a blender to purée, and force through a medium-mesh sieve into a bowl. Set aside.

Preheat the oven to 350°F.

In a small saucepan, heat the lard until rippling over medium-high heat. Add the onion and garlic and cook, stirring frequently, for 2 minutes. Add the poblano strips and cook for 3 minutes longer. Add the tomato purée and cream; season with salt and pepper. Bring to a boil and immediately reduce the heat to low. Cook, partly covered, stirring occasionally, for 10 minutes. Let cool slightly.

Arrange half the sliced tamales in one layer in a greased 1 1/2-quart baking dish deep enough to hold all the ingredients in 2 layers. Pour half the sauce over the tamales. Add another layer of tamales and cover with the remaining sauce. Bake for 15 to 20 minutes, until the sauce is hot and bubbling.

Tamalitos de Cambray
"Chambray" Tamales

Banana leaves for wrapping (page 108), thawed if frozen

12 guajillo chiles (page 47), tops and seeds removed

1 large ripe tomato

3/4 pound beef round, in one piece

3/4 pound pork butt, in one piece

1 small head of garlic

10 whole black peppercorns, bruised

1 tablespoon plus 1 teaspoon salt, or to taste

1 teaspoon dried thyme, crumbled

1 pound 3 ounces (about 2 1/2 cups) lard (preferably home-rendered; page 36)

1 medium onion, chopped

2 ripe plantains (page 39), peeled and cut into 1/4-inch dice

1/4 cup small pitted green olives

1/4 cup dark raisins

Freshly ground black pepper

2 pounds (about 4 cups) coarsely ground fresh *masa* (page 93), homemade or bought from a supplier, or reconstituted *masa* made by mixing 3 1/2 cups *masa harina* (page 94) with 2 1/4 cups chicken stock (preferably home-made; page 74) or water

6 hard-cooked eggs, peeled (optional)

*T*he origin of the name, according to the *Diccionario de Mexicanísmos*, is that at one time these delicate tamales were cooked inside small bags of fine chambray. Now they are wrapped in corn husks or banana leaves. This banana-leaf version is adapted from a recipe I learned from Yolanda Cacho in Juchitán.

If desired, cut the raisins in half and soak in a little warm sherry before adding to the filling. However, this is never done in Oaxaca.

12 tamales (12 servings as first course or light dinner entrée)

Have ready a steamer arrangement.

Remove the banana leaves from the package; unfold carefully and wipe clean as directed on page 108. With kitchen scissors, cut out twelve 14×11-inch rectangles. Tear off long thin strands from the remaining leaves to serve as "string" ties for the leaf packets. Set aside.

Wash and griddle-dry the chiles by the directions on page 45. Place in a deep bowl, cover generously with boiling water, and let soak for at least 20 minutes. Griddle-roast the tomato by the directions on page 26; peel, seed, and chop fine, saving the juices. Set aside.

Place the beef and pork in a medium-size saucepan. Break off and reserve 4 cloves of garlic; add the remaining garlic to the meat. Add the peppercorns, 1 teaspoon salt, and enough water to cover (about 3 cups). Bring to a boil over high heat; at once reduce the heat to low, skim off any foam that accumulates on the top, and cook, partly covered, for 30 to 35 minutes. Remove the meat from the broth (which can be strained and saved for another use). When it is cool enough to handle, tear into fine shreds. Set aside.

Drain the soaked chiles. Peel 2 of the remaining garlic cloves and place in a blender with the chiles and thyme. Process to a purée. With a wooden spoon or pusher, force the mixture through a medium-mesh sieve into a bowl. In a small saucepan, heat 2 tablespoons of the lard over medium-high heat until rippling. Add the chile purée and cook, stirring constantly, for 5 minutes. Set aside.

Peel and mince the remaining 2 garlic cloves. In a large skillet, heat another 2 tablespoons of the lard over medium-high heat until rippling. Add the minced garlic and chopped onion; cook, stirring occasionally, until the onion is translucent, about 3 minutes. Add the reserved chopped tomato with its juices and cook, stirring occasionally, for about 5 minutes, to concentrate slightly. Stir in the plantains, olives, and raisins and the shredded beef and pork; cook for another 5 minutes, to bring out and meld the flavors. Taste for seasoning; add more salt and freshly ground black pepper to taste. Remove the meat filling from the heat and let cool while you prepare the *masa* mixture.

In a small saucepan, gently melt all the remaining lard. Remove from the heat and let cool until lukewarm but still liquid. In a mixing bowl, combine and beat the lard, *masa*, and remaining 1 tablespoon salt by the directions for Basic Tamal Dough (page 110).

Prepare the banana-leaf packets. Briefly hold each of the rectangles over an open flame to soften, or place for a few seconds on a hot griddle. Stack them by the work surface. Place a 1/2-cup dollop of the *masa* mixture on each. With the back of a spoon, flatten out the *masa* slightly into an oval shape. Spoon about 1/3 cup of the meat filling over the center of the *masa*. Spoon 2 to 3 tablespoons of the chile purée over the filling. If using the optional hard-cooked eggs, cut them in half lengthwise and top the filling of each tamal with half an egg. Fold up the banana leaves as directed on page 109 to enclose the filling in neat rectangular packets, then tie shut with the leaf "strings" or kitchen twine. Steam the tamales by the directions on page 109, allowing 1 hour cooking time.

Tamales de Huitlacoche

Huitlacoche Tamales

2 poblano chiles (page 45)

1 1/2 pounds (about 3 cups) coarsely ground fresh *masa* (page 93), homemade or bought from a supplier, or reconstituted *masa* made by mixing 2 3/4 cups *masa harina* (page 94) with about 1 3/4 cups chicken stock (preferably homemade; page 74) or water

8 ounces (about 1 generous cup) lard (preferably home-rendered; page 36)

1/4 cup (approximately) chicken stock (preferably homemade; page 74) or water

1 tablespoon plus 1 teaspoon salt

14 large dried corn husks (page 106)

1 small onion, finely chopped

1 garlic clove, minced

8 ounces *huitlacoche*, fresh, canned, or frozen and thawed

2 tablespoons fresh epazote leaves, stripped from stems and finely chopped, or 2 teaspoons dried epazote, crumbled (page 35)

4 ounces Oaxacan string cheese (page 31) or medium-sharp white cheddar, shredded (about 1 cup)

*T*his is a southern and central Mexican dish that I have often had in Oaxaca and can't resist including here. Now that U.S. cooks have increasing access to *huitlacoche* or *cuitlacoche*, the delectable corn fungus that Mexicans prize like truffles, these are among the simplest as well as best of tamales. Some enterprising growers sell *huitlacoche* at farmers' markets during the corn season, and it is also available frozen by mail order. Once in a while it can be found canned in Mexican groceries (see Mail Order Sources, page 320).

14 tamales (about 7 servings)

Have ready a steamer arrangement.

Griddle-roast the chiles by the directions on page 42. Place in a plastic or paper bag for 10 to 15 minutes to loosen the skins; peel and seed the chiles. Chop the flesh fine. Set aside.

In a mixing bowl, combine the *masa*, all but 1 tablespoon of the lard, and most of the chicken stock by the directions for Basic Tamal Dough (page 110). Beat until very smooth and silky, adding the rest of the stock if necessary to achieve the right consistency. Beat in the salt. Set aside.

Place the corn husks in a deep bowl and cover with hot water. Let soak for 30 minutes while you prepare the other ingredients.

In a medium-size skillet, heat the remaining 1 tablespoon lard over medium heat until rippling. Add the onion and garlic. Cook, stirring frequently, for 3 minutes, until the onion is translucent. Stir in the chopped poblano chiles and cook for 1 minute. Add the *huitlacoche*, epazote, and remaining 1 teaspoon salt. Reduce the heat to low and cook for 5 minutes longer, stirring occasionally. Remove from the heat and let cool to room temperature. Stir in the cheese.

Drain the corn husks and pat dry. Spread 1/4 to 1/3 cup of the *masa* mixture across the wide end of each by the directions for basic corn-husk tamales on page 106 and place about 2 to 3 tablespoons of the *huitlacoche* mixture in the center of the *masa*. Fold and steam the tamales as directed on page 108.

Freshly baked bread cooling in the courtyard by the oven in Juchitán

Tamales de Etla en Hoja de Aguacate

Etla-style Tamales with Avocado Leaves

4 ounces (about 1/2 cup) home-rendered lard (page 36)

1 pound (about 2 cups) best-quality coarse-ground fresh *masa* (page 93), homemade or bought from a supplier

1 tablespoon salt, or to taste

Two 1/4-ounce packages dried avocado leaves (see page 28)

On one of my visits to Juchitán in the Isthmus of Tehuantepec I was introduced to a group of artists who were in town for a major exhibition. I struck up a conversation with the painter Juan Alcázar, who comes from the town of Etla in the Valley of Oaxaca and is as proud of his home's culinary traditions as the Isthmians are of theirs. He described some fascinating Etla specialties to me, including an unusual type of tamal wrapped in fresh avocado leaves. The next time I was in Etla I went looking for the tamales at the market. They were as exquisite as he'd said.

When I came back to New York I sought to recreate the avocado-leaf tamales. I think I've succeeded in capturing the spirit, but the details had to be adapted. The ingredients are so simple that each one makes a tremendous difference.

In the market tamales, the corn *masa* was fantastically good, better than any I've ever found in the U.S. This is one case where reconstituted *masa harina* would just be a travesty. You absolutely must have superior-quality coarse-ground *masa* for these tamales. Also, only home-rendered lard will do (or possibly lard made by a very good Latin American butcher). The hydrogenated version in packages is so flavorless I wouldn't even dream of using it. The other crucial ingredient, the fresh avocado leaves, doesn't exist here. The original tamales were wrapped all over in the fragrant, pliable leaves. Here I improvised by enclosing the tamales in parchment paper and using a small amount of dried avocado leaves (too brittle to be good wrappers) to perfume the *masa*.

8 tamales (8 servings as part of a large party menu, 4 servings as a main dish)

Have ready a steamer arrangement with a rack.

Cut out eight rectangles of parchment paper approximately 7 1/2 × 15 inches.

Combine the lard and *masa* by the directions for Basic Tamal Dough (page 110). Beat in the salt.

Pick over the avocado leaves, trying to choose uniformly sized leaves and allowing 2 large ones per tamal. If they are of very unequal sizes, allow about 6 different-sized leaves per tamal.

Line up the parchment-paper rectangles on the counter like sheets of typing paper. Working with one at a time, place one large avocado leaf lengthwise in the center. (If you have mismatched sizes, place one of the bigger ones just below the center and two or more small ones just above it.) Form about 1/3 cup of the lard-*masa* mixture into an oval about 3×4 inches, centered right on top of the avocado leaf. Place another avocado leaf (or leaves) lengthwise in the center of the *masa*. Fold the sides of the parchment paper together to form one long rectangle; seal by twisting the ends like a party favor.

Once all are done, place the tamales, seam side up, on the steamer rack, arranging in layers as necessary but being sure that they are all lying flat. Using the directions on page 108, steam over medium-low heat for 25 to 30 minutes. Serve at once; unlike most tamales, these lose their tender melting quality after a few minutes.

Tamales de Guajolote con Mole Negro

Turkey Tamales with Mole Negro

Banana leaves for wrapping (page 108), thawed if frozen

2 turkey drumsticks or 1 thigh and drumstick

1 small onion, unpeeled

2 garlic cloves, unpeeled

8 whole black peppercorns

2 1/2 teaspoons salt, or to taste

1 1/2 cups Mole Negro de Oaxaca (page 168) or Mole Negro de Teotitlán (page 164)

8 ounces (about 1 cup) lard (preferably home-rendered; page 36)

1 1/2 pounds (about 3 cups) coarse-ground fresh *masa* (page 93), homemade or bought from a supplier, or reconstituted *masa* made by mixing 2 1/4 cups *masa harina* (page 94) with 1 3/4 cups chicken stock (preferably home-made; page 74) or water

These are one of the most renowned Oaxacan classics: succulent banana-leaf tamales with a fluffy pillow of *masa* infused with the rich flavors of black *mole* and shredded cooked turkey. The meat has to be cooked by a moist-heat method, or it will be tasteless and dry, so I don't recommend using leftover roast turkey. Simmer pieces of turkey in liquid and use the most flavorful parts, not the white breast meat.

Though the black *mole* version of turkey tamales is best-known, the dish is equally good with Mole Rojo, Coloradito, or Amarillo.

8 tamales (8 servings as first course or light dinner entrée)

Have ready a steamer arrangement.

Remove the banana leaves from the package; unfold and wipe clean as directed on page 109. With kitchen scissors, cut out eight 12×10-inch rectangles. Tear off long thin strips from the remaining leaves to serve as "string" ties for the packets. Set aside.

Place the turkey pieces in a medium-size saucepan with the onion, garlic, peppercorns, and 1 teaspoon salt (or to taste). Add enough water to cover (about 4 cups) and bring to a boil over high heat. Reduce the heat to medium-low and cook, partly covered, until the meat is falling off the bones, about 35 to 40 minutes. Remove the turkey pieces from the broth (which can be strained and saved for another purpose); when cool enough to handle, remove the skin and tear the meat into long shreds. You should have about 2 cups. Set aside.

In a small saucepan, heat the *mole* to a boil over medium heat, reduce the heat to low, and cook for 5 minutes. Stir in the shredded turkey. Set aside.

Combine the lard and *masa* by the directions for Basic Tamal Dough (page 110). Beat in the remaining 1 1/2 teaspoons salt.

Prepare the banana-leaf packets. Briefly hold each of the cut rectangles over an open flame to make them more pliable, or place for a few seconds on a hot griddle. Stack them by the work surface. Place a heaping 1/2-cup dollop of the *masa* mixture on each. With the back of a spoon, flatten out the *masa* slightly into an oval shape. Spoon about 1/4 cup of the turkey *mole*-filling over the *masa*. Fold up the banana leaves as directed on page 109 to enclose the filling in neat rectangular packets, then tie shut with the leaf "strings" or kitchen twine. Steam the tamales by the directions on page 109, allowing 1 hour cooking time.

Tamales de Amarillo
Tamales with Yellow Mole

10 large dried corn husks (page 106)

2 large or 4 medium fresh *hoja santa* leaves or 4 to 5 dried leaves, crumbled (page 36)

1 pound (about 2 cups) finely ground *masa* (page 93), either fresh or reconstituted by mixing 1 1/2 cups *masa harina* (page 94) with 1 1/4 cups warm homemade chicken stock (page 74) or water

1 teaspoon salt, or to taste

1 1/2 cups *Amarillo I* (page 142)

1 cup cooked shredded chicken

When the Spanish introduced cooking fats to the New World, they revolutionized the whole concept of tamales. Today virtually all are filled with a mixture of *masa* and lard. Without the added fat the *masa* would be almost inedibly dense. I'd always wondered how the pre-Hispanic peoples could have made tamales without lard to lighten the dough. Insight came from Zoyla Mendoza, the inspired Valley Zapotec cook who has been my mentor in so many ways.

I had come to visit her village, Teotitlán del Valle, during the annual Days of the Dead celebration. Zoyla first took me shopping at the village market and then showed me the secret of the popular *amarillo* tamales. Essentially they are tortilla-tamales—you make a very thin corn tortilla and carefully fold it over a filling of Mole Amarillo and a little plain shredded chicken, then wrap it up in a long corn leaf—not a husk, but the leaf stripped from the cornstalk.

It would be hard to duplicate the same feat unless you could get some big corn leaves and master a somewhat intricate wrapping technique. I have adapted the recipe to use corn husks. For true pre-Hispanic tamales, eliminate the chicken and make Mole Amarillo without cloves or peppercorns.

10 tamales (5 servings)

Have ready a steamer arrangement.

Place the corn husks in a deep bowl, cover well with hot water, and let soak for about 30 minutes.

If using fresh *hoja santa*, tear the leaves into a total of 10 pieces, as equal-sized as possible. Set aside.

In a large mixing bowl, combine the *masa* and salt, working well with your hands to mix evenly. (If using *masa harina*, add the salt before mixing in the stock or water.) Form the dough into 10 ping-pong-size balls.

Drain the corn husks and pat dry. Have them on the counter ready to fill.

Working with one ball of dough at a time and keeping the rest covered with a damp cloth, prepare a tortilla press by the directions on page 100 and press out the dough into a 5-inch round. Gently peel off the plastic liner.

Carefully holding the tortilla in the palm of one hand, place 1 heaping table-spoon of Amarillo in the center. Place several pieces of shredded chicken over it and top with a piece of the reserved *hoja santa*. (If using dried *hoja santa*, sprinkle about 1/2 teaspoon over the chicken.) Fold together the sides of the tor-tilla to enclose the filling; it is not necessary to close the open ends. Carefully place the filled tortilla lengthwise in the center of a corn husk. Fold the sides of the husk together, taking care to keep it seam side up.

Place the tamales on the steamer rack, seam side up, stacking in layers as necessary but making sure that they lie flat on the rack. Steam, tightly covered, over medium-low heat for about 30 to 35 minutes.

Tamales Miahuatecos

Miahuatlán-Style Tamales

16 to 20 large dried corn husks
(page 106)

One 1-inch piece *canela* (page 30)

8 to 9 ounces (about 1 generous cup)
lard (preferably home-rendered;
page 36)

1 1/2 pounds (about 3 cups)
coarse-ground fresh *masa* (page
93), either homemade or bought
from a supplier, or reconstituted
masa made by mixing 2 3/4 cups
masa harina (page 94) with about
1 3/4 cups chicken stock (preferably homemade; see page 74) or
water

1 tablespoon salt

2 cups cooked or canned puréed
pumpkin or winter squash
(drain if very watery)

1/2 cup grated Mexican brown loaf
sugar (*panela* or *piloncillo*; page
40), or 1/2 cup dark brown sugar,
packed

2 to 3 dried Oaxacan pasilla chiles
or dried chipotle chiles (pages 46
to 47), stems and tops removed,
or canned chipotle chiles *en adobo*

2 to 2 1/2 cups black beans, cooked
by the directions on page 234,
or drained canned black beans

5 to 6 garlic cloves, coarsely chopped

6 to 7 large or 8 to 10 medium fresh
hoja santa leaves (page 36)

*M*aría Concepción Portillo de Carballido, the well-known Oaxacan cooking teacher, introduced me to these pumpkin-enriched tamales from the
neighborhood of Miahuatlán in the Sierra Madre del Sur. I included an adapted
version of the recipe in my first book, *Food From My Heart*, but it is so good that
it bears repeating—especially since the anise-scented fresh *hoja santa* leaves are
now becoming more available in the U.S. In the first version I wrapped the
tamales in banana leaves to contribute a little extra fragrance. Now that I can
put *hoja santa* into the filling, I follow Doña Concepción in using corn husks
as wrappers.

If unable to obtain fresh *hoja santa*, either crumble the contents of two 1/4-ounce
packages of dried *hoja santa* and sprinkle about 1 teaspoon over the filling of each
tamal, or make an anise infusion by the directions on page 29 (starting with
2 teaspoons aniseed and 2 cups boiling water) and add to the beans while puréeing, in place of the water.

I use home-cooked beans, but this is a case where canned beans would be
acceptable.

16 to 20 tamales (8 to 10 servings as a first course or light dinner entrée)

Have ready a steamer arrangement.

Place the corn husks in a deep bowl. Cover well with hot water and let soak
for about 30 minutes.

Grind the *canela* in an electric coffee or spice grinder. Set aside.

Set aside 2 to 3 tablespoons of the lard. In a mixing bowl, combine the
remaining lard, the *masa*, and 1 1/2 teaspoons salt by the directions for Basic
Tamal Dough on page 110. When the mixture is smooth and silky, beat in the
pumpkin purée a little at a time, stopping occasionally to scrape down the sides
of the bowl. Beat in the ground *canela*, grated *panela*, and 1 teaspoon salt. Set
aside while you make the bean filling.

Place the Oaxacan pasilla or dried chipotle chiles in a bowl, cover generously with boiling water, and let soak for 10 minutes. (It is not necessary to soak
canned chipotles.) Drain well. Working in batches as necessary, purée the beans

in a blender together with the chiles, garlic, and about 1 cup water (or enough to facilitate blending; alternatively, purée in a food processor, reducing the water to 1/2 cup).

In a large, heavy skillet or wide saucepan, heat the remaining 2 to 3 tablespoons lard over high heat until rippling. Add the bean mixture, watching out for splatters. Reduce the heat to medium and simmer, uncovered, stirring to prevent sticking, until most of the liquid is evaporated, 5 to 7 minutes. Stir in the remaining 1/2 teaspoon salt, or to taste.

Cut or tear the *hoja santa* leaves into 16 to 20 equal-sized pieces.

Drain the corn husks and pat dry. Spread about 1/4 to 1/3 cup of the *masa* mixture across the wide end of each husk and place about 1 1/2 to 2 tablespoons of the bean mixture over the center. Top with a piece of *hoja santa*. Fold and steam the tamales by the directions on page 108, allowing 45 minutes cooking time.

Gueta Bi'ngui'

Baked Unwrapped Tamales with Dried Shrimp

One 3-ounce package small dried shrimp (page 33), tails only

3 medium-size ripe tomatoes

1 jalapeño chile

2 pounds 2 ounces (about 4 1/4 cups) coarse-ground fresh *masa* (page 93) homemade or bought from a supplier, or reconstituted *masa* made by mixing 3 3/4 cups *masa harina* (page 94) with 2 1/2 cups water

1 1/2 teaspoon achiote paste (page 28)

2 1/2 teaspoons salt, or to taste

1/3 cup fresh epazote leaves stripped from stems and coarsely chopped, or 2 tablespoons dried epazote (page 35)

8 ounces (about 1 cup) lard (preferably home-rendered; page 36), gently melted and cooled until lukewarm but still liquid

*T*he Zapotec name refers to various kinds of tamales containing fish or seafood, made throughout the Isthmus of Tehuantepec. Once I bought a *gueta bi'ngui'* in a very poor fishing village of the Isthmus and was handed a large banana-leaf package that I unwrapped to find a whole fish inside—head, eyes, fins, tail, and all—lightly coated with *masa*, in a savory tomato sauce. This dried-shrimp version, which I encountered at a cocktail party in Juchitán, is dramatically different: "naked" tamales consisting of *masa* rounds baked without any wrapping. There was another touch that I've had to omit—the little rounds of *masa* were baked on leaves from the almond trees that grow abundantly in the Isthmus.

The dish as I tasted it in Juchitán contained much more lard, to the point that the baked *masa* was oozing grease. That is the authentic Isthmian style, but I found it heavier than most people would want even for the sake of authenticity. My version reduces the proportion of lard to *masa*.

6 *servings*

Select 36 nicely shaped dried shrimp tails. In a small bowl, soak them in several changes of cold water to remove excess salt. Drain well and set aside.

Meanwhile, make the *molito* (tomato-*masa* mixture). Griddle-roast the tomatoes and jalapeño chile by the directions on pages 26 and 42 respectively. Place the chile in a small plastic or paper bag and let rest for 10 minutes to soften the skin; peel and discard the top and seeds. Peel the tomatoes when cool enough to handle, being careful to save the juices. In a small bowl, mix 1/3 cup of the *masa* to a paste with the juices of the roasted tomatoes. Transfer the mixture to a blender with the tomatoes, chile, achiote paste, and 1/2 teaspoon salt. Process to a smooth purée (about 2 minutes on high). You should have about 1 1/2 cups of the mixture. Set aside in a bowl.

Preheat the oven to 350°F.

Place the remaining *masa* in a large mixing bowl. Add the epazote, lard, and remaining 2 teaspoons salt. Beat with a wooden spoon or your bare hand until smoothly mixed. (Alternatively, combine the ingredients in the large bowl of a standing electric mixer and beat on medium speed for 2 minutes.)

Divide the dough into 12 portions. Place on 1 or 2 baking sheets, forming each portion into a round about 3 inches across and 1/2 inch thick and flattening slightly with the back of a spoon. With your fingers, make a depression about 1 inch wide in each, being careful not to go all the way through to the baking sheet. Place 3 of the dried shrimp in each depression and add about 2 tablespoons of the reserved tomato *molito*. Bake for 20 to 25 minutes, until set like little cookies.

Tamales de Camarón
Shrimp Tamales

8 to 9 ounces (slightly more than 1 cup) lard (preferably home-rendered; see page 36)

1 1/2 pounds (about 3 cups) coarsely ground fresh *masa* (page 93), homemade or bought from a supplier, or reconstituted *masa* made by mixing 2 1/4 cups *masa harina* (page 94) with 1 3/4 cups chicken stock (preferably home-made; see page 74) or water

1 tablespoon plus 1 teaspoon salt, or to taste

2 cups finely crumbled pork cracklings (page 36)

1/2 cup fresh epazote leaves, stripped from stems and coarsely chopped, or 2 tablespoons dried epazote, crumbled (page 35)

12 to 14 large dried corn husks (page 106)

1 cup (4 ounces) hulled pumpkin seeds

2 small ripe tomatoes, coarsely chopped

2 jalapeño chiles, tops and seeds removed, coarsely chopped

1 small onion, coarsely chopped

1 garlic clove, coarsely chopped

1 tablespoon achiote paste (page 28)

24 to 28 medium (20- to 24-count) fresh shrimp, peeled and deveined

*T*his would also qualify for the name *gueta bi'ngui'* (which can apply to any type of seafood tamales), but here the shrimp are fresh, not dried, and the tamales are cooked by the more conventional method of wrapping and steaming. The crumbled pork cracklings add fantastic texture and flavor but also make the dish very rich and filling—I think these are best served as party buffet food, allowing about 1 per person.

Venancia Toledo Hernández gave me this delicious recipe.

12 to 14 tamales

Have ready a steamer arrangement.

Set aside about 3 to 4 tablespoons of the lard. In a mixing bowl, combine the remaining lard, the *masa*, and 1 tablespoon salt by the directions for Basic Tamal Dough on page 110. Beat in the pork cracklings and epazote. Set aside.

Place the corn husks in a large bowl, cover well with hot water, and let soak for about 30 minutes while you make the rest of the filling.

In a medium-size skillet, heat 1 to 2 tablespoons of the reserved lard over medium heat until rippling. Add the pumpkin seeds and cook in the hot fat until slightly puffed and toasted, about 2 to 3 minutes, stirring and shaking the pan constantly to keep them from scorching and turning bitter.

At once scrape out into a small bowl and let cool slightly. Place the pumpkin seeds in a blender with the tomatoes, chiles, onion, and garlic and process to a smooth purée, stopping occasionally to scrape down the sides with a rubber spatula.

In a medium-size saucepan, heat the remaining 1 to 2 tablespoons lard over medium heat until rippling and add the pumpkin-seed purée. Cook, covered, stirring occasionally, for 15 minutes. Add 1 teaspoon salt, or to taste. Dissolve the achiote paste in a little water and add to the pan. Cook uncovered, stirring constantly, for another 10 minutes, until slightly thickened. Remove from the heat and let cool to room temperature.

Drain the corn husks and pat dry. Spread about 1/3 cup of the *masa* mixture across the wide end of each husk, place about 2 tablespoons of the pumpkin-seed purée in the center, and arrange 2 shrimp on top. Fold and steam the tamales as directed on page 108, allowing 45 minutes cooking time.

Other Corn Dishes

Enchiladas Zapotecas del Istmo
Isthmian-style Zapotec Enchiladas

*T*his is based on a recipe in *María's Culinary Secrets* by María Villalobos. It is one of the few dishes where I prefer to use commercial tortillas—they don't tear as easily or absorb as much cooking fat in cooking.

6 servings

Prepare the Mole Rojo and set aside.

Bring a small saucepan of salted water to a boil and cook the potatoes until barely tender, about 11 to 12 minutes. Drain, peel, and cut into 1/4-inch dice. Set aside.

In a large sauté pan, heat the oil to rippling over medium-high heat. Add the garlic and half the onion; cook, stirring, until the onion is translucent, about 3 minutes. Add the plantain and tomatoes; cook, stirring frequently, for 5 minutes. Add the diced potatoes along with the shredded pork, capers, and raisins. Cook, stirring to mix well, for another 5 minutes. Season with 1/2 teaspoon salt (or to taste) and freshly ground pepper. Set aside.

Preheat the oven to 375°F.

Combine the remaining chopped onion with the vinegar, oregano, and 1/2 teaspoon salt or to taste. Set aside.

In a medium-size saucepan, heat the Mole Rojo and keep warm over low heat.

Soften the tortillas: Either pour vegetable oil into a medium-size skillet to a depth of 1 inch, heat to rippling, and cook one tortilla at a time for 30 seconds (lifting out to drain on paper towels as they are done), or omit the oil, place the tortillas 6 at a time in a plastic bag, and microwave for 40 seconds on full power. While they are still warm enough to be pliable, dip the tortillas one

1 recipe (2 1/2 to 3 cups) Mole Rojo del Istmo (page 146)

2 medium-small red potatoes, unpeeled

2 tablespoons vegetable oil

3 garlic cloves, minced

1 medium onion, finely chopped

1 small plantain (page 39), peeled and cut into 1/4-inch dice

2 medium ripe tomatoes, finely chopped

1 1/2 cups cooked shredded pork (page 73)

2 teaspoons capers, drained

1 1/2 tablespoons dark raisins

1 teaspoon salt, or to taste

Freshly ground black pepper

2 tablespoons cider vinegar or distilled white vinegar

1 teaspoon dried Mexican oregano (page 38)

Twelve 6-inch commercial corn tortillas

Vegetable oil for frying (optional; see recipe)

8 ounces *queso fresco*, crumbled, or Oaxacan string cheese, shredded (page 31)

at a time into the warmed *mole*, place about 2 to 3 tablespoons of the pork mixture in the center of each, and roll up into a cylinder. Place them in a heat-proof 8×8-inch baking dish. When all the tortillas are filled and rolled, pour the remaining *mole* over them and top with the crumbled or shredded cheese. Bake for 10 to 15 minutes, until the cheese has melted and the tortillas are heated through. Sprinkle with the onion-vinegar mixture and serve immediately.

Enfrijoladas
Tortillas with Bean Purée

This is one of the standard snacks found at Oaxaca City food stands and restaurants.

4 servings

Place the dried chile in a small bowl and cover with boiling water. Soak for about 20 minutes. Drain well. (It is not necessary to soak canned chipotles.) Coarsely chop half the onion and place in a blender with the drained chile (or canned chipotle chile en adobo), garlic, avocado leaves, beans, and a little of the bean liquid to facilitate blending; reserve the rest. (Alternatively, process in a food processor; the added liquid will not be necessary.) Stir in 1/2 teaspoon salt, or to taste.

In a small saucepan, heat the lard to rippling over medium heat. Add the puréed bean mixture and cook, stirring constantly, for 2 minutes. Gradually stir in enough of the reserved bean cooking liquid to thin the mixture to the consistency of heavy cream. Bring to a boil, reduce the heat to the lowest possible setting, and keep warm, stirring occasionally, while you make the relish.

Mince the remaining half onion. In a small bowl, combine with the vinegar, oregano, and remaining 1/2 teaspoon salt, or to taste. Set aside.

In a small skillet just large enough to hold a tortilla, heat the oil until rippling over high heat. Fry the tortillas, one at a time, about 30 seconds. Lift out onto paper towels to drain. Fold each into quarters while it is still hot enough to be pliable; dip into the hot bean purée and place on a platter. When all are done, sprinkle with the onion mixture and the crumbled cheese. Serve immediately.

1 Oaxacan pasilla chile or dried chipotle chile (pages 46 to 47), top and seeds removed, or use 1 canned chipotle chile en adobo

1 small onion, halved

1 garlic clove, coarsely chopped

2 dried avocado leaves, toasted (page 28)

1 cup cooked black beans (page 234)

3 cups (approximately) bean cooking liquid

1 teaspoon salt, or to taste

2 tablespoons lard (preferably home-rendered; page 36)

1 tablespoon cider vinegar

1/2 teaspoon dried Mexican oregano, crumbled (page 38)

1/2 cup vegetable oil, or as needed

12 corn tortillas, homemade (page 98) or commercial

8 ounces queso fresco (page 31) or young ricotta salata, crumbled

Chilaquiles con Salsa de Hoja Santa

Chilaquiles with Hoja Santa Sauce

1 small whole chicken breast (about 1 pound), skin removed

1 cup chicken stock (preferably homemade; page 74) or water

2 jalapeño or serrano chiles

Twelve 6-inch commercial corn tortillas

2 cups vegetable oil

1 small onion, minced

1 garlic clove, minced

3 large or 5 medium fresh *hoja santa* leaves, or 8 dried (page 36)

1/2 teaspoon salt, or to taste

4 ounces Oaxacan string cheese (page 31) or medium-sharp white cheddar, grated

*I*n Oaxaca City everyone seems to gravitate to the magic square of the *Zócalo*, the big tree-shaded town plaza surrounded by gracious *portales* (arcades). The Hotel Marqués del Valle, named for Cortez, occupies part of one side. It was there that I tasted this marvelous dish on my first trip to Oaxaca. The taste lingered in my memory, and ten years later I finally succeeded in obtaining the recipe.

There is no good English word for *chilaquiles*. The dish can vary a lot but it basically consists of leftover corn tortillas cut into strips and topped with other ingredients like cheese and shredded cooked meat in a sauce. In Oaxaca the tortillas for *chilaquiles* are simply air-dried and need no further cooking. Unfortunately the tortillas available in the U.S. will just get soggy when they touch the sauce. You have to fry them to keep them crisp.

4 servings

Place the chicken breast and the stock in a small lidded saucepan and cook, covered, over medium-low heat until the meat is tender, about 15 minutes. Remove from the heat and let stand until the meat is cool enough to pull into fine shreds. Keep the shredded meat warm; reserve the stock separately.

Griddle-roast the chiles by the directions on page 42. Place in a small plastic or brown paper bag for 10 to 12 minutes until the skins are softened. Peel the chiles, removing and discarding the tops. Set aside.

Cut the tortillas in half. Stack them a few at a time and slice into 1/4-inch strips at right angles to the first cut. Set aside 2 tablespoons of the oil. Pour the rest into a large, heavy saucepan or deep fryer; over medium-high heat, heat the oil to 350°F or until a strip dropped into the hot oil sizzles at once. Fry the tortillas, using no more than a large handful at a time. With a skimmer, rapidly lift out each batch onto paper towels as soon as it stops sizzling and before it can begin to scorch. Let drain well. The tortilla strips can be fried up to 1 day ahead and kept at room temperature, covered well, before you assemble the dish.

In a medium-size skillet, heat the remaining 2 tablespoons oil to rippling over medium-high heat. Add the onion and garlic and cook, stirring frequently, until the onion is translucent, about 3 minutes. Let cool slightly.

Place the sautéed onion and garlic in a blender with the *hoja santa* leaves, roasted chiles, and reserved chicken stock. Process until smooth, return the mixture to the skillet, and bring to a boil over medium-high heat. Add the salt and reduce the heat to low. Cook for 3 minutes more.

Place the fried tortilla strips in a heated serving dish and pour the hot sauce over them. Top with the shredded chicken and cheese; serve immediately.

Young girl on the way to the bakery for the day's bread

Moles and Pepianes:
Main Dish Sauces

To understand *moles* is to understand a basic fact about the kitchen philosophy of Oaxaca as opposed to other cuisines.

At a festive French meal it's self-evident that the main dish will be some kind of meat, poultry, or fish skillfully treated in such-and-such a manner (roasted, grilled, braised, poached, sautéed, etc.) and served with such-and-such a sauce that complements it elegantly. Oaxacans see it the other way. Meats are most often cooked in just a few ways that may at first seem monotonous to diners from other cultures. I would almost say that the meat is incidental in many famous dishes. At any rate, it tends to be a plain, understated foil to the fascinating textures and nuances of the sauces, which are the true *pièce de résistance*.

The Spanish found the indigenous peoples making many elaborate puréed sauces and called them by the Aztec name *molli*, which later got twisted to *mole*. Ever since, the tradition has survived here and there throughout Mexico—everyone knows the *mole poblano* from Puebla—but all Mexicans acknowledge Oaxaca as *mole* capital of the nation. The state is nicknamed "The Land of the Seven *Moles*," though seventy might be more like it.

Just what is a *mole*? I've never heard a definition that fits all cases. The first *mollis* were based on purées of dried chiles and seasonings pounded in a stone mortar, often with seeds and nuts. Some included pumpkin seeds, and these usually acquired the name *pepianes* or *pipianes*.

Today *moles* and most *pepianes* still generally have ground dried chiles, sometimes in elaborate combinations of varieties (though the commonly available anchos and guajillos now seem to be driving out most other chiles even in Oaxaca). The main thickening generally comes from ground seeds or nuts, though the chiles themselves have some thickening effect. *Moles* commonly contain a range of herbs and spices—it would be tempting to say, "If it has 20 ingredients and it's a sauce, it has to be a *mole*!" But really there are no easy rules of thumb. When you come to the poultry and meat chapters you will find many dishes on the *mole* model that bear other names like *almendrado*. Some dishes officially called *moles* are thickened with *masa* or tortillas instead of nuts, and there are others thickened with bread. Some are served as thick pastes and some are more like soups. At least one, the Mole Verde, uses fresh rather than dried chiles. And I have been given *mole* recipes where the herbs and seasonings were no more complex than a little black pepper and cloves with some garlic and onion.

The one generalization that's accurate is that sauces of the *mole* tribe take good logistics. Ironically, cooks in Oaxaca can put together complex sauces more easily than we can here. They can make up preferred combinations of home-roasted chiles and take them to be ground with or without other spices and nuts by *molinos*, small milling operations close to the markets. They can then dip into these mixtures as needed. The market stands also sell different pre-ground *mole* pastes of very good quality that contain everything necessary except the high-moisture ingredients (stock, onions, tomatoes). People buy the paste the day they plan to use it and take it home to be combined with the last strategic elements. So in real life a Oaxacan cook is not faced with a ten-stage marathon when she sets out to do one of the more elaborate *moles*. We in the U.S. are the ones up against these challenges!

It would be wonderful if freshly made *mole* mixtures ever became available here. Meanwhile, there are no real shortcuts for a genuine *mole* or *pepián*. I offer the following suggestions for coping with these and other highly structured Oaxacan puréed sauces that you will find in the poultry chapter and elsewhere in this book.

First: It helps to understand the pre-preparation techniques required by some ingredients. Before trying any *mole* recipe, read and re-read the directions for griddle-drying or frying dried chiles (page 45) and roasting tomatoes, tomatillos, onions, garlic, and fresh chiles (pages 25 to 27). Everyone takes these procedures for granted in Oaxaca. They must become second nature to you before you are at home with *moles*. Once you've mastered this handful of techniques, you will be well on the way to making these wonderful sauces.

Second: Virtually all *moles* and related sauces rest on a grinding/puréeing process that is really several processes. Supposedly primitive Mexican tools like the rough stone metates or *molcajetes* (mortars) can combine the necessary actions better than any single modern electric appliance. They crush whole spices as efficiently as they mash moist ingredients. The metal blades of our appliances neither crush nor mash—they cut and rip. Yet they can handle the job if you reserve each for what it does best. These are the items that you should have lined up before seeking to conquer *moles*:

- **A small electric coffee or spice grinder.** This easily reduces *canela* (soft-stick Mexican cinnamon), cloves, peppercorns, allspice, and dried herbs to a fresh, fragrant powder that can be smoothly combined with other ingredients instead of leaving the hard unprocessed bits that may result if you just try to blend or process them with a lot of other difficult ingredients. My *mole* recipes almost always call for whole spices separately ground in this way, or with a mortar and pestle. (In a few cases I'll just put the whole spices in the blender with the chiles and other ingredients.) If you insist, you can use pre-ground spices from the store. But I can't overstate how much better the freshly ground ones are.

- **A heavy-duty electric blender.** This should be the *only* appliance you use for puréeing dried soaked chiles. The limitation of blenders is that they require some liquid (as specified in the recipes) to encourage the blending action. The advantage is that the short, stubby blades purée soaked ancho, guajillo, and similar chiles more successfully than the curved blades of a food processor. They also seem to be better for emulsifying all ingredients in juicy mixtures with tomatoes, tomatillos and onions. Just be aware that when working with large quantities of sauce, you will have to blend in batches, a few cups at a time. This can slow you down quite a bit.

- **A food processor.** I used to disdain this machine, but now sometimes use it as an adjunct to the blender and grinder. I find that the food processor does a good job on dried chiles that have not been soaked, dried fruits, sesame seeds, and other nuts and seeds. So to help avoid doing endless batches of the more complex *mole* bases in the blender, you can split up the task by using the processor to handle such ingredients and combining them with others that have been separately processed in a blender.

- **A sturdy medium-mesh sieve—or several—and a good pushing implement.** Merely whirling a mixture in a blender or processor won't necessarily give it the right finish for a Mexican sauce. Often the texture must be made even smoother. No machine can substitute for manually forcing the purée through a sieve. If you can find an old-fashioned wooden pusher (the kind shaped like a stubby pestle), it is ideal. My usual tool is a flat wooden spoon. This is one part of the process that takes elbow grease.

Push and rub the puréed mixture to force through every bit you can; discard all the hard or stringy bits that remain in the sieve. Be sure not to use a fine sieve—it will be *too* fine.

As you will see, most of the puréed sauces are fried in a small amount of hot fat before the meats or vegetables are added. Don't be tempted to skip this odd-sounding procedure. It is the secret of deepened, rounded flavor in most Mexican sauces. Just take care—the sauce splatters furiously as you pour it into the rippling hot fat. It will go on sending up splatters throughout cooking, so be sure to cover the pan as the sauce simmers.

For the record, the classic "seven *moles*" of Oaxaca are Mole Amarillo (yellow), Mole Coloradito (reddish), Mole Negro (black), Mole Rojo (red), Mole Verde (green), Chichilo (very dark, but less rich than Mole Negro), and Manchamantel (a fruit-based sauce). I have also included two of the closely related *pepianes*, a version of Chileajo (literally, "chile-garlic" sauce), and the interesting Mole de Castilla.

The recipes are grouped by approximate degree of difficulty. I suggest starting out with the fairly simple Amarillo I or II, Mole Rojo del Istmo, or Mole Verde. At the far end of the spectrum, Chichilo and the two Moles Negros place heavy demands on any cook. If it's any comfort, the demands involve more organizational than culinary skill. No step is really hard to conquer in even the most formidable-looking *mole* recipe. It's the sheer number of steps that can be dizzying. But after you've made several *moles* they will become second nature to you—like riding a bicycle.

There is great flexibility in the use of *moles*, and this is among the hardest things to explain to non-Mexicans. Almost any *mole* can function as a rich, plentiful sauce, semi-soup, or filling for tamales or enchiladas. Almost any can be served by adding some shredded cooked chicken or pork to the *mole* at the last minute, or cooking briefly with such vegetables as green beans, chayotes, and/or potatoes. The *masa* dumplings (Chochoyotes) described in the recipe for Chichilo (page 162) are an attractive addition to other *moles* as well. So please do not be puzzled to see different *moles* receiving various treatments in this chapter. You will notice that I have some standing alone as sauces but write directions for meat and other accompaniments into others. This is more a matter of personal feeling than law. Oaxacan cooks would unhesitatingly thicken or thin a sauce to their own preference, or marry the sauce with the meats, vegetables, and other accompaniments that they had on hand. As you work with these recipes I hope that you will learn to experiment in the same spirit and to feel at home with the Oaxacan concept that *the sauce is the dish*.

To Store Moles

Once the juicy ingredients like tomatoes and onions have been added, a *mole* should be refrigerated and kept tightly covered if it is not to be used at once. All the sauces in this chapter except the Mole Verde can be stored in the refrigerator for at least 4 to 6 days, or in the freezer for up to 6 months. Mole Verde must be used as soon as the purée of herbs has been added.

Grinding cacao for chocolate
on the metate

Amarillo I
Thick Yellow Mole

3 guajillo chiles (page 47), tops and
    seeds removed

1 ancho chile (page 46), top and
    seeds removed

3 large tomatillos, with husks

1 large, hard green tomato

1 small onion, unpeeled

2 garlic cloves, unpeeled

10 black peppercorns

8 whole cloves, or 1/4 teaspoon
    ground

2 tablespoons lard (preferably
    home-rendered; page 36),
    or vegetable oil

1 teaspoon salt, or to taste

2 tablespoons fresh *masa* (page 93),
    or 2 teaspoons *masa harina*
    (page 94) mixed with 2 table-
    spoons water

This is one of the seven major Oaxacan *moles*. There are two main kinds, each with infinite variations. (If you ask ten Oaxacan cooks about Mole Amarillo, you will probably get ten quite different recipes and also realize that no one bothers to use the full name—the informal *amarillo* is enough.) One type, a dense, silky *mole* the consistency of a thick tomato sauce, usually functions as a filling. The other is thinned to any consistency between a heavy batter and a soup, and serves as the basis of stews and braised meat dishes.

Actually, Amarillo is not the only *mole* to be made with a lot of gradations between thick and thin. As you work with all these sauces I hope you will learn to experiment with consistency—Oaxacan cooks usually start with a thick paste as the basis of a *mole* and thin it more or less, depending on the purpose.

The sauce won't really be yellow. It comes out more of an orange shade and then the green tomato dilutes the color a little. It's light, tart and refreshing, in contrast to some of the very rich and intense *moles* given later in the chapter. The chiles amarillos or chilcosles give a yellower color and were once common in this dish. But today I find most people using the fleshier, darker guajillos. If you can't find them, use six to eight chiles amarillos (depending on the size) in place of the ancho.

My Amarillo is based on a recipe from María de los Angeles Lagunas. I like it because all the ingredients are readily available in the United States; also, the sauce has very little fat. The thick version is my favorite. But I follow it with a thin alternative in order to show the ways Oaxacan cooks work with a sauce.

2 1/2 to 3 cups

    Wash and griddle-dry the chiles by the directions on page 45. Place in a small bowl; cover generously with boiling water and let soak for at least 20 minutes. Drain the soaked chiles and reserve.

    While the chiles soak, prepare the vegetables. Using a griddle or cast-iron skillet thoroughly heated over low heat, roast the tomatillos, green tomato, onion, and garlic by the directions on pages 25 to 27. As each is done, remove to a bowl to catch the juices and set aside.

Grind the peppercorns and cloves together in an electric coffee or spice grinder or with a mortar and pestle. When the roasted onion, garlic, and tomato are cool enough to handle, peel them over the same bowl to catch the juices. Remove the husks from the tomatillos. Place the vegetables and their juices in a blender with the drained chiles and ground spices. Process to a smooth purée (about 3 minutes on high). With a wooden spoon or pusher, force the purée through a medium-mesh sieve into a bowl.

In a medium-size saucepan, heat the lard over medium heat until rippling. Add the puréed sauce and cook, covered, for 10 minutes, stirring occasionally. Stir in the salt.

In a small bowl, mix the *masa* with 1/2 cup water and whisk into the sauce. Bring back to a simmer and cook, whisking constantly, until the sauce is somewhat thickened and the flavors are well blended, about 15 minutes.

The Amarillo is now ready to use as a filling, a thick sauce for tamales, or an accompaniment to what strikes your fancy. Mixed with shredded chicken and folded into tortillas, it is the filling for Empanadas de Amarillo (page 104). I love it as a vibrant complement to Tamales de Chepil (page 112), or as a filling for other tamales.

Amarillo II
Thin Yellow Mole

The rich, vivid version of Amarillo that I have just given has a special place in my heart. But if you are starting out to explore the concept of *moles*, please read the following suggestions for experimenting with the other kind, which can fall anywhere between the natures of a thick stew or a soup. The essence of Oaxacan *moles* is that they mold them themselves to circumstances.

3 1/2 to 5 cups of sauce, depending on how much you thin it

Begin with 2 1/2 to 3 cups of the preceding Amarillo I, 1 to 2 cups homemade chicken stock (page 74), and a game plan. The sauce is a chameleon, and you are telling it how to change.

One possibility is to take a simple cooked meat and serve it with the Amarillo, thinned to your taste with stock. When I first brought back the recipe, we used it in quite a few ways at my restaurant in New York. One of the most satisfying scenarios we came up with was to add hot stock little by little to a gently simmering Amarillo until it was light but still had enough body to be pleasing—you have to play this by ear—and then use it to accompany delicate pan-fried sole. (Strong-flavored seafoods seem to overwhelm this *mole*.) In the same vein, you could follow the directions for making either my homemade chicken stock (page 74) or pork stock (page 73) with the resulting bonus of cooked shredded meat. You then use the poaching broth to thin the sauce just to your taste and briefly reheat the meat in the sauce. Or if roast pork strikes your fancy more, cook the meat by the directions in Chileajo de Puerco (page 152) and serve the carved meat with the Amarillo.

Then there are vegetables, or vegetable-meat combinations. The basic Amarillo mixture is the foundation of a delicious stew, a kind of dish that can actually be created with any of several different sauces once you have grasped the principle. Here is the general idea: Thin the *mole* with 2 cups stock. It should be decidedly soupy (add more stock or water if necessary).

Meanwhile, brown about 1 1/2 pounds cubed stewing pork or beef in about 2 tablespoons lard or oil in a large Dutch oven. Pour the hot *mole* over the meat (you can drain excess fat first if desired) and cook, covered, over gentle heat for 20 to 25 minutes.

Have ready about 1/4 pound green beans, trimmed and cut into 1-inch lengths, and 1 chayote, peeled, seeded, and diced; add these to the stew and cook, covered, for another 15 minutes. Serve in soup bowls. This variation also has its variations—for example, you can make it a vegetarian dish for Lent by omitting the meat, maybe adding 2 large red potatoes (peeled and diced), and using water for the stock.

I promise you that most of my *mole* recipes will be more structured than this. But what I've just given you is a key to the way Oaxacans really think about the possibilities of a simple *mole*. Do not feel yourself limited by particular suggestions about using this or that meat cooked by one specific formula. Do not pigeonhole recipes as being either soups, stews, or sauces as if one excluded the others. Just treat the foundation *mole* recipe as the framework for a few different experimental compositions, trying to pay attention to the meats and vegetables I have noted as being staples of Oaxacan cuisine.

Mole Rojo del Istmo
Isthmian Red Mole

1 small day-old French roll (about
    4 ounces), sliced, or 1 thick slice
    day-old challah or brioche

6 large pasilla (page 47) or 4 large
    ancho chiles (page 46), tops and
    seeds removed

6 large unpeeled garlic cloves

1 large ripe tomato

1 small onion, peeled and quartered

One 1-inch piece *canela* (page 30)

1/4 teaspoon black peppercorns

8 whole cloves, or 1/4 teaspoon
    ground

1 teaspoon dried Mexican oregano
    (page 38)

1/2 teaspoon dried thyme

2 bay leaves

1 1/2 cups homemade pork (page 73)
    or chicken stock (page 74)

3 tablespoons lard (preferably
    home-rendered; page 36)
    or vegetable oil

1 teaspoon salt, or to taste

1 1/2 teaspoons sugar

*L*ike Amarillo, Mole Rojo belongs to the lighter, simpler end of the seven-*moles* spectrum. This version from the Isthmus of Tehuantepec is one of my favorites for easy preparation and versatile uses. Like all *moles*, it goes perfectly with pork or chicken and is a great sauce for enchiladas. (See Enchiladas Zapotecas del Istmo, page 129.)

Mole Rojo as I've encountered it in Oaxaca has usually been on the sweet side, typically enriched with raisins. I prefer this fresher-tasting approach, based on a recipe I found in a little English-language pamphlet of recipes by María Villalobos titled *María's Culinary Secrets*.

In Oaxaca many sauces receive part of their thickening from a good-sized slice of Pan de Yema (page 308). Here you may substitute a small roll or—better to reproduce the right sweetness and texture—a slightly sweet egg bread like brioche or good-quality Jewish challah (not the dismal supermarket challah). The bread should be stale enough to make nice dry crumbs.

2 1/2 to 3 cups

Crush the bread to fine crumbs or grind in a food processor. You should have about 1 cup.

Wash and griddle-dry the chiles by the directions on page 45. Place in a bowl, cover generously with boiling water, and let soak for at least 20 minutes.

Roast the garlic cloves by the directions on page 26; when cool enough to handle, peel and set aside.

Bring a small saucepan of water to a boil, add the tomato and onion, and cook over medium heat for 10 minutes. Remove the vegetables. Save 1/2 cup of the cooking liquid, let cool slightly, and place in a blender with the tomato, onion, and roasted garlic. Process until thoroughly puréed (about 2 minutes on high). With a wooden spoon or pusher, force the mixture through a medium-mesh sieve into a bowl. Set aside.

Grind the *canela*, peppercorns, cloves, oregano, thyme, and bay leaves together in an electric coffee or spice grinder or with a mortar and pestle. Set aside.

Drain the soaked chiles. Place in the blender (you don't have to rinse it) with the stock and process until smooth (about 3 minutes on high), stopping occasionally to scrape down the sides with a rubber spatula. With a wooden spoon or pusher, force the mixture through a medium-mesh sieve into a bowl. Combine with the tomato purée.

Now you are ready to combine and cook the ingredients. In a heavy medium-size saucepan, heat the lard over medium heat until rippling. Add the ground spices and cook for 2 minutes, stirring often. Stir in the tomato-chile mixture; cook, covered, for 10 minutes, stirring occasionally. Stir in the bread crumbs and salt and cook for 2 minutes. If the sauce seems overly pasty, thin it with a little water. Add the sugar; taste for seasoning and add a little more salt or sugar if desired. (For serving possibilities, see the suggestions given under Amarillo II [page 144].)

Mole Verde con Puerco
Green Mole with Pork

2 pounds boneless center cut pork loin in one piece, rolled and tied together with the ribs and backbone

1/2 teaspoon black peppercorns, bruised

1 teaspoon salt, or to taste

9 garlic cloves

8 whole cloves, or 1/4 teaspoon ground

1 teaspoon cumin seeds

3 jalapeño chiles, tops removed

6 large tomatillos, husks removed

1 small onion, cut into chunks

2 sprigs fresh thyme

2 sprigs fresh marjoram

1 cup (8 ounces) *masa* (page 93), either fresh or reconstituted by mixing 6 tablespoons *masa harina* (page 94) to a smooth paste with 1 cup water

1 medium bunch Italian parsley

Eight 6-inch sprigs fresh epazote or 1/4 cup dried, crumbled (page 35)

3 large or 5 medium-size fresh *hoja santa* leaves or 6 dried leaves (page 36)

2 cups cooked Great Northern or other white beans

*M*ole Verde, or just Verde for short, is the lightest and freshest-tasting of Oaxaca's "seven *moles*." Of the many variants I've tried, this version served with pork loin at the Oaxaca City restaurant Casa de la Abuela is my favorite.

Fresh herb rather than spice accents are what distinguish a Mole Verde. A purée of green herbs has to be added at the last minute. In other parts of Mexico I've had green *moles* made with various greens, even lettuce leaves. But the Oaxacan Mole Verde uses just three: epazote, *hoja santa*, and parsley. If you can't get the first two you'll have to improvise with what's available, but the results will not be at all Oaxacan. Dried epazote and *hoja santa* are better than none at all, though the fresh herbs are incomparable. Sometimes I've replaced *hoja santa* with an anise tea (page 29). The amount of chiles can be varied to taste; however, this particular sauce is not usually very *picante* (hot).

At Casa de la Abuela they combine the sauce with white beans that have been cooked separately, to keep the flavors simple and distinct. It is very important not to overcook the pork loin, a tender cut that dries out easily. I have devised a way of using boned pork loin that gets some added flavor from the reserved bones. When you have the meat boned, ask the butcher to tie the meat to the backbone and ribs. At serving time, untie and carve it to distribute both meat and rib pieces equally. If this is not practical and you have to get preboned loin without the frame of bones, buy 1 pound of pork neck bones separately and cook them with the meat. It will add some body and flavor.

Mole Verde is also delicious made with chicken instead of pork. In that case, use a 3 1/2-pound chicken, cut into serving pieces, and simmer as directed below for the pork loin, reducing the cooking time to 30 minutes. Remove the skin before serving.

4 to 6 servings

Choose a deep saucepan or Dutch oven large enough to hold the meat comfortably. Place the tied pork loin and bones in it along with the peppercorns, salt, and 4 of the garlic cloves. Add enough cold water to cover by 1 inch (at least 7 cups). Bring to a boil over high heat. Reduce the heat to medium-low and cook, partly covered, for 1 hour, or until a meat thermometer inserted into the center reads 120°F. (Do not worry about the low temperature. The meat will cook more thoroughly in reheating.) Remove the meat and bones from the cooking stock and set aside. Strain the stock; you should have about 6 cups.

Grind the cloves and cumin together in an electric coffee or spice grinder, or with a mortar and pestle. Place the ground spices in a blender with the chiles, tomatillos, onion, thyme, marjoram, the remaining 5 garlic cloves, and 1/2 cup of the strained stock. Process until smoothly puréed (about 2 minutes on high).

Return the remaining strained stock to the pan; bring back to a boil, and adjust the heat to maintain a gentle simmer. Add the puréed mixture to the hot stock and cook, uncovered, for 3 minutes.

Thin the *masa* by mixing with 1 cup water. Whisk the thinned *masa* into the stock mixture; whisking constantly, let the sauce return to the simmer.

Cook, uncovered, over low heat for 10 minutes, whisking occasionally. If lumps form, pass the mixture through a medium-mesh sieve (pushing with a spoon to force through the lumpy bits) and return to the heat. The mixture should thicken to the consistency of whipping cream; if necessary, increase the heat slightly to reduce and thicken it.

Untie the cooked pork and carve into serving pieces. Carve the bones into separate rib sections.

Place the parsley, epazote, and *hoja santa* in a blender or food processor. If using a blender, add a few tablespoons water to facilitate blending. Process to a smooth purée.

Add the cooked beans to the *masa*-thickened sauce and let return to a simmer. Return the carved meat and bones to the pot along with the puréed herbs. Taste and add more salt if desired. Cook until just heated through, 4 to 5 minutes. Give each person a piece or two of rib bone along with the meat and sauce. Serve immediately.

Mole de Castilla
Bread-Thickened Mole

8 ounces coarse, rough-textured whole-wheat bread, sliced and allowed to stale for 1 to 2 days

4 ounces guajillo chiles (page 47), tops and seeds removed

1 head of garlic, unpeeled

2 tablespoons cumin seeds

15 whole cloves

5 allspice berries

2 tablespoons dried Oaxacan oregano or 2 teaspoons dried Mexican oregano, crumbled (page 38)

4 1/2 teaspoons dried thyme

1 small onion, coarsely chopped

8 cups homemade chicken stock (page 74)

1 teaspoon salt, or to taste

*T*hough this unusual sauce is not among the seven classic Oaxacan *moles*, it has become one of my favorites. I learned it from Rufina Montoya of Teotitlán del Valle in the Valley of Oaxaca. Unlike some of the dishes where a small amount of *pan de yema* (sweet egg bread) lends a little body to a sauce along with other thickenings, this one is essentially bread-based. Like some of the Italian bread soups and salads, it's a great way to use up leftover bread.

Rufina used *pan amarillo*, which is hearty enough to keep a good texture when added to the sauce. I usually look for a coarse, dense-textured Italian whole wheat bread—in this case, avoid sweet bread. It should be a day or two old but not rock-hard.

The sauce shows one of the most fascinating qualities of the Valley Zapotec cooking: the use of little or no added fat. This *mole* is virtually fat-free, yet it has a rich, deep flavor and satisfying consistency that no one would associate with that term. I serve it by itself as a soup (as I had it from Rufina), but it would make a lovely sauce for mussels or another slightly assertive seafood.

4 to 5 servings (about 7 to 8 cups)

Crush the bread to coarse crumbs, or pulse very briefly in a food processor (it should not be too fine). Set aside.

Wash and griddle-dry the chiles by the directions on page 45. As they are done, place them in a deep bowl. Cover generously with boiling water and let the chiles soak for at least 20 minutes.

Meanwhile, roast the garlic by the directions on page 26. When it is cool enough to handle, break into separate cloves and peel. Set aside.

Working in 2 batches if necessary, grind the cumin, cloves, allspice, oregano, and thyme together in an electric coffee or spice grinder or with a mortar and pestle.

Drain the soaked chiles. Place half the chiles in a blender with half the ground spice mixture and half the peeled garlic and chopped onion.

Add about 1 1/2 cups of the chicken stock and process until well blended (about 2 minutes on high), adding more stock or a little water if necessary to facilitate blending. Repeat with the remaining chiles, spices, garlic, onion, and another 1 1/2 cups chicken stock.

Set a medium-mesh sieve over a large saucepan. With a wooden spoon or pusher, force the mixture through the sieve into the pan. It may help to pour a little more of the stock into the strainer to rinse the pulp through.

Add the remaining chicken stock to the saucepan, stir to mix evenly, and bring the sauce to a boil over high heat. Immediately reduce the heat to medium-low. Cook, partly covered, for 30 minutes, stirring occasionally. Add the reserved bread crumbs and the salt; cook, partly covered, for another 15 minutes. Taste for seasoning and add more salt if desired. Ladle into soup bowls and serve immediately.

Chileajo con Puerco

Isthmian Chile-Garlic Sauce with Pork

12 garlic cloves, coarsely chopped

1 tablespoon plus 1/2 teaspoon
   dried Mexican oregano, crumbled
   (page 38)

Salt and freshly ground black pepper

4 to 5 pounds pork shoulder or butt,
   bone in

4 thick slices day-old challah or
   brioche, or two 8-ounce French
   rolls

12 guajillo chiles (page 47), tops and
   seeds removed

3 ancho chiles (page 46), tops and
   seeds removed

8 medium ripe tomatoes

1/2 teaspoon achiote paste (page 28)

8 bay leaves

2 teaspoons black peppercorns

One 1 1/2-inch piece *canela*
   (page 30)

1/2 teaspoon dried thyme, crumbled

1/2 teaspoon dried marjoram,
   crumbled

4 cups homemade chicken stock
   (page 74), or more as needed

1 large onion, coarsely chopped

1 teaspoon salt, or to taste

1/2 to 1 teaspoon sugar (optional)

Chileajo figures prominently at weddings in the Isthmus of Tehuantepec. It is customary for the bride's family to make up a big batch and send it to the groom's family. In Oaxaca the sauce would ordinarily be served with plain shredded chicken (page 74) or pork (page 73). I sometimes use this roast-pork variation. Feel free to try other main-dish sauces with pork cooked in the same way.

About 8 servings

Preheat the oven to 475°F.

With a mortar and pestle, crush 8 of the garlic cloves to a paste with 1 tablespoon of the oregano and a little salt and pepper. With the top of a small sharp knife, pierce 1-inch deep gashes all over the roast. Rub the garlic mixture into the meat, pushing it down into the incisions. Season the meat with additional salt and pepper. Place in a roasting pan and bake for 20 minutes. Reduce the heat to 350°F and bake for approximately another 2 hours, until tender and thoroughly cooked. A meat thermometer inserted in the center should read 165°F. While the meat is roasting, prepare the sauce.

Crush the bread to fine crumbs or grind it in a food processor (you should have about 4 cups). Set aside.

Wash and griddle-dry the chiles by the directions on page 45. As they are done, place them in a deep bowl and cover generously with boiling water. Let soak for at least 20 minutes.

Bring a medium-size saucepan of water to a boil. Drop in the tomatoes and cook over medium heat for 10 minutes. Drain the tomatoes; as soon as they are cool enough to handle, peel them over a bowl to catch the juices and set aside.

Place the achiote paste, bay leaves, peppercorns, *canela*, thyme, marjoram, and remaining 1/2 teaspoon oregano in a blender. Add 2 cups of the chicken stock and process until smooth, about 3 minutes on high.

With a wooden spoon or pusher, force the mixture through a medium-mesh sieve into a large saucepan, discarding any coarse bits that won't go through. Bring the purée to a boil over high heat. Immediately reduce the heat to low and cook, covered, for 5 minutes.

Drain the soaked chiles. Working in 2 or more batches as necessary, purée them in a blender with the tomatoes and their juices, onion, remaining 4 garlic cloves, and enough chicken stock to facilitate blending (about 1/3 to 1/2 cup per batch). With a wooden spoon or pusher, force the purée through a medium-mesh sieve into the first mixture. Stir to combine and simmer on low heat, covered, for 15 minutes. Add the salt.

In a bowl, mix the bread crumbs to a paste with the remaining chicken stock. Stir into the sauce, a little at a time, letting the mixture cook for a few minutes between additions, until it reaches a consistency just slightly thinner than a paste. Taste for seasoning; it should be slightly sweet. Add more salt and a little sugar if desired.

Carve the roast pork into thin slices. Pour the hot sauce into a deep serving dish and arrange the meat over it.

Pepián con Pollo
Pumpkin-Seed Sauce with Chicken

4 jalapeño (page 45) or serrano chiles
(page 45)

One 3 1/2-pound chicken, cut into
serving pieces

Salt and freshly ground black pepper

6 tablespoons lard (preferably
home-rendered; page 36)
or vegetable oil

2 cups (8 ounces) hulled pumpkin
seeds, plus a few more for optional
garnish

8 whole cloves, or 1/4 teaspoon
ground

8 allspice berries

2 teaspoons dried Oaxacan oregano
or 1/2 teaspoon dried Mexican
oregano, crumbled (page 38)

6 large garlic cloves

2 cups homemade chicken stock
(page 74)

1 teaspoon salt, or to taste

Five 6-inch sprigs fresh epazote
or 2 tablespoons dried, crumbled
(page 35)

Pepianes or *pipianes* are among the oldest of the pre-Hispanic main-dish sauces. In ancient times they were made with pumpkin seeds, but a modern *pepián* may contain some other type of seed or nut for thickening. This version typifies the uses of a simple *pepián* with cooked meats. You can try it also with the plain shredded chicken on page 75.

4 to 6 servings

Roast and peel the chiles by the directions on page 45; set aside.

Season the chicken with salt and pepper. In a large Dutch oven, heat half the lard over medium-high heat until rippling. Lightly brown the chicken, allowing about 3 minutes per side. Remove from the pan and set aside. Pour off and discard all but about 2 tablespoons fat from the pan; set the pan aside.

Heat the remaining lard in a large, heavy medium-size skillet over low heat. Add the pumpkin seeds and toast in the hot fat until slightly puffed, stirring and shaking the pan constantly. The two dangers are burning them (which makes the entire dish bitter) or being hit by flying seeds as they heat up and pop—watch carefully!

Remove the seeds from the pan and let drain on paper towels. Let cool briefly.

Grind the cloves, allspice, and oregano together in an electric coffee or spice grinder or with a mortar and pestle. Place in a blender along with the garlic, pumpkin seeds, reserved chiles, and chicken stock. Process to a smooth purée. (Alternatively, place the ground spices, garlic, pumpkin seeds, and chiles in a food processor and process to a smooth purée; scrape down the sides with a rubber spatula and with the motor running, add the chicken stock through the feed tube a little at a time.)

Over medium-high heat, reheat the reserved fat in the Dutch oven until rippling. Carefully add the pumpkin-seed mixture; bring just barely to a boil, reduce the heat to medium, and cook, stirring frequently, for 5 minutes. Stir in 1 teaspoon salt, or to taste. Remove 1 cup of the sauce and reserve in a small saucepan.

Add the chicken pieces and epazote to the remaining sauce and cook, covered, over medium-low heat until the chicken is tender, about 20 minutes. Stir frequently. If desired, briefly toast a few extra pumpkin seeds in a small dry skillet over low heat while the chicken is cooking.

When the chicken is done, heat the reserved 1 cup sauce over medium heat, stirring constantly. Arrange the chicken pieces on a serving dish with the sauce from the Dutch oven. It will look curdled and not very appetizing, but don't worry! Pour the reheated 1 cup sauce over the dish; if desired, sprinkle with the extra toasted pumpkin seeds. Serve at once.

Pepián Zapoteco
Zapotec Pumpkin-Seed Sauce

1 cup (8 ounces) dried Great
    Northern or other white beans

3 cups (9 ounces) whole unsalted
    pumpkin seeds in the shell

3 árbol chiles (page 46), tops and
    seeds removed

4 cups homemade chicken stock
    (page 74)

1 medium onion, coarsely chopped

Four 8-inch sprigs fresh epazote
    or 1 tablespoon dried, crumbled
    (page 35)

6 dried avocado leaves (page 28)

3/4 cup (one 1 1/2-ounce package)
    dried shrimp (page 33)

1/4 teaspoon salt, or to taste

Some *pepianes* are smooth, satiny, and very simple to make thanks to modern blenders and food processors. But this one, from Zoyla Mendoza, is closer to the roots of the dish. In fact, it is not far removed from a true pre-Hispanic *pepián*. (The poultry stock and onion are European additions.) You will notice one of the most ancient Oaxacan flavors, the briny and assertive accent of dried shrimp.

The texture is quite different from the preceding *Pepián con Pollo*. This is because of the amount of liquid—*Pepián Zapoteco* is one of the "sauces" that really would be seen as soups by U.S. lights—and also the technique.

At one time whole pumpkin seeds, hulls and all, were used to make a *pepián*, and the fibrous residue was not always strained out. Even today you sometimes find *pepianes* made this way in Mexico. Roasting the seeds in the hull gives an important dimension of flavor, and the coarse stringy texture is accepted as part of the dish.

It should be noted that U.S. pumpkin seeds are much harder-shelled. To get the taste with a smoother texture, I follow a procedure partly streamlined by using a food processor but still somewhat laborious. I toast the whole seeds and grind them in the processor, then remove the hard bits of hull through a combination of straining and skimming. If you don't want to go through this process, by all means use pre-hulled pumpkin seeds—but the dish will lose some of its character.

Pepián Zapoteco is routinely eaten with white beans, which must cook with the sauce for a while to help mingle the flavors. I sometimes stir 3 cups shredded cooked chicken (page 75) or pork (page 73) into the dish about 5 minutes before serving, cooking just to heat the meat through. Potatoes are a delicious meatless alternative.

4 servings

Preheat the oven to 375°F.

Carefully pick over the beans and rinse under cold running water. Place in a medium-size Dutch oven or saucepan and add enough cold water to cover by at least 1 inch. Bring to a boil over high heat and boil rapidly for 1 minute. Remove from the heat at once and let the beans sit in their cooking liquid for 1 hour.

Meanwhile, spread out the pumpkin seeds on a baking sheet in an even layer. Bake until lightly toasted, 10 to 15 minutes. Do not let them scorch or the entire dish will be bitter. Remove from the oven and let cool completely, about 1 hour. Place the pumpkin seeds in a food processor and process with an on/off motion for about 3 minutes. The seeds will break up, but fragments of hard shell will remain. Do not process any longer or the seeds will become pasty.

Working in 2 or 3 batches, turn out the pumpkin seeds into a medium-mesh sieve placed over a bowl and shake to let the fine particles go through. After sifting each batch, pour 1 cup water over the contents of the sieve to rinse through as much as possible. Discard the fibrous residue. Pour the strained seeds and water into a deep, narrow container such as blender jar or narrow pitcher; any bit of shell that went though the sieve will then float to the top and can easily be skimmed off. Add the strained, skimmed liquid to the pot of parboiled beans.

Wash and griddle-dry the chiles by the directions on page 45. (This time it is not necessary to soak them as in most *mole* recipes.) Purée the chiles in the blender with 1 cup of the chicken stock. With a wooden spoon or pusher, force the puréed chiles through a medium-mesh sieve into a bowl. Add the chiles to the beans and pumpkin seeds along with the onion, epazote, avocado leaves, dried shrimp, remaining chicken stock, and salt. Bring to a boil over high heat. Reduce the heat to maintain a low simmer and cook, uncovered, until the beans are thoroughly cooked, about 45 minutes.

Variation: *To make the dish with pre-hulled pumpkin seeds, use 1 1/2 cups (6 ounces) seeds and toast them with 2 tablespoons lard or vegetable oil as directed in Pepián con Pollo (page 154). Let cool briefly and purée in a blender with 2 cups of the chicken stock (or more if necessary). Add to the parboiled beans, stir in the remaining chicken stock, and proceed as above.*

Coloradito

Reddish Mole

3 tablespoons sesame seeds

Half of a 3-ounce tablet Mexican chocolate (pages 277 to 279)

1 thick slice day-old challah or brioche

4 ancho chiles (page 46), tops and seeds removed

4 guajillo chiles (page 47), tops and seeds removed

One 2-inch piece *canela* (page 30)

5 cloves, or 1/8 teaspoon ground

5 whole black peppercorns

1/4 cup lard (preferably home-rendered; page 36), or vegetable oil

1 small onion, coarsely chopped

6 garlic cloves, minced

3 medium ripe tomatoes, coarsely chopped

1/3 small ripe plantain (page 39), or about a 4-inch chunk, peeled and chopped (about 1 cup)

1/2 bunch or 1 small bunch fresh thyme, about 2 dozen sprigs

6 sprigs fresh Mediterranean oregano or 1/2 teaspoon dried Mexican oregano (page 38)

1/4 cup dark raisins

3/4 cup blanched almonds

6 to 8 cups homemade chicken (page 74) or pork stock (page 73), with the resulting 3 cups cooked meat shredded and reserved

1 teaspoon salt, or to taste

Call it Mole Coloradito if you want to stand on ceremony, but everyone in Oaxaca just says Coloradito. There are many versions, some made with chocolate and some without. This one comes from one of my favorite restaurants in Oaxaca City, Casa de la Abuela ("Grandmother's House"), which is named for the grandmother of the present owner, Jaime Martínez. For years she lived and worked at the site on the northwest corner of the *Zócalo*, running a family business in religious articles that she had taken over when she was widowed very young. Her legacy to Jaime and his wife, Olga, was not only the house and store but her recipes. After her death they converted the second floor of the building into a restaurant where they now share the wonderful food of La Abuela with a large and loyal public.

Coloradito is unusual among Oaxacan moles in that it is often served with beef. (You can brown cubes of chuck or another braising cut in a little fat, then finish stewing it in the sauce; cubed red potatoes make a good vegetarian substitute.) But in the Casa de la Abuela version the sauce is mixed with shredded cooked chicken or pork. Turkey parts like wings or legs would also be appropriate; pre-cook in a small amount of water or stock for at least 35 to 40 minutes before simmering in the sauce for another 30 to 40 minutes.

Anyone who has on hand a batch of homemade chocolate blend (page 277) can use it in this mole. Substitute 1 1/2 cakes or 1/2 cup of the mixture for the commercial Mexican chocolate. If you are able to find chilhuacles rojos (page 46), use 8 of them in place of the guajillo-ancho combination. Griddle-roast for only a few seconds.

4 to 6 servings

Place the sesame seeds in a small heavy skillet over medium heat. Cook, stirring constantly and shaking the skillet, for 2 to 3 minutes, just until you see them starting to turn golden. Scrape the seeds out into a small bowl to stop the cooking and set aside.

Grate the chocolate coarsely on a straight-sided grater, or break or chop into small pieces. (If mixture is in granular form, leave as is.) Set aside.

Crush the bread to fine crumbs or grind in a food processor. You should have about 1 cup. Set aside.

Wash and griddle-dry the chiles by the directions on page 45. Place in a bowl as they are done and cover generously with boiling water. Let soak for at least 20 minutes.

Meanwhile, grind the *canela*, cloves, and peppercorns together in an electric coffee or spice grinder or with a mortar and pestle. Set aside.

Drain the soaked chiles and reserve. In a medium-size skillet, heat half of the lard over medium heat until rippling. Add the ground spices and cook, stirring, just until fragrant, 1 to 2 minutes. Add the onion, garlic, tomatoes, plantain, thyme, oregano, toasted sesame seeds, raisins, and almonds. Cook, uncovered, stirring frequently, for 15 minutes.

Let the cooked mixture cool for about 10 minutes, then place half the mixture in a blender with 1 cup chicken stock and half the drained chiles. Process to a smooth purée (about 3 minutes on high). Repeat with the remaining sauce mixture, another 1 cup chicken stock, and the remaining chiles.

In a large Dutch oven or deep skillet, heat the remaining lard over medium-high heat until rippling. Add the puréed mixture, stirring well to prevent splattering. Stir in the remaining stock, a little at a time. Cook, covered, stirring frequently, for 15 to 20 minutes, until the chiles lose the raw edge of their flavor. Stir in the bread crumbs and cook, stirring frequently, until the mixture is lightly thickened, about 10 minutes. Stir in the chocolate and cook, stirring constantly, until it is well dissolved. Add the salt.

Stir in the reserved shredded meat; cook, partly covered, stirring occasionally, just until heated through, 7 to 10 minutes. Taste for seasoning and add another pinch or two of salt if desired.

Manchamantel

"Tablecloth-Stainer"

4 large ancho chiles (page 46), tops and seeds removed

10 guajillo chiles (page 47), tops and seeds removed

2/3 cup vegetable oil

10 unpeeled garlic cloves

1 large or 2 medium unpeeled onions

4 large ripe tomatoes

5 large tomatillos, with husks

5 large sprigs fresh Mediterranean oregano or 1/2 teaspoon dried Mexican oregano, crumbled (page 38)

6 sprigs fresh thyme or 1/2 teaspoon dried

3 bay leaves

One 1-inch piece *canela* (page 30)

1/2 teaspoon cumin seeds

10 black peppercorns

One 3 1/2-pound chicken, cut into serving pieces

1 pound baby back pork ribs, cut into separate ribs

Salt and freshly ground black pepper

1 1/2 to 2 cups fresh pineapple, cut into large (1 1/2-inch) chunks (about 1/3 small pineapple)

2 large, firm green apples, peeled, cored, and cut into 8 wedges each

*I*n my childhood I used to love a wonderful, exciting sweet-and-sour dish called *manchamanteles* that friends from Chiapas shared with my mother. (You'll find the recipe in my first book, *Food From My Heart*.)

The Manchamantel of Oaxaca—considered one of the seven classic moles—is obviously related, but the flavors are spicier and less fruity.

This version is one that I discovered when I was exploring the food counters of the 20 de noviembre market in Oaxaca City. I had asked several people who the best cook there was and they all pointed me in the direction of one stall named La Pereñita. They were right. Now I go there every time I'm in Oaxaca. The owner, Nicolasa Ramírez, is a strong-willed, proud woman who has had the business for the last 48 years and lived to see her daughter, granddaughter, and great-granddaughter all working there. She did not look overjoyed when I asked what made her Manchamantel so special and I think she was surprised to find herself telling me. Perhaps her sense of obligation to give a true record overcame her natural reserve. "You have bewitched me," she said almost in a tone of injury. "I'm sharing all my secrets with you."

Two details make a great difference in Nicolasa's version of the dish. Before combining her spice mixture with the rest of the ingredients, she deepens the flavor by frying it in oil—moreover, oil that is already perfumed with sautéed garlic.

Nicolasa uses fresh pineapple for Manchamantel and I have always followed her. The canned chunks are much too sweet. She uses Oaxacan oregano; fresh Mediterranean oregano is not a close match, but here and in several other recipes I find it better than any type of dried oregano. You want that "green" note.

About 8 servings

Wash and thoroughly dry the chiles. In a heavy medium-size skillet, heat 1/4 cup of the oil over medium heat until rippling. Fry the chiles, 3 or 4 at a time, turning several times with tongs, until they just start to puff, about 30 seconds. Quickly remove them to a bowl as they are done; do not let them burn. Cover generously with boiling water and let soak at least 20 minutes while you prepare the vegetables.

Peel 2 of the garlic cloves and set aside. Using a griddle or medium-size cast-iron skillet, roast the 8 unpeeled garlic cloves by the directions on page 26. Set aside. Roast the onion, tomatoes, and tomatillos by the same procedure, removing each vegetable as it is done and setting it aside in a bowl.

Drain the soaked chiles and place in a blender with 1/2 cup water. Process to a smooth purée, about 3 minutes on high, stopping occasionally to scrape down the sides with a rubber spatula. It may be necessary to add a little more water to facilitate blending (one tablespoon at a time), but be careful not to make the mixture soupy—it should be quite thick. With a wooden spoon or pusher, force the paste through a medium-mesh sieve into a large bowl and set aside.

When the roasted garlic, onion, and tomatoes are cool enough to handle, peel them (being careful to save the juices) and place in the blender. Remove the husks from the tomatillos and add to the other vegetables. If using fresh oregano and thyme, add them and process to a smooth purée (about 1 minute on high). Add to the bowl with the chile purée, stirring well to combine.

Grind the dried oregano and thyme (if using), bay leaves, canela, cumin, and peppercorns together in an electric coffee or spice grinder or with a mortar and pestle. Set aside.

Cut the reserved peeled garlic cloves into thin slices. In a large skillet, heat 2 tablespoons oil over medium heat until rippling. Drop the sliced garlic into the hot oil and cook just until fragrant and golden, one to two minutes; do not allow to burn.

Scoop out and discard the garlic. Add the ground spices and cook for 1 minute, stirring constantly. Add the puréed chile-tomato mixture and cook the sauce, covered, stirring occasionally, until the flavors are blended, about 20 minutes.

Meanwhile, season the chicken pieces and pork ribs with salt and pepper. In a large, deep-lidded skillet or Dutch oven, heat the remaining oil (about 1/3 cup) over medium-high heat until rippling. Brown the chicken well on all sides (about 3 minutes per side); remove and set aside. Brown the ribs on all sides. Discard all but 3 tablespoons of the fat from the pan; add the sauce mixture, stirring constantly to guard against splatters.

Stir in the pineapple chunks and ribs. Reduce the heat to low and simmer, covered, for 15 minutes. Return the chicken to the pan. Add the apple wedges and simmer, covered, until the chicken is cooked through, about 20 minutes.

Chichilo con Chochoyotes
Dark Mole with Masa Dumplings

6 unpeeled garlic cloves

1 unpeeled medium onion, quartered

2 pounds beef round, cut into
1 1/2-inch cubes

2 pounds trimmed pork butt or
shoulder, cut into 1 1/2-inch
cubes

1 teaspoon salt

1 teaspoon black peppercorns

4 guajillo chiles (page 47), tops and
seeds removed

6 chilhuacles rojos (page 46) or
ancho chiles (page 46), tops and
seeds removed

3 packaged corn tortillas

4 whole cloves, or large pinch ground

2 tablespoons dried Oaxacan oregano,
or 1 teaspoon dried Mexican
oregano, crumbled (page 38)

10 dried avocado leaves (page 28)

1 cup (8 ounces) fresh *masa*
(page 93), or 1/2 cup *masa
harina* (page 94) mixed to a
smooth paste with 1 cup water

For the chochoyotes

3 tablespoons lard (preferably
home-rendered; page 36)

1/2 teaspoon salt

1/2 cup (4 ounces) fresh *masa*
(page 93), or 6 tablespoons *masa
harina* (page 94) mixed to a
smooth paste with 6 tablespoons
water

*T*his is one of the "seven *moles*" of Oaxaca—less rich and elaborate than a *mole negro*, but with a more complex intensity than some of the family. The thickening comes from *masa*, not seeds or nuts. It is also one of the few *moles* where specific meats—cubed stewing beef and pork—are a traditional part of the dish. Chichilo is often made with small *masa* dumplings called *chochoyotes* that are formed into a shape a little like old-fashioned "thimble" cookies and added to the sauce at the end.

Chichilo is one of the "burned" dishes of Oaxaca in which some ingredient must be well charred and blackened to give the right flavor. If you have a yard or terrace, burn the tortillas there to avoid filling the kitchen with fumes. Or at least disable the smoke alarm for the duration! The bitterness of the charred tortillas softens when they are soaked and then cooked in the sauce, melding perfectly with the other flavors.

6 to 8 servings

Peel 4 of the garlic cloves and set aside.

Place the remaining 2 unpeeled garlic cloves in a deep soup pot or large Dutch oven along with the onion, beef and pork cubes, and salt. Add the pepper, setting aside 4 peppercorns to be used later in the mixture. Add 9 cups cold water, or enough to cover the meat well. Bring to a boil over high heat, reduce the heat to low, and skim off any foam that forms on top. Simmer, partly covered, for 15 minutes. Remove the meat cubes with a slotted spoon and set aside; let the remaining ingredients simmer another 15 minutes. Strain the stock through a fine-mesh sieve, discarding the solids, and return it to the rinsed-out pot. You should have about 8 cups of liquid. Set aside.

While the stock is cooking, wash and griddle-dry the chiles by the directions on page 45. (If using chilhuacles rojos, griddle-dry for only a few seconds.) Char the tortillas over an open flame or under the broiler until thoroughly blackened and slightly shrunken. Place the tortillas and chiles in a medium-size saucepan and cover generously with water. Bring to a boil over medium heat and let cook for 10 minutes. You will have an unappetizing sight like drenched tortilla charcoal, but don't be dismayed. Drain well, discarding the cooking water. Set aside.

Grind the cloves, reserved 4 peppercorns, and oregano together in an electric coffee grinder or with a mortar and pestle. Set aside.

Place the avocado leaves on a griddle or in a heavy skillet warmed over medium heat. Toast for a few seconds, just until fragrant and very lightly browned; remove at once. Set aside 4 of the avocado leaves; place the rest in a blender together with the ground spices, drained chiles and tortillas, and reserved peeled garlic cloves. Add 1 cup of the reserved stock and process until smooth, stopping occasionally to scrape down the sides with a rubber spatula.

Return the pot of stock to the stove and heat to a low boil over medium heat. Reduce the heat to maintain a gentle simmer. With a wooden spoon or pusher, force the puréed chile-tortilla mixture through a medium-mesh sieve into the stock. Taste for seasoning and add more salt if desired. Add the remaining 4 avocado leaves.

Place the *masa* in a bowl. Add about 1 cup water and mix to the consistency of a smooth pancake batter. (Work in the water little by little; you may need slightly more or less.) Whisk the mixture into the simmering stock a little at a time and continue to whisk over low heat until it thickens to the consistency of heavy cream. If lumps form, press the mixture through a medium-mesh sieve (pushing with a spoon to force through the lumpy bits) and return to the heat. Add the reserved beef and pork cubes to the sauce and simmer, partly covered, stirring occasionally, for 35 minutes or until the meat is fork-tender.

While the stew simmers, make the *chochoyotes*. Place the lard in a mixing bowl with 1/2 teaspoon salt. Add the *masa* and stir the ingredients together with a wooden spoon until thoroughly combined. (Do not beat—this time you want a dense rather than a fluffy mixture.) Roll bits of dough between your palms to form balls the size of small marbles. Poke a deep indentation in each with a finger (this helps them cook faster). From this amount of *masa* you should get about 20 to 25 *chochoyotes*. Add them to the simmering stew, a few at a time. Serve as soon as all have floated to the top, about 5 minutes.

Mole Negro de Teotitlán
Teotitlán-style Black Mole

Mole Negro is the state dish of Oaxaca, the king of *moles*. It also happens to be the most difficult to make. People pride themselves on their own different touches, and family recipes are passed down as heirlooms. Markets stands specializing in *moles* all proclaim that their version is the best.

I have selected two representative recipes for Mole Negro. The first is an adaptation of a version made by my friend and culinary mentor Zoyla Mendoza, who has given me such insight into the cooking of the Valley Zapotecs. When she made it for me at her home in Teotitlán del Valle, she first toasted the chiles, nuts, and spices and sent them out to a nearby mill to be ground. Meanwhile, she pounded the tomatoes and other moist ingredients in her big stone mortar, to be combined later with the nut and spice paste. Less sweet than many other versions, her Mole Negro is spicy and intense—I love the sprightly taste of fresh ginger. Increase the amount of clove and thyme in the recipe if you wish. Zoyla used much more of both than I do.

Though Zoyla's version of Mole Negro is less complex then some, it shows the crucial "blackening" feature of most black *moles*. For years I'd made versions that turned out no blacker than dark red. An offhand remark revealed what I was doing wrong. "*Queman los chiles*" ("They burn the chiles"), a Juchitecan woman casually told me when I asked her. My instinct said that it would turn the whole dish bitter, so I'd just been toasting the chiles lightly. But in Oaxaca it is normal to make Mole Negro by first separating the seeds from the dried chiles, then toasting the chiles to an absolute crisp and literally burning—BURNING—the seeds. Zoyla also follows this procedure. The bitterness disappears through soaking and extended cooking.

Because the pungent fumes can leave you gasping and call down the wrath of neighbors in city apartment buildings, it is wise to attempt this recipe only if you can do the worst part (burning the seeds) outdoors or with a good exhaust fan going full blast. You should also work out an advance plan for the final grinding of the paste. You can either combine all the ingredients and process them in several batches in the blender or assign part of the task (the chiles, nuts, and spices that Zoyla sent out to the mill) to the food processor. Read the recipe through carefully in advance, and decide which strategy you prefer. (The processor alone will definitely give the wrong texture.)

This sauce is popular with enchiladas and shows up in chicken, turkey, or pork tamales (see Tamales de Guajolote con Mole Negro, page 120). But the age-old way of eating black *mole* is with boiled turkey. In this country, use turkey parts like wings or drumsticks and simmer for 35 to 40 minutes in a small amount of stock, then finish cooking in the sauce for another 30 to 40 minutes.

Please note that when served in this manner with poultry or other meats, the sauce should be thinned to a fairly light consistency. When it is used as a filling, it must be dense and thick.

About 3 1/2 to 4 1/2 cups before thinning

4 ounces ancho chiles (page 46)

4 ounces guajillo chiles (page 47)

1 thick slice day-old brioche or challah

1/3 cup pecan meats

1/4 cup blanched almonds

4 unpeeled garlic cloves

1 large or 2 medium unpeeled onions

1 large ripe tomato

4 ounces tomatillos, with husks

2/3 cup (about 3 ounces) sesame seeds

7 tablespoons lard (preferably home-rendered; page 36)

One 6-inch piece *canela* (page 30)

1/2 bunch or 1 small bunch thyme (about 2 dozen sprigs), or 2 teaspoons dried, crumbled

1/4 cup dried Oaxacan oregano or 1 teaspoon dried Mexican oregano, crumbled (page 38)

16 whole cloves

14 allspice berries

1/4 teaspoon freshly grated nutmeg

One 1-inch piece fresh ginger, peeled and minced

1 cup dark raisins

2 to 4 cups homemade chicken stock (page 74), or as necessary

The day before beginning the sauce, remove the stems and tops from the chiles; carefully shake out and reserve the seeds. Rinse the chiles under cold running water. Spread them out in a single layer where they can dry completely. Let stand until the following day, turning occasionally and checking to be sure not a drop of moisture remains.

Crush the bread to fine crumbs or grind in a food processor. You should have about 1 cup. Set aside.

Preheat the oven to 350°F.

Spread the chiles (they must be bone-dry) in one layer on a baking sheet. Toast them in the oven, turning frequently, until crisp and deeply blackened, about 20 minutes. Let the chiles stand at room temperature until completely cooled.

Spread the pecans and almonds on a baking sheet. Toast them in the oven until golden brown, about 10 minutes. Set aside.

Place the crisp toasted chiles in a food processor and process until finely ground. Set aside.

On a griddle or in a small cast-iron skillet, heat the reserved chile seeds over high heat, shaking the pan occasionally, until thoroughly charred and black on all sides, about 5 minutes. (Because of the fumes, this is best done outdoors if you have the means.) You can speed the process by sprinkling a few drops of vegetable oil over the seeds and igniting with a match, standing well back from the flame and taking care to shield your face, clothing, and hair. Place the charred seeds in a bowl, cover with at least 2 cups cold water, and soak for 1 1/2 hours, changing the water twice. Drain and set aside.

Heat a griddle or medium-size cast-iron skillet over low heat. Roast the garlic, onion, tomato, and tomatillos by the directions on pages 25 to 27, removing each kind of vegetable as it is done and setting it aside in a separate small bowl. When they are cool enough to handle, remove the husks from the tomatillos and peel the rest, making sure to save the juices.

Place the sesame seeds in a medium-size heavy skillet over medium heat and toast just until golden (about 3 minutes), stirring constantly and shaking the pan. Immediately scrape out the seeds into a small bowl to stop the cooking. Set aside.

In a small, heavy skillet, heat 1 tablespoon lard over medium-high heat until rippling. Add the *canela*, thyme, oregano, cloves, allspice, nutmeg and ginger. Fry the spices, stirring constantly, until fragrant, about 2 minutes. Set aside.

In a small skillet, heat another 2 tablespoons lard over medium heat until rippling. Add the raisins and bread crumbs; cook, stirring, until the raisins are puffed and the bread is lightly colored, about 2 minutes. Set aside.

Now you are ready to purée all the ingredients, using either a blender/food processor combination or a blender alone.

If using both machines, place the pecans, almonds, sesame seeds, bread-raisin mixture, ground chiles, and drained chile seeds in the food processor (working in batches as necessary). Process to a smooth purée. Next, place the fried spices, peeled garlic, onion, tomatoes, and tomatillos in the blender and process to a smooth purée. Combine the two mixtures in a large bowl.

If using only a blender, line up all the prepared ingredients next to the machine on the counter, place some of each in the blender container, add a few tablespoons chicken stock, and process until smooth, adding more stock as necessary to facilitate blending. (This method requires great patience; small batches will be well puréed in 1 to 2 minutes while large ones may retain coarse bits of the spices. If thoroughly processed, the mixture will not require sieving, so try not to rush things.) Pour each batch into a bowl as it is done and proceed with the next batch.

In a large, heavy saucepan or Dutch oven, heat the remaining 4 tablespoons lard over high heat until rippling. Add the purée, all at once, watching for splatters, and reduce the heat to medium-low. Cover and cook, stirring frequently, until the harshness of the chiles is mellowed, 35 to 40 minutes.

The *mole* should now be a heavy paste like a thick frosting mixture. It can be stored for later use (see To Store *Moles*, page 140) or used at once. In either case, it should be thinned before further cooking. Place the paste in the blender when ready to thin it; add 1 cup chicken stock (or as necessary) and process to combine thoroughly.

Mole Negro de Oaxaca
Oaxaca City-style Mole

Richer and sweeter than the preceding Mole Negro de Teotitlán, this Oaxaca City version is the pinnacle of the Spanish-Zapotec culinary art. It was one of the first Oaxacan dishes I learned, from the well-known cooking teacher María Concepción Portillo de Carballido.

In this Mole Negro, the black color comes not so much from toasting the chiles until dark but because the chiles themselves—chilhuacles negros—are black. Doña Concepción did not toast the chiles to the same dark, brittle stage as cooks I know in other parts of the state, so if you have to use the mulato/guajillo combination your *mole* might not be as black as the name suggests. She also sautéed the sesame seeds and nuts in lard, which seems to send U.S. cooks into fits of terror. This is an unjustified reaction. The idea is just to deepen the flavor of each type of seed or nut by lightly browning it in a little fat. (Start with 2 tablespoons lard per batch and add more if necessary.) You are burnishing a rich sauce with an extra richness, and the true Oaxacan way of doing it is with lard.

The recipe is essentially the same as the one in my first book, *Food from my Heart*, but I have had second thoughts about the procedure. The recipe makes a very large quantity that can easily be halved, but even so it takes such an eternity to purée everything using only a blender that I now prefer to do part of the task in a food processor (after grinding the toasted spices in a coffee mill).

This several-machine method produces a mixture close to the texture of the *mole* pastes that people have ground at special mills in Oaxaca. It is meant to be stored as a paste and diluted with stock just before use. Because of the extreme length of the efforts involved, I have arranged the order of preparation so that some ingredients can be ground or puréed somewhat ahead of time and held for several hours until you are ready for the final tasks and assembly job.

The all-blender method, which I give as an alternative, requires more liquid. Therefore it gives a larger volume of a sauce that is already thinned to the right consistency for serving with meat and poultry. You will be happy to know that rinsing out the blender between different parts of the operation isn't necessary, except after puréeing the chiles.

Combined Appliance Method
About 2 quarts

Heat a small heavy skillet over medium-low heat and prepare to toast the spices. Add the peppercorns and cloves; heat, shaking the pan and stirring constantly, until their aroma is released, about 1 minute. Empty into a small bowl. Add the *canela* to the pan and toast the same way for about 1 minute; add to the pepper and cloves. Toast the dried oregano the same way until fragrant and add it to the other spices.

Grind the toasted spices together in an electric coffee or spice grinder or with a mortar and pestle. Set aside.

Remove the tops from the chiles. Carefully shake out and reserve the seeds. Reserve the chiles separately.

Wipe the skillet clean. Raise the heat to high and add the reserved chile seeds. Cook, shaking the pan occasionally, until charred and black all over. (Because of the fumes, this is best done outdoors if you have the means.) You can speed up the process by sprinkling a few drops of vegetable oil over the seeds and very carefully igniting the oil with a match, standing well back from the flames and taking care to shield your face, clothing, and hair. Place the burned chile seeds in a bowl and cover with cold water. Soak for 1 1/2 hours, changing the water twice. Drain and reserve.

While the chile seeds soak, heat 2 to 3 tablespoons of the lard in a heavy medium-size skillet over medium heat. When the fat ripples, add the sesame seeds and cook about 3 minutes, stirring constantly and shaking the pan, just until lightly golden. Immediately scrape out the seeds into a heatproof bowl. Add a little more lard to the pan, heat, and cook the peanuts in the same way, about 3 minutes or until lightly browned. Add to the bowl with the sesame seeds. Cook the slivered almonds, then the pecans, in the same way, allowing about 3 minutes cooking time for each. Add a little more fat each time and add the toasted nuts to the sesame seeds and peanuts.

If desired, drain off the excess lard from the toasted nuts and reserve 2 tablespoons for cooking the plantain later.

12 whole black peppercorns

6 whole cloves

One 2-inch piece *canela* (page 30)

1/4 cup dried Oaxacan oregano or 2 tablespoons dried Mexican oregano, crumbled (page 38)

1 pound chilhuacles negros (page 46) or 8 ounces each of mulato and guajillo chiles (page 47), tops removed

1/2 to 1 cup lard (preferably home-rendered; page 36) or as needed

1/2 cup (about 2 1/2 ounces) sesame seeds

1/2 cup dry-roasted peanuts

1/2 cup blanched slivered almonds

1/2 cup pecan or walnut meats

1 1/2 cups dry sherry

1/2 cup dark raisins

1 cup pitted prunes, coarsely chopped

1 cup pitted dried apricots, coarsely chopped

2 tablespoons butter (or omit and use part of the lard)

1 large very ripe plantain (page 39), peeled and cut into 1/2-inch slices

3 to 5 cups homemade chicken stock (page 74), or as needed

1/2 unpeeled head of garlic (about 8 large cloves)

1 large or 2 medium unpeeled onions

2 large ripe tomatoes

5 to 6 large tomatillos, husks removed

One 3-ounce tablet Mexican chocolate (pages 277 to 279), or 3 cakes or 1 cup homemade chocolate blend (page 277)

Let the nuts cool to room temperature. Place in a food processor and grind to a smooth paste. Scrape out the ground mixture into a bowl and set aside.

In a small saucepan, heat the sherry until just too hot for your finger. Place the raisins and chopped dried fruits in a bowl. Pour the hot sherry over them and let soak for 30 minutes.

Heat the butter or reserved lard in a medium-size skillet over medium-high heat. When the fat is very hot, add the plantain and cook, turning several times with a spatula, until golden on both sides, about 3 minutes. Set aside.

Working in batches as necessary, rinse and griddle-dry the reserved seeded chiles by the directions on page 45. As they are done, remove them to a deep bowl. Cover generously with boiling water and let soak for about 20 minutes.

Place the plantain, soaked fruits, and sherry in a food processor. Process, in batches if necessary, to a thick purée; scrape out into a bowl and reserve.

Drain the soaked chiles. Working in batches as necessary, place the chiles and chile seeds in a blender, adding 1/2 to 3/4 cup chicken stock per batch, and process until smoothly puréed (4 minutes on high), adding more stock if necessary. Working in convenient-sized batches, turn out the chile mixture into a medium-mesh sieve set over a large bowl. With a wooden spoon or pusher, force the purée through, discarding any bits that won't go through.

Now you have 4 separate mixtures on hand: dry ground spices, ground nuts, puréed fruits, and puréed chiles. If you wish to continue with the recipe later, each of these things can hold for up to 4 hours (the chile mixture should be refrigerated). When you are ready to proceed, heat a griddle or medium-size cast-iron skillet over low heat. Working in sequence, roast the garlic, onion, and tomatoes by the directions on page 26, removing each kind as it is done and reserving it in a small bowl. While the other vegetables roast, bring a small saucepan of water to a boil and drop in the tomatillos. Cook, uncovered, until they change color, about 3 minutes. Drain.

When the garlic, onion, and tomatoes are cool enough to handle, peel them and place (with their juices) in a blender along with the tomatillos. Process until smoothly puréed (about 3 minutes on high).

Combine all the purées and the ground spices in a Dutch oven or saucepan large enough to hold everything. Bring to a boil over medium-high heat and stir in the chocolate. Reduce the heat to medium-low. Cook, covered, stirring often, for 30 to 40 minutes to marry and develop all the flavors.

All-Blender Method
About 3 1/2 quarts

Have 4 to 5 cups homemade chicken stock on hand. Toast all the whole spices as described above and set aside. Seed the chiles and set aside; burn the seeds and leave to soak. Fry the nuts and soak the dried fruits; set aside. Fry the plantain; set aside. Roast, soak, and drain the chiles. (All steps may be done as much as 4 hours ahead to this point.) Roast the garlic, onion, and tomatoes and set aside, peeling when cool and saving the juices; boil the tomatillos and add to the other vegetables.

Choose a Dutch oven or saucepan large enough to hold all the ingredients. Drain the chile seeds. Working in batches as necessary, place the chiles and chile seeds in a blender with the toasted whole spices and enough chicken stock to facilitate blending; start with 3/4 cup stock per batch and increase a little if necessary. Process each batch to a smooth purée (about 5 minutes on high). Working in convenient-sized batches, force the purée through a medium-mesh sieve into the Dutch oven, discarding whatever won't go though. Rinse out the blender to remove any hard and fibrous bits. Then purée all the prepared ingredients (fried nuts, fruits with plantain, roasted vegetables) in any preferred order, working in small batches for best results and adding stock as necessary to facilitate the action of the blades. Add each batch to the pot as it is processed. When all the puréeing has been completed, heat to a boil, add the chocolate, and simmer as described above.

Roosters for sale at the Mercado de Abasto

Chicken

Chicken is the favorite meat of Oaxaca. And no wonder. The chickens that are available there are range-fed, plump, and fresh-killed just before cooking. The quality is indescribably better than what we have in the United States. Not one mass-produced, force-fed, anemic frozen chicken has ever soiled the land.

The difference in quality gave me some problems in translating recipes for use in United States kitchens. As I point out elsewhere, the soul of the great traditional Oaxacan dishes is usually the sauce. Whatever meat or poultry you are serving is often simply boiled or poached, then just placed in the sauce (which may have been made with some of the cooking liquid). Try this with U.S. supermarket chickens! These take only about half as long to cook as chickens do in Oaxaca, but they badly need help in the flavor department.

My way of trying to improve the taste in recipes originally calling for plain boiled chicken is to adopt a braising technique: browning the chicken in a small amount of fat before finishing it in the sauce. (I usually have on hand a batch of separately prepared chicken stock, page 74.) It is some sacrifice of authenticity, but it helps deepen and enrich the flavor.

Some people are lucky enough to have access to free-range chickens through farmers' markets or specialty butchers. You can expect more variation in cooking times than with the standardized supermarket birds. I have experimented with some good-quality free-range chickens and found the browning step is not necessary. Also, the skin (especially on the breast) tends to stick to the pan in browning. The flavor, however, is wonderful. I suggest that you play it by ear—follow the recipe except for the browning step, adding the chicken pieces directly to the hot sauce and starting to test for doneness with a skewer or sharp knife tip after 20 minutes. The meat is done when it yields slightly to pressure and the juices are barely pale pink. The breast pieces may take less time to cook and can be added 5 to 10 minutes after the rest. You may prefer to remove the skin before serving.

Strange to say, in Oaxaca I have never been served turkey, either at restaurants or in private homes. But I see them in the markets and I know that many of the dishes I give in chicken-based versions were traditionally made with turkey, the main pre-Hispanic meat. The sauce dishes like Almendrado or Guisado de Fandango are excellent made with turkey. But please note that the birds in Oaxaca are nothing like our gigantic factory-farm turkeys with acres of dry, tasteless breast meat. It is best to buy turkey parts like wings or drumsticks, which have more flavor (although the skin is never the best part and the dish may look more attractive if you remove it after cooking). Omit the browning step; pre-cook the turkey pieces, covered, in a small amount of water or stock for 30 minutes, then lift out and add directly to the hot sauce. Cook the turkey parts for 40 to 45 minutes in the sauce; you can save the cooking liquid for another use. Allow 1 wing (wing tip removed if you wish) or 1/2 drumstick per serving.

Almendrado de Pollo
Chicken in Almond Sauce

One 3 1/2- to 4-pound chicken, cut in serving pieces

Salt and freshly ground black pepper

1/3 cup vegetable oil

1 cup unblanched almonds

1 large slice (about 1 1/2 inches thick) brioche, challah or other egg bread

1 large unpeeled onion, halved crosswise, roasted (page 26)

4 unpeeled garlic cloves, roasted (page 26)

5 large ripe tomatoes (about 2 1/2 pounds)

1 teaspoon salt, or to taste

8 whole cloves, or 1/4 teaspoon ground

15 black peppercorns, or 3/4 teaspoon freshly ground black pepper

One 2-inch piece *canela* (page 30)

1/2 teaspoon dried Mexican oregano (page 38)

3 cups homemade chicken stock (page 74)

1/3 cup dark raisins

1/2 cup pimiento-stuffed green olives (one 3-ounce jar, drained), cut in thick slices

3 tablespoons drained capers

*T*his was the first dish I ever ate in Oaxaca, at a little stand in the Mercado 20 de noviembre in Oaxaca City. It was the start of my love affair with Oaxacan food. The sauce was rich and full of fragrant nuances I had not tasted elsewhere in Mexico—the warm nutty flavor of the fried almonds, the acidity of the capers and olives, and the sweetness of the raisins and aromatic spices, all melding deliciously with roasted garlic and onion. Later I found an even better version at the restaurant Casa de la Abuela by the corner of the *Zócalo* in Oaxaca City.

The most time-consuming part of the recipe is preparing the almonds, which take a long time to peel *after* frying and 45 minutes of soaking. Substituting blanched almonds saves time but reduces the depth of flavor. To make life easier you may do the almonds first, up to 1 day before the rest of the preparation. Fry, soak, and peel the almonds as directed below. Strain the oil through a fine-mesh sieve; set aside the almonds and the oil until needed.

4 to 6 servings

Season the chicken with salt and pepper. In a large Dutch oven, heat the oil until not quite smoking. Lightly brown the chicken over medium-high heat, allowing about 3 minutes per side. Remove from the pan and set aside.

In the same oil, fry the almonds over medium-high heat until fragrant and slightly darkened, about 2 minutes. Do not scorch. With a slotted spoon, remove the almonds to a small bowl. Cover with boiling water and let soak 45 minutes.

While the almonds soak, fry the bread in the same oil over medium-high heat until golden brown on both sides. Remove from the pan and let drain on paper towels. Pour off and discard about half the fat from the pan; set the pan aside.

Prepare the onion and garlic as directed. While they roast, bring a medium saucepan of water to a boil and add the tomatoes. Cook over high heat for 15 minutes and drain. When the onion, garlic, and tomatoes are cool enough to handle, peel them and process together in a blender until smooth, working in batches if necessary.

Peel the almonds, using a small sharp knife to make the process easier. Set aside.

Over medium-high heat, reheat the reserved fat in the Dutch oven until not quite smoking. Carefully add the tomato mixture—it will splatter—and 1 teaspoon salt or to taste, and cook, covered, over medium-high heat, stirring frequently, until slightly thickened, about 15 minutes.

In a coffee or spice grinder or with a mortar and pestle, grind the cloves, peppercorns, and *canela* to a powder. Process the ground spices, oregano, chicken stock, almonds, and fried bread in a blender or food processor until smooth (about 2 minutes on high). Add to the tomato sauce and stir to combine. Bring the mixture to a boil and add the browned chicken pieces, raisins, olives, and capers. Taste the sauce and adjust the seasoning. Reduce the heat to low and simmer, covered, until the chicken is tender, about 20 minutes.

Alcaparrado de Pollo
Chicken in Caper Sauce

1/8 teaspoon saffron threads

1 1/2 cups warm homemade chicken stock (page 74)

5 to 6 tablespoons vegetable oil

3 ounces (about 3/4 cup) hulled pumpkin seeds (page 39)

1 1/2 tablespoons olive oil

1 small onion, coarsely chopped

1 garlic clove, coarsely chopped

1 small crusty roll (about 3 ounces), cut into slices

4 black peppercorns

3 whole cloves

One 1-inch piece *canela* (page 30)

2 teaspoons dried Oaxacan oregano or 1/2 teaspoon dried Mexican oregano (page 38)

Two 3-ounce jars capers with brine

One 3 1/2-pound chicken, cut into serving pieces

Salt and freshly ground black pepper

*T*his dish, like the Almendrado, is almost entirely Mediterranean with only one major New World ingredient—in this case, the pumpkin seeds replacing the almonds that would have been used in Moorish and Spanish cooking. I originally learned the dish from the Oaxacan cooking teacher María Concepción Portillo de Carballido.

4 servings

Crumble the saffron into the chicken stock and let steep a few minutes.

Heat 2 tablespoons of the vegetable oil in a medium-size skillet until very hot but not quite smoking. Add the pumpkin seeds (carefully, since they tend to pop violently as they hit the hot oil). Cook, stirring constantly, until they are puffed and have a nutty fragrance, about 30 seconds. Do not let them burn or they will turn the whole dish bitter. Scoop out at once and drain on paper towels.

In the same skillet, heat the olive oil until very hot. Add the chopped onion and garlic. Cook, stirring, over medium heat until just wilted, 3 to 5 minutes. Add the sliced roll and cook, turning the pieces, until golden brown on both sides.

Add the peppercorns, cloves, *canela*, and oregano and cook, stirring, until their aroma is released, about 2 minutes longer. Add the capers with their brine and stir well to combine. Simmer, uncovered, for 5 minutes on low heat; add the chicken stock with the dissolved saffron and simmer another 5 minutes. Let cool, then place in the blender and process until well puréed, about 30 seconds. Add the pumpkin seeds and purée until smooth, another 30 seconds.

Preheat the oven to 350°F.

Season the chicken with salt and pepper. In a heavy skillet, heat the remaining vegetable oil until rippling over high heat. Brown the chicken pieces well, a few at a time, about 3 minutes on each side. Drain the chicken pieces on paper towels as they are browned.

Place the chicken pieces in a lidded casserole large enough to hold the pieces and sauce comfortably. Pour the sauce over the chicken, cover the casserole, and bake until the chicken is tender, about 40 minutes.

Note: *The sauce is also delicious with grilled or broiled fish. Cook the fish separately and serve the sauce on the side.*

Estofado de Frutas
Chicken and Fruit Stew

*I*t's fascinating how Oaxacan cooks give so many different spins to European-inspired sauces thickened with nuts or seeds. Tomatoes and chocolate are the native American accents in this truly sophisticated dish from Lucila Zárate de Fuentes in Oaxaca City.

This is one case where I probably would use fresh Mediterranean oregano—it is not quite right as a substitute for Oaxacan oregano, but the fresh herb is closer in effect than the dried.

If you have made up a batch of my homemade chocolate blend (page 277), substitute 3 small cakes or 1 cup of the mixture for the commercial chocolate tablet.

4 to 6 servings

Grate the chocolate on a straight-sided grater or break it into small pieces; set aside. (It is easier to incorporate if grated.)

Season the chicken with salt and pepper. In a large Dutch oven, heat the oil over medium-high heat until not quite smoking. Lightly brown the chicken, allowing about 3 minutes per side. Remove from the pan and set aside. Pour off and discard all but 2 tablespoons of fat from the pan; set the pan aside.

Place the sesame seeds in a medium skillet or sauté pan over medium heat. Toast just until golden, about 3 minutes, stirring constantly and shaking the pan. Immediately scrape the seeds into a small bowl before they darken and overcook.

Place the roasted tomatoes, onions, garlic, and toasted sesame seeds in a blender with the herbs and spices and process until smooth. Over medium-high heat, reheat the reserved fat in the Dutch oven until rippling. Add the puréed mixture and bring to a boil, stirring frequently to keep it from splattering. Add the chocolate and stir well to combine. Lower the heat and simmer, covered, stirring occasionally, for 15 minutes. Thin with some chicken stock or water if the sauce has gotten too thick and pasty.

Return the chicken pieces to the Dutch oven. Add the apple wedges and plaintain rounds, spacing them evenly. Scatter the almonds over the top. Cover and cook over medium heat until the chicken is tender, about 20 minutes. Alternatively, you can transfer the dish to a lidded casserole and bake it in a preheated 350°F oven for 35 to 40 minutes.

One 3-ounce tablet Mexican chocolate (pages 277 to 279)

One 4-pound chicken, cut in serving pieces

Salt and freshly ground black pepper

1/4 cup vegetable oil

1 cup sesame seeds (about 5 ounces)

4 large ripe tomatoes (about 2 pounds), roasted and peeled (page 26)

2 medium onions, roasted and peeled (page 26)

8 garlic cloves, roasted and peeled (page 26)

6 large sprigs fresh thyme, or 1 teaspoon dried

4 sprigs fresh marjoram, or 1/2 teaspoon dried

4 sprigs fresh Mediterranean oregano, or 1/2 teaspoon dried Mexican oregano (page 38)

1 teaspoon freshly ground black pepper

One 1 1/2-inch piece *canela* (page 30)

1/4 teaspoon ground cloves

1/4 to 1/2 cup homemade chicken stock (page 74) or water, as needed

2 tart, firm green apples, peeled, cored, and sliced into 8 wedges each

1 large ripe plantain (page 39), peeled and sliced into 1/2-inch rounds

1/2 cup blanched almonds

Guisado de Fandango
Wedding Stew

One 3 1/2- to 4-pound chicken, cut
   in serving pieces

Salt and freshly ground black pepper

1/4 cup lard (preferably
   home-rendered; page 36)
   or vegetable oil

1 small crusty roll (about 3 ounces),
   cut into slices

4 large ripe tomatoes (about
   2 pounds), roasted and peeled
   (page 26)

1 large onion, coarsely chopped

2 garlic cloves, peeled

2 cups homemade chicken stock
   (page 74)

1/2 cup pimiento-stuffed green olives
   (one 3-ounce jar), drained

One 3-ounce jar capers, drained

1/2 cup dark raisins

8 pickled serrano chiles, drained

3 tablespoons chopped fresh Italian
   parsley leaves

*A*s the name indicates, this dish from the Valley of Oaxaca is a traditional specialty at village weddings there (made in quantities to serve a large party). It is often made with turkey, sometimes pork. You can see the family resemblance to other Spanish-influenced dishes like the Almendrado de Pollo (page 176) or Estofado de Frutas (page 179), but this time the sauce is thickened only with bread instead of nuts and the pickled chiles create a totally new balance of flavors.

4 to 6 servings

Season the chicken with salt and pepper. Heat the lard in a large Dutch oven over medium-high heat; brown the chicken pieces until golden, about 3 minutes on each side. Remove from the pan and set aside. In the same fat fry the bread slices over medium-high heat until golden on both sides. Drain on paper towels. Pour off and discard all but about 3 tablespoons of fat from the pan; set the pan aside.

Place the peeled tomatoes in a blender with the onion, garlic, and bread; process to a smooth purée (about 2 minutes on high).

Return the Dutch oven to the stove and heat over medium-high heat until the fat ripples. Add the tomato mixture and cook, covered, over medium-high heat, stirring frequently, for 10 minutes. Stir in the chicken stock, olives, capers, raisins, pickled chiles, and parsley. Bring the sauce to a boil and add the chicken pieces. Reduce the heat to medium and cook, covered, until the chicken is tender, about 20 minutes.

Gallina en Tesmole

Braised Chicken in Masa-Thickened Sauce

"Gallina" is a hen, and probably this simple but excitingly flavored dish would have been originally made with a stewing fowl. For best flavor, use fresh *masa* and fresh epazote.

4 to 6 servings

Season the chicken with salt and pepper. In a large Dutch oven, heat the oil over medium-high heat until not quite smoking. Lightly brown the chicken, allowing about 3 minutes per side. Remove from the pan and set aside. Pour off and discard about half the fat from the pan; set the pan aside.

Drain the soaked chiles and place in a blender with the peeled tomatoes and garlic. Process until smooth, about 2 minutes on high. With a wooden spoon or pusher, work the mixture through a medium-mesh sieve into a bowl.

Return the Dutch oven to the stove and heat over medium heat until the fat is rippling. Add the chile-tomato mixture and cook, stirring frequently, for 5 minutes to concentrate slightly.

In a medium bowl, mix the *masa* to a thin paste with the chicken stock. Add the *masa* mixture to the sauce along with the epazote, 1 teaspoon salt or to taste, and the lime juice. Stir to blend well; taste the sauce and add more salt or lime juice if desired. Add the chicken pieces and cook, covered, over medium heat until the chicken is tender, about 20 minutes.

One 3 1/2-pound chicken, cut in serving pieces

Salt and freshly ground black pepper

3 tablespoons vegetable oil

5 costeño (page 46) or 3 guajillo chiles (page 47), seeds and tops removed, soaked in boiling water to cover for 20 minutes

4 medium ripe tomatoes (about 1 pound) roasted and peeled (page 26)

2 large garlic cloves, peeled

1/2 cup *masa* (page 93), fresh or reconstituted by mixing 3 tablespoons *masa harina* (page 94) with 1/2 cup water

2 cups homemade chicken stock (page 74)

6 large sprigs fresh epazote or 2 tablespoons dried, crumbled (page 35)

1 teaspoon salt, or to taste

Juice of 2 limes, or to taste

Pollo con Oregano
Chicken with Oregano

5 garlic cloves, unpeeled

One 3 1/2- to 4-pound chicken, cut in serving pieces

2 bay leaves

1 small onion, unpeeled

1/2 teaspoon black peppercorns

1 teaspoon salt, or to taste

2 teaspoons dried Oaxacan oregano or 1 teaspoon dried Mexican oregano (page 38)

1/4 cup vegetable oil

*T*his is a favorite dish at food stalls in the markets. It is also popular with home cooks, since it can be marinated until just before the final sautéing and fits easily into any schedule. The combination of flavors is typical of simple, everyday Oaxacan cooking.

4 to 6 servings

Peel 3 of the garlic cloves and reserve.

Place the chicken, bay leaves, onion, remaining 2 unpeeled garlic cloves, peppercorns, and salt in a medium-size saucepan or small stock pot with just enough cold water to cover by 1 inch. Bring to a boil over high heat; immediately reduce the heat to low and skim off any foam that rises to the top. Cover the pot and simmer just until the chicken is cooked through, about 20 minutes.

Remove the chicken from the pot and place in a deep, narrow glass or stainless-steel bowl just large enough to hold the pieces and part of the liquid.

Strain the stock through a medium-mesh sieve and let cool. Mince one of the peeled garlic cloves; scatter the minced garlic and oregano over the chicken. Add enough of the cooled stock to cover the chicken by one inch. Let marinate, refrigerated, for 4 hours. (Any leftover stock can be saved for another purpose.)

At serving time, lift the chicken pieces from the marinade, drain, and pat dry with paper towels. (Strain the marinade and reserve for another purpose.) If desired, salt lightly. Slice the remaining peeled garlic cloves. In a large skillet, heat the oil over medium-high heat until not quite smoking. Add the garlic cloves and sauté until golden, pressing down on the garlic with the back of a spoon or spatula to release its flavor. Remove and discard the garlic before it darkens and turns bitter. Add the chicken pieces and brown lightly, turning once or twice, allowing about 3 minutes per side. Serve immediately.

Pollo Enchilado

Chicken in Chile Sauce

I learned this tasty dish from Rosa Estrada, who owns the Restorán Rosita in the Mazatec mountain village of Huautla de Jiménez. It is an example of a very basic but vivid dried-chile sauce.

4 to 6 servings

Rinse and griddle-dry the chiles by the directions on page 45; soak in boiling water to cover for 20 minutes.

Season the chicken with salt and pepper. In a large Dutch oven or deep skillet, heat the oil over medium-high heat until not quite smoking and lightly brown the chicken, allowing about 3 minutes per side. Pour off and discard all but about 2 tablespoons of fat from the pan; set the pan aside.

Drain the soaked chiles. Place in the blender with the onion, garlic, peppercorns, cloves, and *canela*. Process until smooth, about 2 minutes on high, stopping occasionally to scrape down the sides with a rubber spatula. With a wooden spoon or pusher, work the purée through a medium-mesh sieve into a bowl.

Return the Dutch oven to the stove and heat over medium heat until the fat is rippling. Add the chile purée and cook, covered, stirring occasionally, for 10 minutes. Add the chicken stock, stirring well to combine. Add the chicken pieces and reduce the heat to low. Cook, covered, until the chicken is tender, about 20 minutes.

5 large ancho chiles (page 46)

One 3 1/2- to 4- pound chicken, cut in serving pieces

Salt and freshly ground black pepper

1/4 cup vegetable oil

1 small onion, peeled and coarsely chopped

2 garlic cloves, peeled

12 black peppercorns

6 whole cloves

One 2-inch piece *canela* (page 30)

2 cups homemade chicken (page 74) or pork stock (page 73)

Pollo Relleno de Papas
Potato-Stuffed Oven-Braised Chicken

6 guajillo chiles (page 47), tops, seeds, and veins removed

1 teaspoon salt or to taste, plus more for the stuffing

2 tablespoons achiote paste (page 28)

2 teaspoons dried Oaxacan oregano or 1 teaspoon dried Mexican oregano (page 38)

1 teaspoon freshly ground black pepper

1/4 teaspoon ground cloves

3 dried avocado leaves (page 28), crumbled

One 4 1/2- to 5-pound chicken

2 large Red Bliss or other waxy boiling potatoes (about 1 pound)

2 tablespoons vegetable oil

1 small onion, finely chopped

2 large garlic cloves, minced

1 large ripe tomato, peeled and chopped

1/4 cup cider vinegar diluted in 2 cups water

Every time I've been to the market at Juchitán I've found quite a few women selling this dish—except, for some reason, on my most recent 1996 visit, when I heard stories of shortages and hardly a chicken was to be found anywhere. The traditional presentation is very dramatic. The *juchitecas* like to use hens with unborn eggs inside them. They sell the cooked chickens split open lengthwise to reveal the eggs, which have taken on the earthy red of the achiote mixture used to coat the birds. Unless you know a poultry farmer who will sell you such a chicken, you won't get this colorful effect, but the dish is wonderful nonetheless.

This version was given to me by Margarita Miguel of Fonda Margarita at the market.

If you cannot find avocado leaves, substitute a tea made by boiling 1 teaspoon aniseeds with 1 cup water in a small saucepan until reduced by half and straining out the seeds. Omit the 1/2 cup water used to blend the spice mixture.

6 to 8 servings

Rinse and griddle-dry the chiles by the directions on page 45. Soak in boiling water to cover for 20 minutes. Drain the chiles and place in a blender with the salt, achiote paste, oregano, pepper, cloves, avocado leaves, and 1/2 cup water. Process, stopping occasionally to scrape down the sides with a rubber spatula, until smooth (about 4 minutes on high). Taste for seasoning and add more salt if desired. Slather the mixture all over the chicken, inside and out. Set aside while you make the stuffing.

Bring a medium-size saucepan of salted water to a boil. Cut the unpeeled potatoes into quarters, drop into the saucepan, and cook until done, 15 to 20 minutes. Drain the potatoes thoroughly, return to the pan, and shake dry. Peel and mash coarsely with a fork or masher.

Preheat the oven to 350°F.

In a medium-size skillet, heat the vegetable oil over high heat until not quite smoking. Add the onion and garlic and cook, stirring frequently, until slightly browned, about 2 minutes. Stir in the tomato and cook, uncovered, stirring occasionally, until the juice is partly evaporated, 5 minutes longer. Add the mixture to the potatoes and stir to combine thoroughly. Taste for seasoning and add salt to taste (about 1 teaspoon).

Stuff the potato mixture into the chicken (it is not necessary to truss). Choose a Dutch oven or lidded ovenproof casserole just large enough to hold the bird snugly. Place the chicken in the pan, add the vinegar-water mixture, and cover tightly. Bake until tender, about 2 hours. Carefully carve the chicken into serving pieces and place in soup bowls, distributing some of the stuffing in each. Ladle about 1 cup of the cooking liquid over each helping.

A typical juchiteca (woman of Juchitán)
with clay vessels and beaters used to mix
bread dough

Pollo Pilte
Mazatec-style Steamed Chicken Packets

This is another specialty of Rosa Estrada of the Restorán Rosita in Huautla. She steams the chicken in banana leaves, which add a beautiful fragrance to the anise-like flavor of the *hoja santa*.

Before beginning the dish, figure out a steamer arrangement large enough to hold four sizable packets of chicken in one layer on a rack well above the boiling water.

4 servings

If using banana leaves, cut out four 12-inch squares with kitchen scissors; pull off additional long thin strips to serve as "string" ties. Set aside.

Prepare the chiles as directed above. Bring a small saucepan of water to a boil and add the tomatoes and serrano chiles. Cook over medium heat for 10 minutes; drain. When cool enough to handle, peel the tomatoes. Place them in a blender with the serrano and guajillo chiles, garlic, onion, and *hoja santa*. Process until smooth (about 2 minutes on high). You should have about 2 1/2 cups.

In a medium-size saucepan, heat the lard over medium heat until rippling and add the purée. Cook, covered, stirring occasionally, for 5 minutes. Let cool slightly.

Soften the banana-leaf wrappers by holding over a gas burner one at a time (use tongs) just until they change color and become pliable. (If you have an electric stove, place the leaves, one at a time, on a preheated griddle or large cast-iron skillet over high heat; remove as each piece darkens slightly and becomes pliable.) Place the softened wrappers on the work surface.

Season the chicken pieces with salt and pepper; dip each piece into the sauce, turning to coat all sides, and place on a banana-leaf square. Spoon the remaining sauce over the chicken. Fold over the four sides of each leaf to make as square a packet as possible and tie shut with banana-leaf "strings" or kitchen twine. Arrange, seam side up, on a steamer rack in a single layer.

Over high heat, bring water to a boil in the bottom of the steamer. Arrange the rack at least 2 to 3 inches above the surface of the water. Arrange the chicken packets on the rack, distributing evenly. Cover the steamer tightly; reduce the heat to medium and steam for 45 minutes. Check occasionally to make sure that the water has not boiled away, and add more boiling water if necessary. Place each packet on a serving plate; each guest will open his or her own.

Banana leaves for wrapping, thawed if frozen (page 29) or four 12-inch squares of aluminum foil or parchment paper for wrapping

2 guajillo chiles (page 47), tops and seeds removed, soaked in boiling water to cover for 20 minutes

2 medium ripe tomatoes (about 1/2 pound)

2 fresh serrano or jalapeño chiles, tops removed

2 garlic cloves, peeled

1 small onion, peeled

4 fresh or 8 dried *hoja santa* leaves (page 36)

2 tablespoons lard (preferably home-rendered; page 36) or vegetable oil

One 4-pound chicken, quartered

Salt and freshly ground black pepper

Pollo Asado Aquilino
Aquilino's Grilled Chicken

2 tablespoons achiote seeds (page 28)

2 tablespoons black peppercorns

1 tablespoon whole cloves

3 tablespoons cumin seeds

1/4 cup dried Oaxacan oregano, crumbled, or 1 tablespoon Mexican oregano (page 38)

1 teaspoon dried thyme

4 large garlic cloves, coarsely chopped

1/3 to 1/2 cup cider vinegar, or as needed

One 4-pound chicken, quartered

3 tablespoons vegetable oil

1 teaspoon salt, or to taste

I met Aquilino on my first trip to the Isthmus, when I was looking for a knowledgeable guide to introduce me to the local Zapotec culture. Someone in Salina Cruz came up with the name of a young *declamador*, one who recites poetry. Aquilino shared much beautiful Zapotec poetry and song with me—and also this recipe, with its typical southern Mexican achiote-tinted spice rub. Try the spice paste also with fish.

I have had to adjust Aquilino's original directions, which were for a whole spit-roasted chicken. If you have an electric rotisserie, you may follow this method by coating the chicken (inside and out) with the spice rub and marinating as directed, then spit-roasting for 1 1/2 hours or until the juices run clear. The chicken may also be cooked on a charcoal grill. Since the breast meat of U.S. chickens tends to dry out with this method, I suggest using 4 whole chicken legs and grilling over the prepared charcoal for 20 to 25 minutes, or until cooked through at the joint.

4 servings

Grind the achiote seeds in an electric coffee mill or spice grinder and set aside. (Achiote seeds are ground separately because they are extremely hard.) Working in batches as necessary, grind the peppercorns, cloves, cumin, and oregano. Combine with the thyme and the ground achiote; mix thoroughly in a small bowl. You should have about 2/3 cup of the mixture.

Place the garlic in a blender with 1/3 cup of vinegar and blend to a paste, adding another 1 or 2 tablespoons of vinegar to thin it if it is too sticky. Scrape out into a small bowl and stir in enough of the ground spice blend to achieve a consistency a little lighter than a thin barbecue sauce. Thin with a small amount of vinegar if it is too pasty, but remember that it should be thick enough to coat the chicken. Reserve any leftover spice blend for another occasion.

Choose a glass or stainless-steel bowl large enough to hold the chicken pieces. Rub the spice-vinegar mixture liberally all over the chicken. Brush with the oil, season with salt to taste, and arrange the pieces in the bowl. Let marinate for at least 1 hour at room temperature or (preferably) overnight in the refrigerator.

Preheat the oven to 350°F.

Place the chicken on a rack in a shallow baking dish and bake for 35 to 40 minutes, or until tender.

Variation: I also like to bake the chicken whole. Rub it inside and outside with spice-vinegar mixture and proceed as directed above, baking it on a rack at 350°F for about 1 hour and 20 minutes or until done.

Variation: For a sweeter but still sprightly flavor, substitute fresh orange juice for half the vinegar.

Market vendor with donkey. The flowers are cempasuchil *(marigolds) for the Days of the Dead*

Meats

Oaxaca was never one of the great meat regions in Mexico. The Spanish brought their own livestock—cattle, pigs, sheep, goats—and proceeded to raise them on unsuitable soils that soon became eroded from misuse. Today meat is raised on a fairly small scale and is not everyday fare for most families. Many people in the poorer areas of the state cannot afford meat more than a few days a year. But even affluent families tend to consider meat more a special treat than a daily necessity. When an animal is butchered, every part of it is thriftily used—there is nothing like the U.S. fixation on just a few tender cuts.

It makes sense that the cuisine doesn't contain an abundance of meat recipes matching our menu preferences. I found Oaxacan butcher shops took some getting used to, especially in the villages. Instead of beautifully trimmed steaks and roasts in nice refrigerated display cases, what you see is enormous hunks or odd-shaped pieces of meat just hanging unceremoniously on hooks suspended from a wire or iron bar strung above a long flat counter. Much of the beef that is sold is *retazos* (literally "remnants")—amorphous chunks of backbone or bony joints with a little meat attached, used in soups—or *chuletas*, which theoretically means "cutlets" but really refers to thin, sinewy steaks cut from the leg. There will usually be a huge whole beef liver, fried until the outside is hard and crusty. People buy it by the slice. Overall, the beef dishes of Oaxaca are an acquired taste.

Pork is another story. The quality is wonderful, and the meat cooks up moist and full of flavor. Most of the favorite Oaxacan meat recipes are based on pork. In this country pork is very lean and must be cooked delicately to avoid drying out, so I had to adjust the cooking times accordingly. If you are near a good farmers' market where you can find pork from small local producers, by all means try it. It may be closer to the richness of Oaxacan pork.

I have hit on one trick that seems to bring out the flavor of pork loin, a tender but sometimes bland cut. (It was inspired by a visit to the Isthmus of Tehuantepec where I saw the skilled Luis Armando Hernández roasting the boned loin along with the bones.) I ask the butcher to bone the meat and give me the frame of ribs and backbones. I then use this as a platform to place the meat on, and at serving time I carve up and distribute the bones along with the sliced meat. To make this easier, you can ask the butcher to partly crack the backbone without completely detaching the ribs.

Pork in Oaxaca also furnishes delectable products like the chile-marinated, lightly air-dried ribbons of meat called *cecina*, round links of spicy chorizo sausage, and the fresh, light, not at all greasy *chicharrones* (fried pork rinds). The other important meats are goat and lamb. They usually don't show up in butcher shops. Instead, people are likely to go to the farm where the animals are raised and buy them on the hoof, to be slaughtered for the purpose of a *barbacoa*.

Barbacoa is directly descended from an ancient Zapotec way of cooking a turkey in a covered pit. Today the idea of the dish is still the same. It is a true barbecue, nothing to do with charcoal grills and syrupy "barbecue" sauces. The goat or lamb is purchased with the idea of using everything. The blood is saved for *morcilla* (blood sausage, with a portion of the intestine saved to serve for casings). The rest of the carcass is prepared for cooking in the barbecue pit lined with large, smooth stones that many Oaxacans have in their backyards.

The first step is to build a wood fire in the pit. When it has died to ashes and the stones are red hot, two large earthenware pots are set in the pit. One holds the meat, cut into large pieces (the head is considered the choicest part). The other has the makings of a rich broth using the innards. The meat, either simply seasoned with salt and a few flavorings or slathered with a red chile *adobo* (marinating paste), is arranged in its pot with layers of fresh avocado leaves or *hoja santa*, either of which gives a beautiful anise-like perfume. A thick metal slab is placed over the covered pots and the whole thing is then sealed with a mound of earth. Six to twenty-four hours later (depending on the size of the animal) they uncover the pit to reveal the treasure trove of succulent meat and aromatic broth. It's an incomparable cooking technique for concentrating the intense, sensuous meat flavors without drying up the natural juices or boiling everything to death.

This kind of barbecue obviously has to be reserved for rare family celebrations and other special occasions. I have not tried to duplicate the process in its entirety—when a ceremonial dish springs from a whole way of life, you can only try to recreate a small part of it. But I do cook goat and lamb in my New York kitchen to make an improvised version of a Oaxacan barbecue, and I hope you will explore this link with the ancient culture.

Estofado Verde
Braised Pork Chops with Tomatillo Sauce

1 cup sesame seeds (about 5 ounces)

2 pounds tomatillos, with husks

2 medium onions, unpeeled

6 large garlic cloves, unpeeled

Six 8-ounce center loin pork chops, with ribs

Salt and freshly ground black pepper

2 tablespoons vegetable oil

One 1 1/2-inch piece *canela* (page 30)

1/2 teaspoon freshly ground black pepper

1/8 teaspoon ground cloves

2 sprigs fresh thyme, or 1/4 teaspoon dried

2 sprigs fresh Mediterranean oregano, or 1/4 teaspoon dried Mexican oregano (page 38)

3 tablespoons capers, drained

1/2 cup pimiento-stuffed green olives (one 3-ounce jar)

1/2 cup blanched almonds

*L*ucila Zárate de Fuentes shared this useful dish. The Mediterranean accents like capers and almonds are typical in much Oaxaca City cooking.

6 *servings*

Place the sesame seeds in a heavy medium-sized skillet over medium heat. Toast just until golden (about 3 minutes), stirring constantly and shaking the pan; immediately scrape out into a small bowl and set aside.

Griddle-roast the tomatillos by the directions on page 27. Set aside in a bowl to catch the juices. Roast the onions and garlic in the same manner, saving the juices; set aside.

Season the pork chops with salt and pepper. In a large Dutch oven, heat the oil over high heat until rippling. Quickly brown the chops, 2 or 3 at a time, allowing about 2 minutes per side. Remove to a platter as they are browned and set aside. If more fat has accumulated in the pan, pour off all but about 2 tablespoons; set aside.

When the roasted vegetables are cool enough to handle, remove the husks from the tomatillos over a bowl to catch the juices. Peel the onions and garlic. Working in batches as necessary, place the vegetables in a blender with the reserved sesame seeds, *canela*, pepper, cloves, thyme, and oregano. Process to a purée (about 3 minutes on high).

Over medium-high heat, reheat the reserved fat in the Dutch oven until rippling. Add the puréed sauce and bring to a boil. Stir in the capers, olives, and almonds. Return the pork chops to the pan, reduce the heat to low, and cook, covered, just until the meat is done, about 10 minutes.

Costillas de Puerco
Fritas en Seco
"Dry-Fried" Pork Ribs

This cooking technique is a little like braising with a different wrinkle. You start by cooking the meat in liquid which is allowed to evaporate. By then enough fat will have rendered out that the pork is on the point of "frying" in its own fat. It finishes cooking in a simple chile sauce. The extra-lean U.S. pork has to be watched lest it dry out—do not overcook.

The dish goes well with refried beans (make them on the soupy rather than dry side) and sliced plantains fried in a little lard or vegetable oil.

4 servings

3 guajillo chiles (page 47), tops and
   seeds removed

8 garlic cloves, unpeeled

2 large ripe tomatoes

1 medium onion

2 1/2 pounds country-style pork ribs,
   bone in

1/2 teaspoon salt, or to taste

Freshly ground black pepper

Wash and griddle-dry the chiles by the directions on page 45. Place in a small bowl and cover generously with boiling water. Let soak for at least 20 minutes; drain.

Peel 3 of the garlic cloves and set aside. Roast the tomatoes, onion, and remaining 5 garlic cloves by the directions on page 26. When the vegetables are cool enough to handle, peel them (coarsely chopping the onion) and place them in a blender with the drained chiles. Process to a smooth purée (about 3 minutes on high). With a wooden spoon or pusher, force the mixture through a medium-mesh sieve into a bowl. Set aside.

Crush the reserved garlic cloves to a paste with the flat side of a knife blade or using a mortar and pestle. Season the pork ribs with salt and pepper. Place in a shallow pan large enough to hold them in one layer. (I use a 4-quart Dutch oven.) Add cold water to barely cover the meat. Add the crushed garlic. Bring to a boil over high heat, then lower the heat to medium and cook, uncovered, for 20 minutes, until the water has evaporated and you can see a little film of rendered fat in the pan. Watch carefully as it gets to this stage, turning the ribs occasionally.

Pour the chile mixture over the ribs. Reduce the heat to low and cook, covered, over low heat, stirring occasionally and spooning the sauce over the ribs to keep them moist.

Pastel de Carne del Istmo
Isthmian-style Meat Loaf

1/2 cup brined green olives (one 3-ounce jar), either pitted or pimiento-stuffed, finely chopped

One 2 1/2-ounce jar pimientos, drained and finely chopped

2 canned chipotle chiles en adobo (page 46), minced

2 canned pickled jalapeño chiles (page 45), seeds removed, minced

1/2 cup blanched almonds

4 ounces slab bacon, or 2 to 3 thick slices, cut into 1/3-inch dice

4 ounces boiled ham, cut into 1/3-inch dice

4 ounces smoked sausage (I use kielbasa), finely chopped

1 large onion, finely chopped

3 garlic cloves, minced

2 cups plain dry bread crumbs

One 5-ounce can evaporated milk

1 pound lean ground pork

1 pound lean ground beef

1 large egg, lightly beaten

One 3 1/2-ounce can deviled ham

3 tablespoons mayonnaise

1 tablespoon prepared mustard

3 tablespoons minced Italian parsley (leaves only)

*N*o one can say that this meat loaf is boring! It absolutely explodes with intense flavors, including various smoked, canned, or pickled ingredients that are popular in the Isthmus of Tehuantepec. This dish is a favorite there at the parties accompanying the *velas* (patron saints' fiestas) of the neighborhoods and towns in and around Juchitán.

The demanding part of this dish is dicing and chopping almost a dozen ingredients. Luckily most of them—everything from the olives through the almonds—can be chopped a few hours ahead and set aside until you need them.

About 10 servings

Preheat the oven to 350°F.

Combine the olives, pimientos, chipotles, and pickled jalapeños; set aside.

Spread the almonds on a baking sheet and bake until fragrant and lightly browned, 10 to 15 minutes. Remove from the oven and chop coarsely. Set aside.

If desired, these prepared ingredients can be left at room temperature for 3 to 4 hours and the oven again preheated to 350°F when you resume work.

Place the bacon in a heavy medium-size skillet with 2 tablespoons water. Cook over medium-high heat, stirring frequently, for 5 minutes, until the water has evaporated and some of the fat has rendered out. Scoop out the bacon and set aside. Strain the fat from the first pan (which will now have a salty residue on the bottom) into a large clean skillet set over medium-high heat. Add the partly cooked bacon along with the ham and sausage. Cook, stirring frequently, until lightly browned, about 3 minutes. With a slotted spoon or spatula, scoop out the cooked mixture into a bowl, letting as much fat as possible drain back into the pan. Pour off and discard all but about 2 tablespoons of the fat. Add the onion and garlic; cook over medium-high heat, stirring often, until the onion is translucent, about 5 minutes. Add to the mixture.

Place the bread crumbs in a medium-size bowl, add the evaporated milk, and let sit for 5 to 10 minutes to absorb the liquid while the cooked mixture cools slightly.

Place the ground pork and beef in a very large mixing bowl. Add the soaked bread and beaten egg; mix lightly. Add all the other ingredients and mix as thoroughly as possible with your hands.

Shape the mixture into two roughly oval loaves and place on a baking sheet or on a rack set in a roasting pan. (Alternatively, you can pack the mixture firmly into two 9×5-inch Pyrex loaf pans.) Bake until golden brown, about 1 hour. Serve hot or (as in the Isthmus) at room temperature.

Puerco en Chirmole
Pork with Roasted Tomato-Green Chile Sauce

1 head of garlic, separated into cloves and peeled

2 pounds pork shoulder or butt with some fat left on, cut into large (2-inch) cubes

2 pounds spareribs with some fat left on, cut into 2-inch lengths

1 1/2 teaspoons salt, or to taste

1 tablespoon coarsely ground black pepper

6 poblano (page 45) or Anaheim chiles (page 43)

2 jalapeño chiles

5 large ripe tomatoes (about 2 pounds)

*T*his is another example of the *frito en seco* ("dry-fried") technique (see Costillas de Puerco Fritas en Seco, page 195). But in this case the meat is also covered with coarsely ground pepper, almost like for steak au poivre. You need meat that will render out enough fat for browning, so be sure *not* to have the butt and ribs completely trimmed. Ask the butcher to cut the spareribs into short nuggets.

6 servings

Set aside half of the garlic cloves. With a mortar and pestle or the flat of a large knife blade, mash the rest of the garlic to a paste.

Season the meat lightly with salt and coat as evenly as possible with the pepper. Choose a large, heavy pan wide enough to hold the meat in one layer. (I use a 6-quart Dutch oven.) Add the cubed pork and the rib pieces. Add enough water to barely cover the meat; add the mashed garlic. Bring to a boil over high heat, then reduce the heat to medium and cook, uncovered, until the water is on the point of completely evaporating, about 20 minutes. (Watch carefully toward the end.) Season the meat with 1/2 teaspoon salt, or to taste. Reduce the heat to medium-low and let the meat continue to cook in its own rendered fat until golden brown, about 5 to 7 minutes; turn frequently and scrape up the browned bits. Remove the meat and set aside. Pour off and discard all but about 2 tablespoons of the remaining fat; set the pan aside.

While the pork cooks, griddle-roast the chiles by the directions on page 42. Remove from the heat and place in a paper or plastic bag to loosen the skins for about 15 minutes while you roast the tomatoes in the same manner. Peel the chiles and slit them lengthwise. Remove and discard the tops and seeds. When the tomatoes are cool enough to handle, peel them, saving the juices.

Place the chiles, tomatoes with their juices, and reserved garlic cloves in a food processor or blender. Process briefly, to keep a slightly chunky texture. Over medium-high heat, reheat the reserved fat in the Dutch oven until rippling. Add the purée; stir in the remaining salt. Taste for seasoning and add salt to taste, if needed.

Lower the heat and simmer, covered, for 20 minutes, stirring occasionally. Add the reserved pork and cook, covered, just until heated through, 5 to 7 minutes. Serve at once with freshly made corn tortillas (page 98).

Carne de Res
con Chipotle y Nopalitos
Braised Beef with Chipotle and Cactus Paddles

L ucila Zárate de Fuentes makes this easy but unusual stew—one of the few beef dishes I found in Oaxaca. Serve with rice; Arroz con Elote (page 237) makes an especially lovely accompaniment.

4 to 6 servings

Season the meat with salt and pepper to taste. In a large Dutch oven, heat the oil over medium-high heat until not quite smoking. Add the meat and brown quickly, about 2 minutes per side. Pour off as much fat as you can and set aside the pan with the browned meat.

Roast the tomatoes by the directions on page 26. When they are cool enough to handle, peel them, saving the juices. Add to a blender with the chiles, onion, and garlic and process to a smooth purée (about 2 minutes on high).

Return the Dutch oven to the stove over medium-high heat. Pour the puréed sauce over the meat. Add the epazote and 1 teaspoon salt or to taste. Stir well, reduce the heat to low, and cook, partly covered, for about 1 hour, or until the meat is fork-tender.

When the stew has cooked for about 40 minutes, bring a small saucepan of water to a boil and add the diced nopalitos. Cook, uncovered, over medium heat for 5 to 10 minutes. Transfer to a sieve and rinse under hot and then cold running water. (This removes some of the sticky juice.) Drain well, stir into the stew, and let the nopalitos cook with the beef, partly covered, for another 10 to 15 minutes, or until the nopalitos are tender.

2 pounds stewing beef such as chuck, cut into 1 1/2-inch cubes

Salt and freshly ground black pepper

3 tablespoons vegetable oil

3 large tomatoes

2 canned chipotle chiles en adobo (page 46)

1 small onion, quartered

2 garlic cloves

Three 6-inch sprigs of fresh epazote or 1 tablespoon dried, crumbled (page 35)

1/2 teaspoon salt, or to taste

3 nopalitos (cactus paddles; page 29), cleaned and cut into 1/2-inch dice

Cecina Enchilada
Half-Dried Pork Strips in Chile Marinade

2 cups Adobo para Cecina (page 201)

8 boneless pork cutlets (about 2 ounces each), cut as long and thin as possible

1/2 teaspoon salt, or to taste

3 tablespoons lard (preferably home-rendered; page 36) or vegetable oil

*I*n Spanish and Mexican cooking *cecina* can refer to many jerky-like or salt-cured meats. In Oaxaca, it usually means long, thin pork strips almost like ribbons of meat, allowed to air-dry for a few hours before being pan-broiled. Sometimes *cecina* is seasoned just with lime juice and salt before drying, but most often it is covered in an *adobo* (chile seasoning paste). The dish is featured on the menu of practically every market food stand in the state. As you walk past butcher stands you see long pieces of *cecina* drying, draped on lines like funny-shaped scarves.

This version is based on a recipe given to me by Luis Armando Hernández. There is a special knack to whittling the meat along the grain into narrow, even strips, and I have not tried to duplicate this. In the U. S. the simplest substitute is to ask the butcher for pork cutlets as delicate as veal scaloppine, cut from the leg. If possible, allow a brief period of air-drying after rubbing in the *adobo*, to help approximate the texture of Oaxacan *cecina*. You can hang the pieces to dry over a wooden pasta drier or clothes rack, or even a string tied like a clothesline between two corners of the kitchen. The room should be as cool and airy as possible.

Serves 4

Make the *adobo* and slather it thickly over the cutlets. Carefully drape them over a clothes rack or anything that will let air circulate around the meat; let the *cecina* air-dry for 2 to 3 hours. Refrigerate overnight, preferably laid flat and stacked with plastic wrap between the layers.

When ready to cook, sprinkle the salt over the cutlets. In a large skillet, heat the lard over high heat until almost smoking. Add the cutlets and rapidly fry, not more than 3 to 4 at a time, allowing about 2 minutes per side. Serve immediately with Frijoles Negros Colados (page 235).

Adobo para Cecina
Chile Marinade for Cecina

This useful *adobo* also works well with other cuts. It makes a great marinade for pork chops. The purée should be the consistency of a heavy paste, not a sauce. It can be made up to 2 days ahead and stored in the refrigerator, tightly covered.

About 2 cups

Wash and griddle-dry the chiles by the directions on page 45. As they are done, place in a deep bowl and cover generously with boiling water. Let soak for at least 20 minutes.

Drain the chiles and place in a blender with all the remaining ingredients. Add 1/3 cup water, or just enough to facilitate blending. Process to a smooth purée, about 5 minutes on high, stopping occasionally to scrape down the sides with a rubber spatula. With a wooden spoon or pusher, force the mixture through a medium-mesh sieve into a bowl.

4 ounces guajillo chiles (page 47; about 16 large chiles), tops and seeds removed

3 large garlic cloves

1 1/2 to 2 tablespoons cider vinegar

1/2 teaspoon dried thyme

2 bay leaves

2 dried avocado leaves, toasted (page 28)

2 teaspoons dried Oaxacan oregano or 1/2 teaspoon dried Mexican oregano, crumbled (page 38)

1 teaspoon black peppercorns or freshly ground black pepper

One 1-inch piece *canela* (page 30)

Cochinito con Picadillo de Frutas

Roast Suckling Pig Stuffed with Chopped Fruit Mixture

One of my proudest moments as a cook was taking a picture-perfect roast suckling pig out of the oven the first time I attempted to make this gorgeous dish as I'd seen it done in the Isthmus of Tehuantepec. My teachers there were Venancia Toledo Hernández and her son Luis Armando, both superb cooks. Venancia has a stand at the market in the town of Ixtepec, an amazing enterprise that sells embroidered blouses, *huipiles* (sleeveless tunics), and skirts along with fresh cuts of meat butchered in the rough-and-ready Oaxacan manner, and—on Sundays—an assortment of local dishes. One of the best is this succulent roast pig stuffed with a fruit and vegetable mixture. The intense sweet-and-sour seasonings (including Worcestershire sauce and pickled olives) typify the bold Isthmian approach to flavoring.

Since the original dish as Venancia prepared it may not be an option for everyone, I have experimented with some variations. The *picadillo* (chopped fruit mixture) in her version contained the innards of the pig such as spleen, lungs, and heart, finely chopped and sautéed with the other ingredients. Without these, the stuffing is different but still delicious. I also tried the recipe with and without the fresh orange juice that Venancia adds to the baking pan. It's good both ways—a matter of rich citrus-flavored roasting juices versus the wonderful crisp skin you get by leaving out the liquid. (She uses *naranja agria*, or Seville-type "bitter oranges"; if you can find these in a Latin American market, they will add a lot of flavor. Or squeeze a bit of fresh lime into United States sweet orange juice.)

Venancia and Luis also make this dish with roast loin of pork instead of suckling pig. I have included this version (using boned pork together with the reserved bones) for those who cannot manage a suckling pig. Measure your oven and roasting pan and consult local butchers before deciding which version to use. A 12- to 15-pound suckling pig will probably be 18 to 20 inches long, and you need to figure in at least 2 or 3 more inches to clear the sides of the oven. I do not recommend trying to roast a pig larger than 16 pounds.

Venancia used a deep oval clay pot just large enough to hold the pig—the snugger and deeper the roasting pan, the better. The most time-consuming part of the preparation is dicing the ingredients for the *picadillo*. It is worth taking the trouble to cut everything into neat 1/4- to 1/3-inch dice that will keep both their shape and texture in cooking.

8 to 10 servings

Slather the *adobo* thickly over the pig, inside and out, and marinate, refrigerated, overnight or for at least 4 hours. Remove from the refrigerator 2 hours before roasting. Let it come to room temperature while you prepare the remaining ingredients to make the stuffing; all that is to be chopped or ground should be done before you proceed further.

In a large Dutch oven or deep skillet, heat the oil to rippling over medium-high heat. (It may be necessary to divide the work between two skillets or work in 2 batches.) Add the onions and garlic and cook, stirring, until slightly translucent, 2 to 3 minutes. Add the chopped tomatoes and cook, stirring, for 5 minutes to evaporate the juices slightly. Add the remaining ingredients except for the optional orange juice; reduce the heat to medium and cook, uncovered, for 15 minutes, stirring often. Let the mixture cool to room temperature.

Preheat the oven to 350°F.

Season the pig generously with salt and pepper, inside and out. Stuff it with the cooled fruit and vegetable mixture and close the opening with skewers.

If not using the optional orange juice, arrange the pig in a large roasting pan so that it is lying on all fours and roast for approximately 3 hours, or until a meat thermometer inserted in the thigh reads 160°F. Reduce the heat to 200°F and let the pig rest at this temperature for 15 minutes or until ready to serve (but no longer than 40 minutes). Otherwise lay the pig on one side and pour the orange juice over it. Roast as directed but baste occasionally with the juice and turn the pig onto the other side halfway through cooking. If the liquid seems to be evaporating too fast, add small amounts of water (not more than 1/4 cup at a time) to the pan juices.

Carve the pig. Arrange the stuffing on a serving platter with the carved meat on top. If enough orange juice is left to serve as gravy, strain it and skim off the fat; pass separately in a gravy bowl.

4 cups Adobo para Cochinito (page 204)

1 suckling pig, about 12 to 15 pounds

1/3 cup vegetable oil

3 medium onions, cut into 1/4-inch dice

6 garlic cloves, minced

3 large ripe tomatoes, finely chopped

1/2 medium pineapple, peeled, cored, and cut into 1/4-inch dice (about 2 to 3 cups)

3 firm, tart green apples, peeled, cored, and cut into 1/3-inch dice

6 medium carrots, peeled and cut into 1/4-inch dice

6 large Red Bliss or other waxy potatoes, peeled and cut into 1/4-inch dice

1/2 cup dark raisins

3/4 cup small pimiento-stuffed green olives

3 canned pickled jalapeño chiles, plus 1/3 cup of the pickling juice

1 1/2 tablespoons dried Oaxacan oregano or 2 teaspoons dried Mexican oregano, crumbled (page 38)

1 tablespoon freshly ground *canela* (page 30), from about one 1 1/2-inch piece

1 1/2 teaspoons freshly ground black pepper, plus additional for seasoning the pig

12 bay leaves

12 sprigs fresh thyme or 2 teaspoons dried

1 1/2 tablespoons Worcestershire sauce

2 teaspoons salt, or to taste

2 cups freshly squeezed orange juice, preferably from Seville oranges (optional)

VARIATION

Lomo de Puerco con Picadillo de Frutas
Roast Loin of Pork with Chopped Fruit Mixture

8 to 10 servings

Follow the directions for suckling pig, but substitute a whole loin of pork that has been boned (8 to 10 pounds weight before boning). Ask the butcher to give you the ribs and backbone in one piece, partly cracking through the backbone but leaving the ribs attached. Slather the meat and bones with the *adobo* and let rest in the refrigerator for 4 hours.

Choose a long, narrow roasting pan and spread the chopped fruit and vegetable mixture evenly across the bottom. Place the frame of bones on this bed, ends curving up to cradle the roast. Arrange the meat on the bones and pour the orange juice (which you will definitely need for moisture) over it. The liquid should come about halfway up the sides of the meat; add more orange juice or water if necessary. Cover the pan as tightly as possible (using several layers of aluminum foil unless you have a proper lid). Bake in the preheated 350°F oven for 1 hour, then uncover and bake 30 minutes longer to brown the meat and concentrate the flavor. The internal temperature on a meat thermometer inserted into the center should read 140° to 150°F.

Remove from the oven and let rest for 5 to 10 minutes. Carve the meat into neat slices and cut the platform of bones into separate ribs. With a slotted spoon, remove the fruit and vegetable mixture to a serving platter, letting as much liquid as possible drain back into the pan. Arrange the carved pork on top, with the ribs around the edges of the platter. Strain the remaining pan juices, skim off the fat, and pass separately in a gravy boat.

Adobo para Cochinito
Chile Marinade for Suckling Pig

About 4 cups

Wash and griddle-dry the chiles by the directions on page 45. As they are done, place them in a large deep bowl. Cover generously with boiling water and let soak for at least 20 minutes. Drain.

For a very fine-textured *adobo*, grind the *canela*, peppercorns, bay leaves, oregano, avocado leaves, and dried thyme (if using) to a powder in an electric coffee or spice grinder or with a mortar and pestle, then process in a blender (working in batches as necessary) with the drained chiles and remaining ingredients. Otherwise, simply process all ingredients (in batches as necessary) in the blender until puréed (about 5 minutes on high), stopping occasionally to scrape down the sides with a rubber spatula. If necessary, add a few tablespoons of water to facilitate blending, but the mixture should remain thick and pasty.

8 ounces guajillo chiles (page 47; about 30 chiles)

One 2-inch piece *canela* (page 30)

12 black peppercorns

10 bay leaves

4 large dried avocado leaves (page 28)

10 large sprigs fresh thyme or 1 1/2 teaspoons dried

4 tablespoons dried Oaxacan oregano or 1 tablespoon dried Mexican oregano, crumbled (page 38)

8 large garlic cloves

4 tablespoons cider vinegar

Lomo de Puerco Adobado
Roast Loin of Pork in Chile Marinade

8 guajillo chiles (page 47), tops and
  seeds removed

2 garlic cloves

One 1-inch piece *canela* (page 30)

10 whole black peppercorns

1 teaspoon dried thyme, crumbled

1/2 to 1 teaspoon salt (or to taste),
  plus more for seasoning roast

3 tablespoons vegetable oil

One 5-pound center-cut loin of pork,
  boned after weighing, ribs and
  backbone reserved

3/4 to 1 ounce dried avocado leaves
  (about 30 leaves; page 28)

Freshly ground black pepper

The village of Zaachila, about six miles south of Oaxaca City, is known for one of the most unique enterprises I saw anywhere in the state—a wood market set up in a big, nondescript lot, completely dedicated to the buying and selling of firewood. (Many people still depend on wood for varied purposes.) Zaachila also has a reputation as a good place for wonderful grilled and roast meats, which are not a specialty in most parts of Oaxaca. At La Capilla restaurant—an open-air place with long benches—they bring out big platters of grilled chorizo and pan-seared *cecina* (pages 208 and 200) together with the air-dried beef strips called *tasajo*, irresistible *carnitas* (delectable chunks of crisp "dry-fried" pork), crunchy *chicharrones* (fried pork rinds), and simple accompaniments like guacamole, a vivid salsa, and lime wedges. The menu also features this succulent chile-slathered pork, fragrant with the aroma of fresh avocado leaves. (Here you will probably have to substitute the dried leaves.)

Once more I have used the technique of roasting boned pork on a platform made from the bones. For an extra fine-textured *adobo* you can grind the *canela* and peppercorns together in an electric coffee grinder before adding them to the other marinade seasonings, but I have had good results just putting the whole spices in the blender with the rest of the ingredients.

6 to 8 servings

Wash and griddle-dry the chiles by the directions on page 45. Place in a bowl and cover generously with boiling water. Let soak for at least 20 minutes.

Drain the chiles and place in a blender with the garlic, *canela*, peppercorns, thyme, salt, and 1/3 cup water. Process to a purée, stopping occasionally to scrape down the sides with a rubber spatula and adding a few more tablespoons water if necessary to facilitate blending. With a wooden spoon or pusher, force the mixture through a medium-mesh sieve into a bowl. With the tines of a fork or the tip of a small, sharp knife, pierce holes all over the pork loin. Slather the meat all over with 3/4 of the *adobo* mixture, pushing it into the gashes as much as possible. Rub the rest of the mixture over the reserved bones. Refrigerate the meat and bones, covered, overnight or for at least 4 hours. Remove from the refrigerator at least 1 hour before cooking, to let warm up to room temperature.

Preheat the oven to 350°F. Arrange a rack in a roasting pan. Place half the avocado leaves on the rack to make a bed for the meat. Season the pork loin with salt and pepper. Place the frame of ribs and backbone over the bed of leaves, with the meat resting on it like a cradle. Scatter the remaining avocado leaves over the meat. Roast for about 1 hour, or until a meat thermometer inserted in the center reads 140°F. Carve the meat into thin slices and cut up the platform of bones into separate ribs. Distribute the ribs as equally as possible with each serving.

Chorizo

*A*t the big Juárez market in Oaxaca City I passed the Carnicería Teresita and had to stop. Behind the counter were Hermenegildo Berinstaín Camacho and his wife and son, all sitting on wooden stools eating a lunch of rice, refried beans, and a Mole Amarillo with green beans freshly made and fetched from home by his wife in an enamelware *portaviandas* (the standard Mexican three-tiered lunch box), with each dish in its own compartment. Above their heads were round links of chorizo like necklace beads hanging from butcher hooks fastened to the ceiling, and strips of chile-slathered *cecina* (air-dried seasoned pork; see page 200) draped like clothes over a wire stretching from side to side of the busy little stand. It was the enticing aroma of the chorizo that stopped me in my tracks. We struck up a conversation and Hermenegildo was kind enough to share his recipe with me.

I have made this wonderful sausage in the form of links, and also as a bulk mixture to be frozen in small portions in plastic bags. If you choose the first option, buy hog casings (available most of the time from many ethnic butchers or by special order from other butchers) and prepare them by letting cold water run through them to rinse off as much as possible of the salt in which they are usually packed, then soaking in a large bowl of cold water for half an hour. For this amount of the chorizo mixture you will need 5 feet of 1/2-inch-diameter hog casings. Check them for leaks while rinsing them.

Do not buy packaged pre-ground pork, which will be too fine. If you have a meat grinder, buy about 1 1/2 pounds of fairly lean pork meat (shoulder, rib end of loin) and grind it with the coarse disk; otherwise ask the butcher to give you 2 pounds of pork in a 3:1 ratio of lean to fat, coarsely ground for sausage.

The uses of chorizo are limitless. It can go into fillings like the one for Molotes (page 67) or soups like Cocina de Coles (page 77). It is wonderful with fried potatoes or scrambled eggs. Having a few links or portions in the freezer is like money in the bank.

About 2 pounds sausage mixture

If using whole ancho and Oaxacan pasilla chiles, wash and griddle-dry by the directions on page 45. Place in a deep bowl as they are done; cover generously with boiling water and let soak for 20 minutes. If using ancho chile powder, combine it in a bowl with 1 cup water and mix to a paste.

Working in batches if necessary, grind the cloves, bay leaves, peppercorns, and *canela* together with the oregano, thyme, and marjoram in a electric coffee or spice grinder or with a mortar and pestle.

Drain the soaked chiles. Place them (or the chile powder mixture) in a blender with the ground spice mixture, garlic, salt, vinegar, wine, and the canned chipotle chile (if using). Process until thoroughly puréed, about 3 minutes on high.

Place the ground meat in a large non-aluminum bowl. Add the chile mixture and mix thoroughly with your hands. Cover with plastic wrap and refrigerate for up to 2 days, to let the flavors mingle and develop.

If using sausage casings, prepare them as described above. If you have a grinder with a sausage-stuffing attachment, follow the manufacturer's directions for attaching and filling the casings. You can also fill the casings with the aid of a helper: One person firmly pushes a few inches of casing over the spout of a large funnel and holds it in place (a rubber band may help) while the other uses a long wooden spoon to stuff the mixture into the casing. In either case, use kitchen twine to tie off the filled casing into short round links the size of ping-pong balls. Hang up the sausages to air-dry for about 4 hours, preferably in a cool airy room. (You can drape them over a pasta dryer or clothes rack, or a string stretched between two corners of the kitchen.)

If you are not working with sausage casings, simply scoop 1-cup portions of the chorizo mixture into small plastic freezer bags. Sealed tightly, they can be refrigerated for up to 2 days or frozen for up to 4 months.

10 ancho chiles (page 46), tops and seeds removed, or 3 ounces powdered ancho chile

1 Oaxacan pasilla chile (page 47), tops and seeds removed, or 1 canned chipotle chile en adobo (page 46)

4 whole cloves

2 bay leaves

1 teaspoon black peppercorns

One 1-inch piece *canela* (page 30)

1 teaspoon dried Oaxacan oregano or 1/2 teaspoon dried Mexican oregano, crumbled (page 38)

1/2 teaspoon dried thyme, crumbled

1/2 teaspoon dried marjoram, crumbled

3 large garlic cloves, coarsely chopped

2 teaspoons salt

1/4 cup cider vinegar

1/4 cup dry red wine

2 pounds coarsely ground pork (3 parts lean to 1 part fat)

5 feet of 1/2-inch diameter pork casings (optional)

Barbacoa de Carnero con Masita

Lamb with Cracked Corn, Pit-Barbecue Style

The market in the village of Etla, a few miles from Oaxaca City, is full of surprises. Here I found some unusual foods bearing a distinct Zapotec influence. And here I met Susana Taurino Jiménez Rojas at a little stand where she sells nothing but a lamb barbecue that I had to learn the secret of.

Susana makes this dish with a whole lamb, which is pit-cooked overnight in one pot while a delectable broth made from the innards is cooking in another pot. At the market, she dishes out the meat from a big tin tub and cups of the broth from another container. The customers devour it at the one or two tables by her tiny stand. I can't reproduce the broth in this country and buying a whole lamb is impractical. But I have devised a partial copy of the original.

This dish belongs to the lightly seasoned rather than the *adobo*-marinated type of Oaxacan barbecue. Here avocado leaves lend both a delicate aroma and flavor. The juices of the baking/steaming meat drip onto a layer of corn kernels that you must first prepare by the *nixtamal* process described on pages 92 to 95. Failing that, you can use the large lime-treated corn kernels called *mote* sold in Colombian and Ecuadorian markets. (Use the white variety only, not the yellow.) The cracked corn is mixed with some of the lamb fat for extra richness and flavor, so be sure to buy a leg or shoulder with enough fat to trim some for this purpose. After cooking with the lamb juices, the cracked *nixtamal* kernels become *masita*. It's quite unlike anything I have ever eaten before—starchy and chewy at the same time and to me, wonderfully comforting.

Before starting to cook, you must rig up an arrangement for holding the ingredients. Where a real barbecue has everything buried in a pit, my improvised U.S. version combines the baking/steaming actions by actually putting a steamer in the oven. I have a big rectangular hotel restaurant pan with a steamer liner that will accommodate a whole leg of lamb. The nearest equivalent would be a lidded turkey roaster. Make a steamer platform out of a wire rack covered with a layer of cheesecloth and balanced on supports such as empty cans with tops and bottoms cut off. If the lid won't fit over the meat, cover the roaster as tightly as possible with several layers of aluminum foil.

Preheat the oven to 300°F.

With a small, sharp knife, trim all visible fat from the meat. Reserve enough of the fat to make about 1/2 cup.

With a mortar and pestle, crush the garlic to a paste together with the pepper and 1 1/2 teaspoons of the salt. With the tip of a small, sharp knife, pierce 1-inch-deep gashes all over the leg of lamb. Rub the garlic paste over the meat, pushing it down into the incisions.

Working in batches as necessary, place the *nixtamal* or *mote* in a food processor and pulse briefly, just long enough to break the corn kernels into coarse pieces the size of chopped walnut meats. With a heavy knife, chop the reserved lamb fat almost to a paste. In a large bowl, mix the fat, cracked kernels, and remaining 1 teaspoon salt. Add 6 cups water and stir to mix.

Prepare to set up your steamer arrangement (see above).

Place 3 of the avocado leaves in the bottom of the steamer and pour the *nixtamal* mixture over them. Spread half the remaining avocado leaves on the prepared steamer liner or platform; place the leg of lamb on it and arrange the remaining leaves over the lamb. Cover the steamer tightly and place in the preheated oven. Let the meat steam/bake, undisturbed, until tender enough to fall off the bone, 3 1/2 to 4 hours.

Remove the steamer from the oven and lift the meat to a carving platter. Check to see whether the cooked corn (*masita*) has absorbed all the water; if not, place over medium heat and cook, stirring constantly, to evaporate any remaining liquid. Carve the lamb and serve with the *masita*. This dish should be accompanied by a spicy table sauce like Salsa de Chile Pasilla (page 254) or Salsa de Chile Serrano con Limón (page 255) and freshly made corn tortillas.

One 6- to 7-pound leg of lamb, bone in, untrimmed or 6 pounds lamb shoulder, bone in

6 large garlic cloves

1 teaspoon freshly ground black pepper

2 1/2 teaspoons salt, or to taste

1 1/2 pounds (about 4 cups) *nixtamal*, drained (page 92), or one 15-ounce package of white South American *mote*, about 3 1/2 cups

40 large dried avocado leaves, about 2/3 ounce (page 28)

Barbacoa de Cabrito
Goat in Chile Marinade, Pit-Barbecue Style

*T*he preceding Barbacoa de Carnero con Masita is an example of a simply flavored barbecue where the meat juices themselves predominate. Another approach is to let the meat absorb an *adobo*, a fragrant, spicy marinade of dried chiles and other seasonings. This goat barbecue typifies the second kind.

I watched Zoyla Mendoza make the dish in her village, Teotitlán del Valle. Though she and her family can well afford to eat meat, they usually save it for special occasions, so they rejoiced when I asked them to teach me their favorite *barbacoa*. It was beautiful, breathing the scent of fresh avocado leaves and other herbs. The meat becomes unbelievably tender without drying out or getting mushy.

When I came back to my New York kitchen, I set to work to find other methods close to the tender savor of a true pit barbecue. For the type that Zoyla showed me, I feel the best results come from packing the marinated meat in a tightly covered pan just large enough to hold the ingredients and baking it for a long time in a moderate oven. A turkey roaster is good. If you don't have a big enough pan with a tight-fitting lid, wrap several layers of aluminum foil very snugly around the pan to seal in the steam.

I make the *barbacoa* as Zoyla made it, with young goat (kid). Goat is available in some Greek, *halal* Muslim, and West Indian butcher shops and can sometimes be ordered from other butchers. Ask the butcher to cut it into quarters. Oaxacans always include and specially value the head, which has some extra-tender nuggets of meat. (This is optional for the doubting.) If goat is not available, lamb is the best substitute. At my restaurant, we use lamb shoulder. The dish can also be made with a whole fresh ham or a pot-roasting cut of beef such as round, though you may have to reduce the amount of marinade slightly and experiment with a shorter cooking time. Of course true pre-Hispanic *barbacoa* was made with turkey—not used as frequently nowadays, but still a notably authentic choice.

When the meat is cooked in an authentic pit it yields a lot of rich juices that never develop using the oven method. At my restaurant in New York we approximate this as follows: When the adobo (chile paste) is made, set aside 1 1/4 cup of the mixture and rub the meat with the rest. Cook as described below. When the meat is done, skim the fat from the pan juices and deglaze the roasting pan with 2 cups homemade chicken broth over medium-high heat, scraping up the browned bits. Stir in one 28- to 32-ounce can tomatoes, breaking them up with a spoon. Add the reserved adobo and simmer, stirring frequently, for about 30 minutes, or until reduced to about 4 cups. Let cool slightly and purée in a blender (working in batches as necessary) until smooth. Serve with the carved meat.

8 to 10 servings (more for the lamb version)

Wash and griddle-dry the chiles by the directions on page 45. Place in a deep bowl and cover generously with boiling water. Let soak for at least 20 minutes.

Grind the cumin, cloves, allspice, oregano, and dried thyme (if using) together in an electric coffee or spice grinder or with a mortar and pestle.

Drain the soaked chiles. Working in batches as necessary, place them in a blender with the ground herbs and spices (add fresh thyme at this point if using), garlic, onion, vinegar, salt, and about 1/2 cup water (or enough to facilitate the action of the blades). Process to a smooth purée (about 3 minutes on high), stopping occasionally to scrape down the sides with a rubber spatula. With a wooden spoon or pusher, force the purée though a medium-mesh sieve into a bowl. It should have the consistency of a thick but still moist paste.

Season the pieces of goat or lamb with salt and pepper. Slather the seasoning paste all over the meat. Arrange in a large bowl (or any non-reactive container that's large enough), cover tightly with plastic wrap, and refrigerate overnight or for at least 4 hours. Remove from the refrigerator about 2 hours before beginning the cooking, to let the meat come to room temperature.

Preheat the oven to 325°F.

Choose a deep roasting pan or baking dish large enough to hold the meat snugly. Scatter half of the avocado leaves across the bottom of the pan and arrange the meat on them. Scatter the remaining leaves over the meat. Cover the pan (wrapping very tightly with several layers of foil if there is no lid) and bake 6 to 7 hours (4 to 4 1/2 hours for the lamb). The meat should be almost falling off the bone.

4 ounces guajillo chiles (about 16 large chiles; page 47), tops and seeds removed

2 teaspoons cumin seeds

1 teaspoon whole cloves, or 3/4 teaspoon ground

10 allspice berries

1/3 cup dried Oaxacan oregano or 1 tablespoon dried Mexican oregano, crumbled (page 38)

12 to 15 large sprigs fresh thyme (leaves only), or 2 teaspoons dried

10 garlic cloves

1 large onion, coarsely chopped

1/2 cup cider vinegar

1 teaspoon salt or to taste, plus additional for seasoning goat

Freshly ground black pepper

One 16-pound goat, quartered, or 6 to 8 pounds lamb shoulder, bone in, trimmed

1/2 to 3/4 ounce dried avocado leaves (page 28), about 30 large leaves

Woman holding corn tortillas and clayudas

Estofado de Res de Ixtepec
Ixtepec-style Stewed Beef with Fruits

*M*y friend Venancia Toledo Hernández is a *tehuana*. Everyone in Oaxaca would know just what I mean by that. Venancia is a woman of the Isthmus of Tehuantepec, where the women mean business and business means women—men tend to be relegated to lesser positions in family-owned businesses.

This is what you expect of a *tehuana*: A big, bold-featured woman whose clothes are as commanding as her presence. She usually has a flower in her hair and lots of jewelry. On ordinary days she wears long, flowing cotton skirts in brilliant flowered prints, with gorgeous embroidered blouses and chain-stitched *huipiles* (square tunics). On the days of town *velas* (the Isthmian name for saints' day fiestas) she dresses in magnificent velvet regalia. When she enters a room, she sweeps into it. She radiates strength and entrepreneurial spirit.

All this is Venancia to the life. She's always taken charge of everything. At the age of twenty-eight, with small children, she threw out her faithless husband, declaring, "I adore you, I will die without you, but if you love me so little, get out and never come back." You don't mess with *tehuanas*! I met her in her home town of Ixtepec, where she has an amazing establishment that is half butcher shop (the meat is supplied from her cattle herd in Veracruz State) and half dress shop (she sells very good machine-embroidered copies of traditional Isthmian costumes). I had stopped to look at the clothes while on a recipe-research trek, and found that I'd hit the jackpot: Venancia and her son, Luis Armando Hernández, are great cooks and make some of the most delicious regional dishes to sell on Sunday.

We felt an immediate bond. Venancia threw herself into my project with imperious enthusiasm. We became fast friends in the days I spent cooking and talking and laughing with her. When I think of her I always think of her prompt answer when I asked if she knew how to make Estofado de Res, a slow-cooked beef dish that is one of the most renowned specialties of the area. "Well," began Doña Venancia, "you take a whole cow and bone it. . . ."

I had to explain that in the United States no one has pots like the enormous pinecone-shaped earthenware cooking jars that are made in the area and set on racks over fires in all the yards of the town just for preparing Estofado de Res.

5 guajillo chiles (page 47), tops and seeds removed

3 ancho chiles (page 46), tops and seeds removed

1 small, tart green apple, peeled and cored

1 thick slice (1 1/2 to 2 inches) ripe pineapple, peeled and cored

1 large onion

4 large ripe tomatoes

3 ripe plantains, peeled (page 39)

3 bay leaves, lightly bruised

One 1-inch piece *canela* (page 30)

1 teaspoon dried Mexican oregano (page 38)

1 dried avocado leaf (page 28)

2 1/2 pounds beef chuck, cut into 2-inch cubes

2 teaspoons salt, or to taste

1 cup lard (preferably home-rendered; page 36), warmed just to the melting point

1 cup fine, dry brioche or challah crumbs

Eventually Venancia, Luis, and I arrived at a scaled-down version that can be done in a home oven and a slightly quicker variation that Venancia developed using a pressure cooker.

Estofado ordinarily means a stew or braised dish, but in this case there is no good English translation. The Ixtepec beef Estofado is one of those dishes like real New England baked beans that depend on slow, slow cooking in a special vessel. People there cook it overnight, stirring the meat frequently until everything turns into a velvety paste. It isn't exactly comparable to any other dish I know except pork rillettes—the way they might be if you added fruits and Oaxacan seasonings and served everything straight from the pot instead of shredding the meat and straining the fat over it.

For the bread crumbs that help thicken and bind the dish, use several day-old slices of a sweet, eggy bread like Pan de Yema (page 308), brioche, or challah, crushed into fine, dry crumbs. The slight sweetness is an important part of the flavor. The fruits and vegetables should be very finely chopped so that they will dissolve completely in cooking; you can streamline things a little by chopping (*not* puréeing) the apple, pineapple, and onion together in a food processor. The authentic accompaniment is Clayudas (page 102), but any good homemade corn tortillas will do.

6 to 8 servings

Wash and griddle-dry the chiles by the instructions on page 45. As they are done, place in a deep bowl. Cover generously with boiling water and let soak for about 20 minutes.

While the chiles soak, chop the apple, pineapple, and onion together very fine. Set aside in a deep bowl. Chop the tomatoes very fine and add to the fruits. Chop the plantains very fine and add to the other chopped ingredients. Add the bay leaves and stir to mix everything thoroughly.

Drain the soaked chiles and place in a blender with the *canela*, oregano, avocado leaf and enough water to facilitate blending (about 1 cup). Process until smooth (about 3 minutes on high) stopping occasionally to scrape down the sides with a rubber scraper. With a pusher or wooden spoon, force the purée through a medium-mesh sieve into a bowl.

Preheat the oven to 275°F.

In a heavy lidded Dutch oven with ovenproof handles, arrange the ingredients in three layers as follows: Spread one third of the fruit-onion mixture over the bottom of the pot. Scatter one third of the meat cubes over the fruit, season with a little of the salt, and top with one third of the chile purée. Repeat with the remaining ingredients. Pour the melted lard evenly over the top layer of chile purée.

Cover the pan and bake for 8 hours, stirring about every 30 minutes to redistribute the ingredients. At the end of the baking time, the meat will have disintegrated into fine shreds and the other ingredients will have dissolved into a luscious paste. Add the bread crumbs and stir until they are no longer visible. Serve with fresh corn tortillas.

Variation: For a less time-consuming estofado, Venancia sometimes does part of the cooking in a pressure cooker. Proceed as directed above, but layer the fruit-onion mixture, beef, and chile purée in a pressure cooker. Seal the lid by the manufacturer's directions, place over medium heat, and cook at 10 pounds of pressure for 40 minutes. Remove from heat and let stand until the pressure is released. Transfer the contents of the pot to a large, heavy saucepan or Dutch oven. Pour half of the melted lard over the meat and bring just to a boil over medium heat. (Watch out—it will splatter dangerously.) Reduce the heat to low and cook, covered, stirring every few minutes, for about 1 1/2 hours, or until the meat has disintegrated into very fine shreds. Add the remaining lard and stir to mix well. Add the bread crumbs and stir until they are no longer visible.

The classic flowered skirt
of the Isthmian women

Fish and Shellfish

Oaxaca is not a fish lover's paradise. I have eaten delicious fresh-caught seafood there, but certainly not as often as chicken, pork, or vegetable-based dishes. Many freshwater fish, which were supposed to have been wonderful at one time, disappeared in the Valley of Oaxaca when the Atoyac river dried up from overuse for irrigation. Ocean fish are not as abundant as they once were.

When I did find fresh seafood being served, it was often very simply cooked—too simply to be captured in recipes. Oddly, you rarely see people picturesquely grilling fish on sticks on the beach they way they do near some of the famous resort towns in other states. What you do find are approaches common all over Mexico, like griddle-searing or frying fish to be served with garlic sauce. There doesn't seem to be a wealth of specifically Oaxacan fish dishes— though the fish themselves are often so specifically Oaxacan that it's hard to know how to identify them in English translation.

Though there is some commercial fishing to supply fresh seafood to the markets, it isn't a big industry. A more important role is played by dried fish and shrimp. The popularity of the dried products doesn't seem to be just a matter of making do without refrigeration. Even where refrigerators and refrigerated transport are fairly common, dried fish and shrimp are loved for their own sake. Unfortunately, Oaxacan-style smoked dried fish is not available in the U.S. However, good dried shrimp is sold here in Latin American markets. I have used it in many dishes—soups, sauces, appetizers—and hope you will learn to enjoy its briny, strangely penetrating flavor.

The following are some of the seafood dishes I have enjoyed in coastal Oaxaca—except for Pescado en Nogada de Mostaza, a historical recipe that caught my eye in a book.

Pescado Estilo el Estero
Whole Baked Fish, Estero-style

A few miles north of Juchitán in the Isthmus of Tehuantepec is a spot called just El Estero ("The Estuary," after some tidal inlet). It consists of several restaurants that are unprepossessing huts on the outside and even worse inside, with dirt floors that at the time of my visit (the rainy season) were ankle-deep in mud. At one of these hovels I had a most delicious chipotle-seasoned fish baked in a *calabacero*, a type of masonry and adobe oven. It was unbelievably simple, but worth the muddy trek. The mayonnaise in the sauce releases enough oil to baste the fish and keep it moist.

In this case, commercial mayonnaise is more "authentic" than trying to make your own.

2 to 3 servings

Preheat the oven to 400°F.

Combine the mayonnaise, chipotle chile, and garlic in a small bowl. With a pastry brush or icing spatula, spread the mixture all over the fish, inside and outside. Sprinkle lightly with salt. Place on a baking pan and bake for 20 to 25 minutes, or until just barely opaque at the thickest part of the fish. Serve with Salsa de Chile Pasilla (page 254) or any preferred table sauce. Ensalada de Verduras (page 248) is a good accompanying dish.

1/2 cup mayonnaise

1 canned chipotle chile en adobo (page 46), minced

1 garlic clove, minced

One whole 2-pound sea bass, striped bass, or red snapper, cleaned and scaled, gills removed

1/2 teaspoon salt, or to taste

Pescado en Hoja de Plátano
Fish Baked in Banana Leaves

Banana leaves for wrapping
(page 29), thawed if frozen

2 tablespoons vegetable oil

1 medium onion, finely chopped

2 large garlic cloves, minced

2 large ripe tomatoes, chopped

4 fresh *hoja santa* leaves or 6 dried
leaves (page 36)

2 large semi-ripe plantains (page 39),
peeled and sliced into thin (1/8-
to 1/4-inch) rounds

4 small fish (about 8 ounces each)
such as ocean perch, porgy,
rouget, or spot, scaled and gutted,
gills removed

1 teaspoon salt, or to taste

Freshly ground black pepper

*I*n Oaxaca, this dish is made with *mojarra*, a fish resembling ocean perch that I have never seen in this country. Luckily the wrapping technique works well with several fish that are widely available here. The natural oil in the banana leaf helps the fish steam inside the packet without drying out, and the fragrance of the leaves seems to have an affinity with fish. Parchment paper is a possible substitute, but frankly not a real equivalent.

If you can possibly find fresh *hoja santa* leaves, use them. The delicate anise-like perfume is an important element of the dish. Look for plantains that are not fully ripe. They should just be changing from solid green to green-yellow, not black.

4 servings

Unwrap the package of banana leaves and choose pieces with no visible tears. With kitchen scissors, cut out four 12×12-inch squares. Tear off long thin strands from the remaining leaves to serve as "string" ties. Set aside.

Preheat the oven to 400°F.

In a medium-size skillet, heat the oil over medium-high heat until rippling. Add the onion and garlic and cook, stirring frequently, for 2 minutes. If using dried *hoja santa* leaves, add 2 of them along with the tomatoes. Cook for 5 minutes, stirring occasionally.

If the banana-leaf squares are too stiff to bend without cracking, briefly hold them over an open flame or place for a few seconds on a hot griddle to make them more pliable. Place the 4 squares side by side on the counter. Place 1 fresh *hoja santa* leaf in the center of each and arrange one quarter of the plantain slices over it. (If using the dried herb, put a mound of plantain on each leaf and crumble the remaining 4 *hoja santa* leaves on top.) Season the fish all over with salt and pepper. Place on top of the plantains; spoon the onion-tomato mixture over the fish. Fold up the banana leaves to enclose the fish in square packets with the seam uppermost, then tie like gift packages with the leaf "strings" or kitchen twine.

Place the packets on a baking pan and bake for 15 minutes. Serve immediately, in the packets (each person unwraps his or her own).

Variation: *To make the dish for 4 people with one larger fish weighing about 3 pounds, cut out a banana-leaf rectangle of about 12×18 inches. Proceed as directed above, arranging 2 of the fresh* hoja santa *leaves on the banana leaf and 2 on top of the fish. Bake at 400°F for 35 to 40 minutes. Unwrap the packet and distribute the fish, plantains, and sauce equally on each serving plate.*

Escabeche de Pescado
Marinated Fried Fish

1/2 cup olive oil

1 firm-textured French roll, cut into thin slices

5 sprigs Italian parsley

3 large garlic cloves

1 large onion, thinly sliced into half-moons

1/2 teaspoon black peppercorns

8 cloves

5 bay leaves

1 cup distilled white vinegar

4 fillets (about 6 to 8 ounces each) firm white-fleshed fish such as sea bass or red snapper, skin on

1/2 teaspoon salt

Freshly ground black pepper

10 large pimiento-stuffed olives, sliced

1 tablespoon capers, drained

2 pickled jalapeño chiles, tops and seeds removed, thinly sliced

*T*his is a composite of several typical versions of a standard Latin American and Spanish dish that I sampled in Oaxaca with local fish varieties from the Isthmian coast. Unlike many versions, it omits the step of coating the fish in flour before frying.

If preferred, grill or broil the fish and marinate in the same way.

4 servings

In a skillet, heat 3 tablespoons of the oil over medium-high heat until not quite smoking. Add the sliced bread and fry, turning, until deep golden on both sides, about 2 to 3 minutes in all. Remove from the oil and drain well on paper towels.

Place the slightly cooled bread in a food processor with the parsley and process to coarse green-flecked crumbs. Set aside.

In a medium-size skillet, heat 3 tablespoons of the remaining oil over high heat until rippling. Add the garlic cloves and cook just until golden, pressing down with the back of a spoon to release their flavor. Remove and discard the garlic. Reduce the heat to medium-high. Add the onion and cook, stirring, for 3 minutes, until translucent. Add the bread-parsley mixture, peppercorns, cloves, and bay leaves. Cook, stirring, for 5 minutes. Add the vinegar and cook, stirring, for 1 minute longer. Remove from the heat and let cool to lukewarm.

Season the fish fillets with the salt and pepper to taste. In a large skillet, heat the remaining oil over medium-high heat until rippling. Add the fish fillets and pan-fry until golden, 2 to 3 minutes on each side. (Do not overcrowd the pan; work with 2 fillets at a time if necessary.) Carefully transfer to a serving dish large enough to hold the fish in one layer with the prepared vinegar marinade. Scatter the olives, capers, and jalapeños over the fish and pour the marinade over it. Refrigerate, covered, for at least 4 hours. Let come to room temperature before serving.

Pescado en Nogada de Mostaza

Fish in Almond-Mustard Sauce

While reading Alejandro Méndez Aquino's history of Oaxaca City Christmas and other holiday traditions in *Noche de Rábanos* (published by a Oaxaca state cultural agency in 1990), I came on a tantalizingly brief description of a fish dish, one of many formerly served on meatless days (*vigilias*). It was taken from a ninenteenth-century cookbook and featured *bobo*—the best Oaxacan freshwater fish, now virtually extinct—in an oil and vinegar sauce with a base of ground almonds and mustard. I haven't tried to reconstruct the original from the skimpy directions. I think the fish was served cold and the sauce was served on the side—but the combination of ingredients appealed to my imagination. I did some experimenting and created a delicious mustard and almond paste that I find makes a nice crust when the fish is baked.

4 servings

Preheat the oven to 400°F.

Grind the almonds very fine in a Mouli grater or food processor. Set aside in a mixing bowl.

Grind the *canela* in an electric coffee or spice grinder and add to the almonds. Grind the mustard seeds as fine as possible in the coffee grinder and sift them through a fine-mesh sieve, discarding any bits of chaff. Add the sifted mustard seeds to the almonds and *canela*; add the cloves and pepper and stir well to combine.

Add the vinegar to the dry ingredients and mix well. Add the oil in a thin stream, whisking constantly, until you have a smooth paste. Stir in the capers, olives, and jalapeños. Set aside about 1/4 cup of the mixture. Spread the rest of the paste over both sides of the fillets and place in a baking pan. Mix the reserved paste with 1 cup water and pour into the pan. Bake for for 10 to 12 minutes, or until the flesh is just opaque. Serve at once, spooning some of the pan juices over each serving. Plain rice is the best accompaniment.

1 cup blanched almonds

One 1-inch piece *canela* (page 30)

1/4 cup mustard seed, or 1 tablespoon powdered mustard

1/4 teaspoon ground cloves

1/2 teaspoon freshly ground black pepper

2 tablespoons red wine vinegar or sherry vinegar

1/4 cup olive oil

2 tablespoons capers, drained

1/2 cup pitted green brined olives, minced

2 pickled jalapeño chiles, tops and seeds removed, minced (page 45)

4 fillets (6 to 8 ounces each) from firm white-fleshed fish such as sea bass, red snapper, tilefish or grouper

Camarones con Nopalitos
Dried and Fresh Shrimp with Cactus Paddles

1/2 cup hulled pumpkin seeds

1 cup whole dried shrimp (about 2 to 2 1/2 ounces), cleaned, or 2 tablespoons ground dried shrimp (page 33)

2 large ripe tomatoes, coarsely chopped

1 medium onion, coarsely chopped

2 garlic cloves, coarsely chopped

3 to 4 jalapeño chiles (or to taste), tops removed, coarsely chopped

1 teaspoon achiote paste (page 28)

2 tablespoons vegetable oil

6 large fresh epazote sprigs or 1 tablespoon dried (page 35)

4 large nopalitos (cactus paddles), cleaned and cut into 1/2-inch dice (page 29)

1/2 pound fresh "large" shrimp (16 to 20 count per pound), peeled and deveined

*T*his is an example of an Isthmian *molito*, or "little mole" with a fairly simple puréed sauce less demanding than a full-fledged *mole*. I like to serve it with some straightforward rice dish.

The fresh shrimp are the size called "large" at my fish store, but designations may vary by retailer.

4 servings

Heat a griddle or medium-size cast-iron skillet over low heat. Add the pumpkin seeds and whole dried shrimp and cook, stirring frequently, until lightly toasted, 5 to 7 minutes. (If using ground dried shrimp, do not toast.) Remove from the heat and let cool slightly.

Place the pumpkin seeds and dried shrimp in a blender along with the tomatoes, onion, garlic, jalapeños, and achiote paste. (If using ground dried shrimp, add it now.) Process to a smooth purée (about 3 minutes on high). With a wooden spoon or pusher, force the mixture through a medium-mesh sieve into a bowl.

In a medium-size Dutch oven or saucepan, heat the vegetable oil over medium-high heat until it ripples. Pour in the puréed mixture and bring to a boil, stirring frequently (it will splatter). Cover and reduce the heat to medium-low; cook, stirring frequently, for 5 minutes. Add 1 cup water. When it boils, add the epazote, reduce the heat to low, and cook, covered, stirring occasionally, for 30 minutes.

When the mixture has cooked for about 20 minutes, bring a small saucepan of water to a boil and add the diced nopalitos. Cook over medium heat, uncovered, for 15 minutes. Transfer to a colander and rinse first under hot and then cold running water to remove some of their sticky juices. Drain well. Stir into the sauce along with the fresh shrimp and cook, stirring, just until the shrimp are cooked through, 3 to 4 minutes. Serve immediately with plain steamed rice or Arroz con Elote (page 237).

Camarones Enchilados
Shrimp in Chile Sauce

This lusty dish is adapted from the wonderful chile shrimp served at one of my favorite Isthmian restaurants, Bar Jardín in Juchitán. Odilia Román, the chef, makes a related but differently seasoned dish with crabs, Jaibas en Chile Chipotle (page 228).

For the right flavor, use whole unpeeled shrimp with the heads on. In this country shrimp are almost always frozen before they get to the retailer and sold without the heads. You have to beg a fishmonger to sell them to you with the heads, or find a Chinese market where they routinely come this way. The heads are the most flavorful part. Each diner snaps the shrimp in two and sucks out the delicious juices. If you cannot find shrimp with the heads intact, substitute 1 pound shrimp tails but be sure to cook them in the shell to retain as much flavor as possible. Everyone peels his or her own when they are served.

4 servings

5 guajillo chiles (page 47), tops and seeds removed

1 dried chipotle chile (page 46), top and seeds removed, or 1 canned chipotle chile en adobo

3 tablespoons olive oil

1 pound large whole shrimp in the shell, with heads

2 large garlic cloves, minced

2 tablespoons mayonnaise

Wash and griddle-dry the guajillo chiles (and the dried chipotle, if using) by the directions on page 45. Place in a bowl, cover generously with boiling water, and let soak for 20 minutes.

In a large, heavy skillet, heat the oil over medium-high heat until rippling. Add the shrimp and cook, turning rapidly, for 1 minute. Lift out the shrimp into a bowl, using a slotted spoon and letting the oil drain back into the pan. Set aside the skillet with the oil.

Drain the soaked chiles and place in a blender (along with the canned chipotle chile, if using). Add 2/3 cup water and process until thoroughly puréed (about 3 minutes on high). With a wooden spoon or pusher, force the purée through a medium-mesh sieve into a bowl.

Return the skillet to the stove over medium-high heat until the oil ripples. Add the minced garlic and cook, stirring constantly, for about 30 seconds. Pour in the chile purée. Add the mayonnaise and cook, whisking to combine, for a few seconds. Reduce the heat to low and cook, covered, stirring occasionally, for 15 minutes. Raise the heat slightly, add the shrimp, and cook, stirring to combine, until they are heated through, 2 to 3 minutes. Serve immediately with Arroz con Tomatillos (page 239) or another rice dish.

Jaibas en Chile Chipotle
Crabs in Chipotle Chile Sauce

4 guajillo chiles (page 47), tops and
    seeds removed

6 canned chipotles chiles en adobo
    (page 46)

10 cloves garlic

1 to 1 1/2 teaspoons salt

12 live blue crabs or rock crabs,
    or 24 large stone crab claws

1/3 cup olive oil

Odilia Román's chile-shrimp dish, Camarones Enchilados (page 227), is only one of several variations she likes to play on the shellfish-and-chile theme. The exact makeup of the sauces varies with her mood. I was there once when she produced this fiery crab entree. The dish should be quite hot, but if you want to temper it a little, change the proportion of chiles to 8 guajillos and 2 canned chipotles.

4 to 6 servings

Wash and griddle-dry the guajillo chiles by the directions on page 45. Place in a bowl and cover generously with boiling water. Let soak for at least 20 minutes. Drain and place in a blender along with the canned chipotles. Process until smoothly puréed. With a wooden spoon or pusher, force the purée through a medium-mesh sieve into a bowl. Set aside.

With a mortar and pestle, mash the garlic and salt to a paste.

If using whole crabs, chop them in half with a heavy sharp knife or cleaver. In a large, heavy skillet, heat the oil over medium-high heat until rippling. Add the garlic paste and crabs; cook the crabs for 3 minutes on each side. Lift out onto a plate, using a slotted spoon and letting the oil drain back into the pan. Set aside.

Pour the chile purée into the pan and bring to a boil over medium-high heat. Reduce the heat to medium and cook, covered, for 15 minutes, stirring occasionally. Return the crabs to the pan and cook until heated through, about 2 minutes.

Variation: *I have had a dish very like this in which the crabs were marinated in the juice from more than a dozen small local limes. Here I suggest chopping the crabs in half (or cracking the crabs claws) and placing them in a bowl with the freshly squeezed juice of 4 to 6 limes. Let marinate, refrigerated, for 15 minutes. Drain well and pat dry before sautéing in the hot oil and adding to the chile sauce as directed above.*

Colas de Langosta
Lobster Tails

Seafood and cheese sounds like an unorthodox combination; adding Mexican chocolate sounds like pure lunacy, but it works! I have adapted the recipe from one by María Edith Sánchez Sumano in an anthology of the best Oaxacan recipes collected by the Banco Rural (which has done a whole series on the cooking of all 31 Mexican states). Her recipe used the meat of a local spiny lobster, removed from the shell. I have had good results with rock lobster tails cooked in the shell, but if you prefer you could substitute the shelled uncooked meat of two 1 1/2-pound Maine lobsters. The cheese in the original was *queso menonita*, a sort of cheddar from the northern state of Chihuahua.

4 servings

1 small onion, finely chopped

2 garlic cloves, minced

2 tablespoons chopped Italian parsley leaves

4 ounces medium-sharp white cheddar cheese, shredded

Half of a 3-ounce tablet Mexican chocolate (pages 277 to 279), grated

1/4 teaspoon freshly grated nutmeg

Freshly ground black pepper

1/2 teaspoon salt, or to taste

1/4 cup olive oil

Four 6- to 8-ounce lobster tails in shell, thawed if frozen

2 cups dry white wine

Combine the onion, garlic, and parsley in a small bowl. Add the cheese, chocolate, nutmeg, pepper, and salt; stir well to mix.

In a large, heavy lidded skillet, heat the oil over medium-high heat until it ripples. Add the lobster tails and cook for 2 minutes, turning once. Remove the pan from the heat. Arrange the lobster tails with the convex outer side up and distribute the onion-cheese mixture over each, mounding neatly on the shell. Pour the wine into the pan. Return the pan to the stove and bring to a boil over medium-high heat. Immediately cover, reduce the heat to medium, and cook until the lobster is cooked through, about 3 to 4 minutes. Arrange the lobster on serving plates, pouring some of the pan juices over each serving. Serve with plenty of plain steamed rice to soak up the savory juices.

The market in Juchitán

Vegetables and Side Dishes

When I started searching for Oaxacan vegetable dishes my first impression was that there weren't any. After a while I knew better. It's written formulas with official titles that are hard to find. In fact, vegetables are a huge part of the cuisine. They are so taken for granted, and used with such instinctive skill, that the general attitude would be, "Who needs recipes?"

Certain vegetables like tomatoes, squashes, and beans have been known as long as people have lived in the region. European produce such as cauliflower, cabbage, globe onions, carrots, radishes, beets, cucumbers, asparagus, and pulses (chickpeas, lentils) was mostly brought in the early years of the Conquest by the Dominican friars. They started all kinds of seeds of flowers, herbs, and vegetables in a town—now a neighborhood of Oaxaca City—named for its Church of the Trinity, *Trinidad de las Huertas* (*huerta* is "garden"). This became a local center for horticulture, where the friars taught the native peoples how to plant and cultivate the new specialties. They were so successful that by 1547 local farmers are said to have been exporting seeds to Guatemala. Eventually rice was introduced to Oaxaca and became a popular staple, often in combination with native herbs and vegetables.

The pre-Hispanic diet had been a largely vegetarian one, and most people continued to eat very little meat except on special occasions. If any additional stimulus to develop the art of vegetable cookery was necessary, it came from the many days of abstinence from meat in the Church calendar. As well as abstaining from meat throughout Lent, people were expected to eat meatless meals on *vigilias*, times of fasting and abstinence on the eves of feast days. One *vigilia*—Christmas Eve—gave rise to one of Oaxaca's best-known traditions. Because Christmas Eve supper grew to be an important and elaborate event, a special market was held before the date on the site of the present *Zócalo*. The produce-sellers would set up stands with lavish displays of vegetables. Sometimes they would even be decorated with sculptures made from vegetables. Around the turn of the century a promotion-minded mayor started a contest for the best displays. The market is gone, but part of the contest lingers on: *Noche de Rábanos*, an annual exhibit of sculptures made from radishes! Should you happen to be in the city on the night of December 23, head for the *Zócalo* and there you will see the beautiful and amusing radish tableaux, all that remains of the old December *mercado de vigilia*.

The *comida de vigilia*, or the meatless meal marking religious observances, is still very much a part of Oaxacan life, as is everyday thrifty vegetable-based cooking. The truth is that many of the sauces I present in the chapters on *moles*, meats, and poultry would be cooked with stewed vegetable medleys at least as often as with meat. No one would bother to write down a special recipe—it's simply a matter of using whatever happens to be best and most abundant at the moment.

The same is true of the vegetable *escabeches*—the mixed-vegetable pickles that people love as snacks or relish-like side dishes. If you really want to make them "authentic" you will throw in some of this and some of that, being guided by the state of your garden or the nearest farmers' market. Look through the list of suggested vegetables in Ensalada de Verduras and experiment with any selection you prefer in other pickled recipes or to replace meats in the big sauce-based dishes.

Salads of uncooked leafy greens are nearly unknown in Oaxacan cooking. Indeed, it would be most uncommon to serve raw vegetables of any sort except in the form of salsas.

Frijoles Cocidos
Basic Cooked Beans

1 pound (about 2 1/2 cups) dried
    beans, picked over and rinsed to
    remove stones or grit

1 large sprig fresh epazote (page 35),
    optional

2 teaspoons to 1 tablespoon salt,
    or to taste

*D*ried beans are one of the core foods in the Oaxacan diet—and no wonder, since the beans are so fine. I did not find a panoply of exciting, unusual dishes. That is not the Oaxacan way. People seldom stray far from the plain, simply cooked beans that are a part of most meals. It's the beans themselves that give the good flavor. Black beans are the most popular, especially a very large variety called *ayocotes* that I've even seen in New York.

No matter what kind of beans you are working with, the basic method is the same. However, depending on the size and age of the beans, the cooking time must be played by ear. Remember to choose a deep rather than wide cooking pot so that the beans stay well covered with water.

About 7 to 8 cups

    Place the beans and optional epazote in a large, deep saucepan or Dutch oven. Add enough cold water to cover by at least 2 inches (the exact amount will depend on the shape of the pot). Bring to a boil over high heat, reduce the heat to low, and cook, partly covered, for about 25 minutes before adding the salt. (Salting at the beginning tends to toughen them.) Continue to cook, partly covered, keeping a kettle of boiling water in reserve to replenish the cooking liquid as necessary so the beans are always covered by at least 1 inch. After about 45 minutes test for doneness by eating a bean; continue to cook, adding boiling water to cover as necessary, until they are tender. The oldest and toughest may take 1 1/2 hours or longer. Basic boiled beans are supposed to be a little soupy and are usually eaten with some of the cooking liquid, so do not drain unless they are to be used for another recipe.

Frijoles Negros Colados
Puréed Black Beans

*T*his is an exciting variation on the theme of refried beans. The taste immediately brings Oaxaca to my mind—the fragrant, anise-like avocado
leaves and the delicate spiciness of the chiles are so characteristic.

Made with oil, this is an excellent vegetarian dish. However, I usually use home-
rendered lard for deeper flavor.

About 6 servings

Cook the beans by the basic method for Frijoles Cocidos on page 234,
adding the garlic and unpeeled onion to the saucepan along with the beans.
Start testing for doneness 45 minutes after adding the salt. When the beans are
tender, discard the onion and garlic and let the beans cool in the cooking liquid.

When the beans are partly cooled, griddle-roast the chiles by the directions
on page 42. Place in a small bowl and cover well with boiling water. Let soak for
20 minutes. Lightly toast the avocado leaves on the hot griddle (just a few seconds, until the aroma is released). Crumble when cool enough to handle.
Set aside.

Drain the beans, reserving about 1 to 1 1/2 cups of the cooking liquid. Drain
the soaked chiles. Working in batches as necessary, purée the beans, chiles,
and avocado leaves together in a blender, adding enough of the reserved cooking liquid to facilitate blending. The mixture should be about the consistency of
peanut butter. (Alternatively, process in a food processor, adding enough liquid
to achieve the right consistency.) With a wooden spoon or pusher, force the
mixture through a medium-mesh sieve into a bowl, discarding any fibrous parts
that will not go through.

Cut the remaining 3 onions into thin slices. In a large, heavy saucepan or
Dutch oven, heat the lard over medium-high heat until rippling and add the
onions. Cook, stirring frequently, until they are well browned, about 8 minutes.
Do not scorch. Scoop out and discard the onions, letting as much of the fat as
possible drain back into the pan. Add the puréed beans to the seasoned fat,
stirring vigorously to mix. Reduce the heat to low and cook, covered, stirring
frequently to prevent sticking, for 30 minutes.

1 pound (about 2 1/2 cups) black
   beans, picked over and rinsed to
   remove stones or grit

1 whole head of garlic, unpeeled

4 medium onions, 1 left unpeeled

2 teaspoons to 1 tablespoon salt,
   or to taste

3 árbol chiles (page 46), tops
   removed

12 dried avocado leaves (page 28)

1/2 cup lard (preferably
   home-rendered; page 36)
   or vegetable oil

Arroz con Camarones Secos
Rice with Dried Shrimp

2 cups long-grain rice

4 ounces (about 2 cups) dried shrimp (page 33), cleaned, tails and heads separated

2 large ripe tomatoes, coarsely chopped

2 garlic cloves, coarsely chopped

1/2 small onion, coarsely chopped

2 fresh green chiles such as serranos or jalapeños (or more to taste), stems and tops removed, coarsely chopped

1/2 teaspoon achiote paste (page 28)

1/4 cup vegetable oil

3 cups homemade chicken stock (page 74) or water

Pinch of salt (optional)

*T*his recipe comes from Bertha Dolores de Liljehult, whose son Fidel Liljehult owns Casa Grande in Juchitán, one of the few restaurants that try to showcase regional Isthmian dishes. Because of the assertive flavor of the shrimp, it's a dish best served with some fairly simple meat (like Costillas de Puerco Fritas en Seco, page 195, or Puerco en Chirmole, page 198) or as a one-dish meal with plain cooked beans and a salad.

In dishes like this, where the rice is sautéed in oil or lard before being cooked in liquid, I often like to coat it generously with the fat at the beginning and discard the excess before proceeding. This seems to work better than starting with a smaller amount of fat. Incidentally, converted rice will not give the right result here or in any other of my rice recipes.

6 to 8 servings

In a deep bowl, carefully rinse the rice in several changes of cold water until no starchy residue is visible. Drain very thoroughly in a large sieve, shaking to eliminate as much water as possible.

Soak the dried shrimp tails in several changes of cold water to remove some of the salt; drain well.

Heat a cast-iron skillet over medium-high heat until a drop of water sizzles on contact. Add the shrimp heads and toast, stirring constantly, until fragrant, about 2 minutes. Transfer to a bowl and set aside to cool slightly. Place in a blender along with the tomatoes, garlic, onion, chiles, and achiote paste. Process as smooth as possible (about 2 minutes on high). With a wooden spoon or pusher, force the mixture through a medium-mesh sieve into a bowl, discarding bits of shell or fiber that will not go through. Set aside.

In a heavy medium-size saucepan, heat the oil until rippling. Add the rice and cook, stirring constantly, until it colors slightly and sounds like sand as you stir it. Carefully pour off and discard the excess fat. Add the puréed mixture and cook, stirring occasionally, for 3 minutes. Stir in the chicken stock and drained shrimp tails. Add a little salt if desired (the stock and shrimp will contribute some). Cover tightly. Reduce the heat to very low and cook for 15 to 18 minutes. Remove from the heat and let sit for about 5 minutes, tightly covered, before serving.

Arroz con Elote
Rice with Sweet Corn

*L*ucila Zárate de Fuentes of Oaxaca City supervises the cooking in the household of the well-known artists Justina Fuentes and Juan Alcázar, her daughter and son-in-law. This is a favorite family side dish at lunch. It goes well with Lucila's Estofado de Frutas (page 179), or actually just about anything else.

The corn used in the original is a white variety. In this country I suggest old-fashioned shoepeg corn if you can find it.

4 servings

In a deep bowl, carefully rinse the rice in several changes of cold water until no starchy residue is visible. Drain thoroughly in a large sieve, shaking to remove as much water as possible.

In a medium-size saucepan, heat the oil to rippling over medium-high heat. Add the rice and cook, stirring constantly, until it colors slightly and sounds like sand as you stir it. Add the garlic, onion, and corn kernels and cook, stirring constantly, until the onion is translucent, about 5 minutes. Stir in the parsley, chicken stock, milk, and salt. Cover tightly. Reduce the heat to very low and cook for about 12 to 13 minutes. Lift the lid just long enough to drizzle the *crema* over the top; cover at once and cook for another 5 minutes. Let sit off the heat, tightly covered, for about 5 minutes before serving.

1 cup long-grain rice

3 tablespoons vegetable oil

1 large garlic clove, minced

1 medium onion, sliced into thin half-moons

1 cup fresh or frozen corn kernels, preferably white

3 large sprigs parsley

1 cup homemade chicken stock (page 74) or water

1 cup whole milk

1/2 teaspoon salt, or to taste

1/4 cup Mexican *crema* (page 33) or heavy cream

Arroz con Chepil
Rice with Chepil

1 cup long-grain rice

3 tablespoons lard (preferably
home-rendered; page 36)
or vegetable oil

2 garlic cloves, minced

1 small onion, finely chopped

2 cups homemade chicken (page 74)
or pork stock (page 73)

3 tablespoons *chepil* leaves stripped
from stems (from defrosted
package of frozen *chepil*; page 32)

1/2 teaspoon salt, or to taste

*T*his is one of the most popular Oaxacan rice dishes. There is no substitute for the *chepil*, but luckily good frozen *chepil* can be found in many Latin American groceries under the name *chipilín*. It has become one of my favorite herbs.

4 servings

In a deep bowl, carefully rinse the rice in several changes of cold water until no starchy residue is visible. Drain thoroughly in a large sieve, shaking to remove as much water as possible.

In a heavy medium-size saucepan, heat the lard over medium-high heat until rippling. Add the rice and cook, stirring constantly, until it colors slightly and sounds like sand as you stir it. Carefully pour off and discard any excess fat. Add the garlic and onion; cook, stirring, for about 1 minute. Stir in the stock, *chepil*, and salt. Cover tightly, reduce the heat to very low, and cook for 15 to 18 minutes. Remove from the heat and let sit for about 5 minutes, tightly covered, before serving.

Arroz con Tomatillos

Rice with Tomatillos

This is a typical rice dish that I have had everywhere in Oaxaca. I first learned it from María Concepción Portillo de Carballido. The handling of the tomatillos is a little fussy—only the outer portion is used. This is because the pulp with the seeds would tend to give the whole dish a sticky consistency.

4 servings

Cut the tomatillos into quarters. Place in a bowl, cover with cold water, and let soak for 30 minutes (to make the pulp easier to remove). Scrape out the pulpy interior with a grapefruit spoon or small sharp knife. Discard the pulp. With a heavy sharp knife, coarsely chop the soaked outer portion. Set aside.

In a deep bowl, carefully rinse the rice in several changes of cold water until no starchy residue is visible. Drain very thoroughly, shaking out as much excess water as possible.

Place the onion, garlic, and cilantro in a blender and process until smoothly puréed, about 1 minute on high.

In a medium-size saucepan, heat the oil over medium-high heat Add the rice and cook, stirring constantly, until it colors slightly and sounds like sand as you stir it. Add the chopped tomatillos and puréed onion mixture. Cook, stirring frequently, for 3 minutes. Stir in the chicken stock; taste and add salt. Cover tightly and reduce the heat to very low. Cook for 15 to 18 minutes. Let sit off the heat, tightly covered, for a few minutes before serving.

8 ounces tomatillos, husks removed

1 cup long-grain rice

1 small onion, coarsely chopped

1 garlic clove, coarsely chopped

1/2 cup fresh cilantro leaves, stripped from stems

3 tablespoons vegetable oil

2 1/4 cups homemade chicken stock (page 74)

1/2 teaspoon salt, or to taste

Especie Mixteca

Mixtec-style Rice

2 cups long-grain rice

One 1/2-inch piece *canela* (page 30)

1 large ripe tomato, coarsely chopped

1 teaspoon dried Mexican oregano, crumbled (page 38)

1/8 teaspoon ground cloves

4 tablespoons lard (preferably home-rendered; page 36) or vegetable oil

1 medium onion, finely chopped

4 garlic cloves, minced

4 cups homemade chicken stock (page 74)

1 teaspoon salt, or to taste

Freshly ground black pepper

10 to 12 strips of pickled jalapeño chiles (preferably red)

*T*his spicy rice dish from the Mixtec regions is especially pretty when made with pickled red jalapeño strips. If you can't find the pickled red strips, use pickled green jalapeños cut into strips.

About 8 servings

In a deep bowl, carefully rinse the rice in several changes of water until no starchy residue is visible. Drain as thoroughly as possible in a strainer, shaking to remove excess water.

Grind the *canela* in an electric coffee or spice grinder. Place the tomato in a blender or food processor with the *canela*, oregano, and cloves and process to a purée. Set aside.

In a medium-size saucepan, heat the lard over medium-high heat until rippling. Add the rice and cook, stirring constantly, until it colors slightly and sounds like sand as you stir it. Add the onion and garlic and cook, stirring constantly, for 2 minutes. Add the puréed tomato mixture and cook, stirring constantly, for 2 minutes longer. Add the chicken stock, salt, and pepper, and bring back to a boil.

Cover the pan tightly, reduce the heat to very low, and cook for about 10 minutes. Lift the lid and quickly arrange the chile strips over the rice in a spoke pattern. At once replace the lid and cook for another 5 to 8 minutes. Remove from the heat and let sit, tightly covered, for about 5 minutes before serving.

Macarrones Estilo Luis Armando

Luis Armando's Pasta in Creamy Sauce

*I*talian pasta is variously called "macarrones" or "espaguetti" in Mexico and cooked in ways that an Italian might not recognize! Creamy macaroni dishes with cheese are very popular. This version comes from Luis Armando Hernández in Ixtepec. He and his mother, Venancia Toledo Hernández, serve it on all their special occasions. They make it with cream cheese (*queso crema*) and Oaxacan string cheese, which is a wonderful melting cheese.

4 servings

Place the tomatoes, onion, garlic, half the cilantro, and the *crema* in a blender or food processor; process until smooth. Add the cream cheese and process until thoroughly combined. Season with salt and pepper. In a large saucepan, heat the oil until rippling over medium-high heat. Add the tomato-cream cheese mixture and the remaining cilantro. Bring to a boil, stirring constantly to prevent splattering. Reduce the heat to low and cook, partly covered, for 15 minutes, until slightly thickened.

Preheat the oven to 350°F.

Cook the pasta according to package directions. Drain well and return to the well-dried cooking pot. Add the sauce and toss to mix thoroughly. Transfer to a 1 1/2-quart baking dish and sprinkle with the shredded cheese. Bake until the cheese is bubbling and the pasta is heated through, about 10 minutes.

4 large ripe tomatoes or 10 to 12 large ripe plum tomatoes (about 2 pounds), coarsely chopped

1 medium onion, coarsely chopped

3 garlic cloves, coarsely chopped

10 sprigs fresh cilantro or Italian parsley

1/2 cup Mexican *crema* (page 33) or heavy cream

One 3-ounce package cream cheese, cut into bits

1/2 teaspoon salt, or to taste

Freshly ground black pepper

2 tablespoons olive oil

1 pound rigatoni or elbow macaroni

1 cup shredded Oaxacan string cheese (page 31) or medium-sharp white cheddar

Purée de Papas
Potato Purée

6 medium russet or other starchy potatoes (about 2 1/2 to 3 pounds), scrubbed and quartered but unpeeled

2 medium carrots, peeled and cut into 1/4-inch dice

1 cup tiny new peas, fresh or frozen

3/4 cup Mexican *crema* (page 33) or heavy cream

1 large egg, beaten

2 teaspoons prepared yellow mustard, or to taste

4 tablespoons (1/2 stick) unsalted butter

1 medium onion, finely chopped

1/4 cup minced Italian parsley leaves

One 3-ounce jar pickled pearl onions, drained

One 3-ounce jar (1/2 cup) pitted green brined olives, drained and sliced

1/4 cup (or to taste) pickled jalapeño chiles, drained and finely chopped

Freshly ground black pepper

1/2 teaspoon salt (optional)

When I visited the Isthmus of Tehuantepec at the season of spring parties accompanying the local *velas* (saints' day festivals), I found this vividly seasoned dish being served everywhere. It also turned out to be one of the regular Sunday offerings at Venancia Toledo Hernández's food stand in the Isthmian town of Ixtepec. She gave me her recipe and now everyone I've served it to in New York is in love with the brassy, sensuous flavors.

6 servings

Prepare the vegetables: Have ready a medium-size saucepan of boiling salted water. Add the potatoes and cook until barely tender, 12 to 15 minutes. Lift out, letting them drain well, and peel. Set aside. Add the diced carrots to the water and cook just until crisp-tender, about 4 minutes. Scoop out with a strainer or slotted spoon, letting them drain well, and set aside. Add the peas and cook until barely tender, about 3 minutes; remove and drain.

In a large bowl, mash the potatoes with a potato masher. Add the *crema* and beat with a wooden spoon to eliminate most of the lumps. Add the egg and mustard, continuing to beat until the mixture is smooth and fluffy.

Preheat the oven to 350°F.

In a medium-size skillet, melt the butter over medium-high heat until fragrant and sizzling but not browned. Add the onion and cook, stirring, until the onion is translucent, about 3 minutes. Add the parsley, cook for 1 minute longer, and beat the mixture into the mashed potatoes. Stir in the carrots, peas, pickled onions, olives, and jalapeños. Taste for seasoning and add the pepper and optional salt. Transfer the mixture to a buttered 2-quart baking dish and bake 20 minutes. Serve at once.

Budín de Nopalitos

Cactus Paddle Casserole

This savory pudding makes a nice luncheon dish or hearty side dish for a simple dinner menu. It is also an excellent vegetarian main dish. When I had it in various parts of Oaxaca, the proportion of eggs to vegetables was higher. You can adjust it to your taste as you prefer. My mother reports that the dish is very good prepared with fresh ricotta cheese, which makes it moister.

4 to 6 servings

Bring a small saucepan of water to a boil and add the diced nopalitos. Cook, uncovered, over medium heat for 10 to 12 minutes. Turn out into a colander and rinse under hot and then cold running water to remove some of the sticky juices. Set aside.

Griddle-roast the tomatoes by the directions on page 26. When they are cool enough to handle, peel, saving the juices. Place in a blender with 1 of the onions, the garlic, and the canned chipotles. Process to a smooth purée. With a wooden spoon or pusher, force the mixture through a medium-mesh sieve into a bowl. Set aside.

Preheat the oven to 350°F. Grease a 2-quart baking dish.

In a medium-size saucepan, heat the oil to rippling over medium-high heat. Add the puréed tomato mixture and cook, covered, stirring frequently, for 5 minutes. Season with freshly ground pepper, add the nopalitos, and cook for 3 minutes longer. Remove from the heat and let cool.

In a mixing bowl, combine the cheese with the eggs, cilantro, cornstarch, and remaining onion and salt. Beat with a wooden spoon until very smooth. Stir in the nopalitos mixture. Pour into a buttered baking dish and bake until set like a quiche, about 20 to 30 minutes.

6 nopalitos (cactus paddles), cleaned and cut into 1/2-inch dice (page 29)

2 large ripe tomatoes

2 small onions, chopped

2 garlic cloves, coarsely chopped

2 canned chipotle chiles en adobo (page 46), coarsely chopped

3 tablespoons vegetable oil

Freshly ground black pepper

4 ounces crumbled *queso fresco* (page 31) or young ricotta salata, or 1 cup fresh ricotta cheese

3 large eggs, beaten

1/2 cup cilantro leaves stripped from stems

1 tablespoon cornstarch

1 teaspoon salt, or to taste

Calabacitas Rellenas
Stuffed Summer Squash

Six 6- to 8-ounce summer squash
(see headnote)

2 teaspoons salt, or to taste

1/4 cup freshly grated *queso cotija*
or *queso añejo* (page 31)
or Parmesan cheese

1/2 cup plain dry bread crumbs

2 tablespoons vegetable oil

2 tablespoons minced onion

1 garlic clove, minced

1 large ripe tomato, peeled and finely
chopped

3 ounces boiled ham, minced

3 pickled jalapeño chiles, tops and
seeds removed, minced

Freshly ground black pepper

2 tablespoons unsalted butter, cut
into small bits

*A*s common in Oaxaca as our cucumber-shaped zucchini is a type of zucchini as round as a little melon. This is what would be used for stuffing, since it's easy to scoop out while keeping the shape intact. Something like this is sold in the U.S. under the name roly-poly squash; if unable to find it, substitute another type of summer squash such as pattypan, regular zucchini, or yellow squash.

6 *servings*

Place the squash in a Dutch oven or saucepan large enough to hold them without crowding (preferably in one layer). Cover with cold water, add 2 teaspoons salt (or more to taste), and bring to a boil over high heat. Reduce the heat to medium and cook, uncovered, until about half-cooked (5 to 8 minutes, depending on their shape and size). Drain and let stand until cool enough to handle. Trim off the stem end with a sharp knife. Carefully scoop out the fleshy pulp, leaving the hollowed-out walls intact. Set aside the pulp and shells separately.

Preheat the broiler.

In a small bowl combine the cheese and bread crumbs; set aside.

In a large skillet, heat the oil to rippling over medium-high heat. Add the onion and garlic; cook, stirring, for 2 minutes. Add the tomato, ham, jalapeños, and squash pulp; cook, stirring, until the mixture is slightly reduced, another 2 to 3 minutes. Season with pepper to taste and a little more salt, if desired (the ham and cheese have some salt). Carefully fill the mixture into the hollowed-out squash. Place on a baking sheet, sprinkle with the cheese and bread crumb mixture, and dot with the butter. Run under the broiler until the topping is golden, about 3 minutes.

Serve plain or with a flavorful sauce such as Salsa de Tomate para Tortitas (page 69).

Chayotes Guisados
Sautéed Chayotes

I love this versatile side dish that Nicolasa Ramírez serves at La Pereñita, the always busy stand in the 20 de noviembre market in Oaxaca City. It's a basic, almost effortless technique more than a recipe. I find it great for party menus because I can do everything ahead except the final sautéing of the vegetables. The same approach works well with many vegetables, though you must adjust the cooking time and size of the pieces depending on what you're working with.

4 servings

3 chayotes

2 large garlic cloves, coarsely chopped

1 teaspoon Mexican oregano, crumbled (page 38)

1 teaspoon salt, or to taste

2 tablespoons vegetable oil

Peel and seed the chayotes and cut into 1/2-inch dice. Place in a medium-size saucepan, cover with cold water, bring to a boil over high heat, and cook for 5 minutes. Have ready a large bowl filled with ice water. Drain the chayotes and quickly plunge into the ice bath to stop the cooking. Drain well. Set aside in a bowl.

With a mortar and pestle or the flat of a heavy knife blade, crush the garlic to a paste with the oregano and salt. Toss well with the diced chayotes. Let stand until ready to serve.

In a medium-size skillet, heat the oil over medium-high heat until rippling. Add the chayotes with the garlic mixture that clings to them and cook, stirring constantly, until the moisture has evaporated, about 5 minutes. Serve at once.

Ejotes Guisados
Braised Green Beans

1 pound young green beans, strings removed if necessary

2 garlic cloves, coarsely chopped

1/2 teaspoon salt, or to taste

2 tablespoons vegetable oil

1 small onion, finely chopped

1 large ripe tomato, peeled, seeded, and finely chopped

1/2 cup freshly squeezed orange juice

2 tablespoons freshly squeezed lime juice

Freshly ground black pepper

*T*he always resourceful Venancia Toledo Hernández introduced me to this unusual combination of flavors at breakfast before one of our cooking marathons. She cooked the beans longer than I do—feel free to vary the timing if you prefer them softer or crunchier.

I use a combination of orange and lime juice to approximate the flavor of *naranja agria* ("bitter orange," though it's not really that bitter) used in Oaxaca. (It is also called "Seville orange.") If you can find *naranja agria* in a Latin American grocery, use 1/2 cup of the freshly squeezed juice, omitting the lime juice.

4 servings

Trim the beans and cut into 1-inch lengths; set aside.

Using a mortar and pestle or the flat of a heavy knife blade, mash the garlic to a paste with the salt. In a medium-large skillet, heat the oil until rippling over medium-high heat. Add the crushed garlic and the onion; cook, stirring frequently, for 3 minutes. Add the beans and chopped tomato and cook, stirring occasionally, for 5 to 7 minutes. Add the orange juice and lime juice, stirring well to combine. Add the pepper and more salt if desired. Raise the heat to high and cook, stirring frequently, until the liquid is nearly evaporated, another 2 to 3 minutes.

Chiles Jalapeños en Escabeche
Pickled Jalapeño Chiles

*I*n Oaxacan marketplaces there are always plastic bags full of freshly pickled jalapeños—very good, but the ones that diligent cooks usually prefer to make at home are fantastic. It's a good way to preserve a bumper crop of jalapeños. Whenever my recipes call for pickled jalapeños, the canned variety will do but the homemade version will transform the dish.

About 3 cups of solids

Prick the chiles in several places with the tines of a fork, or use a small sharp knife to cut a small X at the tip of each. (This will help the marinade penetrate better.) Place in a large saucepan, cover with cold water, and bring to a boil over high heat. Cook for 1 minute; at once drain in a colander and allow to cool to room temperature.

In a large, deep non-reactive skillet or sauté pan, heat the oil over medium-high heat until not quite smoking. Add the onions and garlic; cook, stirring frequently, for 2 to 3 minutes. Add the oregano, thyme, marjoram, peppercorns, and bay leaves. Cook, stirring, for 1 minute longer. Add the chiles, vinegar, and salt. Bring to a boil, stirring. Remove from the heat and let cool completely. Transfer to storage containers, distributing the solids and liquid as equally as possible. (Glass jars, non-aluminum storage bowls with tight-fitting lids, or leak-proof zipper-fastened plastic bags are all good.) Refrigerate for at least 3 days to let the flavors develop. The pickled chiles will keep in the refrigerator, tightly covered, for up to 2 months.

1 pound fresh green chiles such as jalapeños (preferably) or serranos (page 45)

1/4 cup olive oil

2 large onions, sliced into thin (1/8-inch) half-moons

20 large garlic cloves

8 sprigs fresh Mediterranean oregano or 1 teaspoon dried Mexican oregano, crumbled (page 38)

8 sprigs fresh thyme or 1 teaspoon dried thyme, crumbled

8 sprigs fresh marjoram or 1 teaspoon dried marjoram, crumbled

1 teaspoon black peppercorns, bruised

6 bay leaves

1 cup distilled white vinegar

1 tablespoon kosher salt

Ensalada de Verduras
Vegetable Salad

For the vegetables

6 small waxy red potatoes, unpeeled, thinly sliced

8 ounces young green beans, strings removed if necessary, cut into 1-inch lengths

2 medium carrots, peeled, cut into 1/4-inch dice

1 small cauliflower, separated into small florets

1 chayote, peeled, seeded, and cut into 1/3-inch dice

One 10-ounce basket pearl onions, peeled

For the dressing

3 tablespoons olive oil

1 medium onion, minced

8 garlic cloves

1 teaspoon ground allspice

8 sprigs fresh thyme or 1 teaspoon dried thyme, crumbled

1/2 cup cider vinegar or distilled white vinegar

1/3 cup pickled jalapeño chiles (page 45), sliced, with some of their juice

1/2 cup chopped scallions, white part only

1/2 to 3/4 teaspoon salt, or to taste

Freshly ground black pepper

*T*his robust salad is often served at big events and the parties accompanying village fiestas. It's a practical dish where refrigeration is scanty, since it can be prepared ahead of time and will keep well even in the torrid Isthmus of Tehuantepec. Venancia Toledo Hernández gave me her recipe.

About 6 servings

When you have prepared the separate vegetables as directed above, have ready a large pot of boiling salted water and a large bowl or saucepan of ice water, with more ice in reserve. Add the potatoes to the boiling water and cook until just tender, about 6 minutes. Lift out and drain. Add the beans and cook until barely crisp-tender, about 5 to 7 minutes. Scoop out with a strainer or slotted spoon and at once plunge them into the ice bath to stop the cooking. Remove and drain well. Follow the same cooking, chilling, and draining procedure for the carrots (cooking for about 4 minutes), cauliflower (3 to 4 minutes), chayote (about 3 minutes), and pearl onions (5 to 8 minutes, depending on their size).

Set the well-drained vegetables aside in a large bowl while you make the dressing. In a medium-size skillet, heat the oil over medium-high heat until rippling. Add the minced onion, whole garlic cloves, ground allspice, and thyme. Cook, stirring frequently, until the onion is translucent and the garlic colors slightly, about 3 minutes. Add the vinegar, pickled chiles with juice, and 1/2 cup water. Bring to a boil, remove from the heat, and let cool to room temperature.

Add the chopped scallions to the reserved cooked vegetables. Add the vinegar mixture and toss to combine well. Taste for seasoning; add salt if desired (the pickled chiles will contribute some) and pepper. Let stand for at least 4 hours at room temperature before serving. It will keep well for a week or longer in the refrigerator, stored in tightly covered non-reactive containers.

Rajas y Verduras Curtidas
Pickled Green Chile Strips and Vegetables

I found this useful, vivid-tasting side dish in the Mexican regional cookbook series published by the Banco Rural. The original version, which I have adapted slightly, was contributed by Socorro Castillejas de Martínez. You may use poblano chiles if Anaheims are unavailable.

About 6 servings

Griddle-roast the chiles by the directions on page 42. Place in a paper or plastic bag for 10 to 15 minutes to loosen the skins. Peel the chiles; remove and discard the tops and seeds. Cut into long thin strips. Slice the onions into thin half-moons; place in a non-aluminum bowl with the chile strips. Add the vinegar and salt; season generously with pepper. Let stand at room temperature for 6 hours or in the refrigerator (tightly covered) up to 2 days.

Bring a saucepan of salted water to a boil. Peel the potatoes and cut into 1/2-inch dice. Cook for 5 to 7 minutes, until just tender. Scoop out with a strainer or slotted spoon and set aside to drain. Peel the carrots, cut into 1/2-inch dice, and cook until tender, about 4 minutes. Scoop out and drain in the same way.

In a large skillet or Dutch oven, heat the oil over medium-high heat until it ripples. Add the garlic, bay leaves, thyme, marjoram, and cloves. Cook, stirring constantly, for 1 minute. Add the chiles and onions with the vinegar marinade. Bring to a boil, reduce the heat to medium, and cook for 3 minutes. Add the reserved carrots and potatoes; cook for 5 minutes longer.

Serve warm or at room temperature. The pickle will keep in the refrigerator, tightly covered, for up to 1 month. I find it gets better week by week.

6 fresh Anaheim chiles (page 43)

3 large onions

2 cups distilled white vinegar

1 1/2 to 2 teaspoons kosher salt, or to taste

Freshly ground black pepper

1 pound waxy red potatoes

3 large carrots

1/4 cup olive oil

4 garlic cloves

3 bay leaves

4 sprigs fresh thyme or 1/2 teaspoon dried thyme, crumbled

4 sprigs fresh marjoram, or 1/2 teaspoon dried marjoram, crumbled

2 cloves

Traditional greeting in Teotitlán del Valle

Accompanying Sauces

As I've explained earlier, *moles* and other major Oaxacan sauces are considered dishes in themselves. They are unrelated to the other category of simple, quickly prepared mixtures meant to be added to the food at the table. Like U.S. bottled sauces, these are condiments that can go with practically anything, and I have not always thought it necessary to give serving suggestions.

The Oaxacan table sauces are often very plain though subtly varied from cook to cook—everyone has their own favorite variation on a few themes. The soul of these simple creations is in the quality of the ingredients, not in complex seasonings. These sauces are meant to add spiciness without competing with the other flavors of the finished dishes.

Where green chiles like jalapeños or serranos are called for, I urge you to look for ones grown by local farmers in your region. The freshness makes an incredible difference. Usually they will be milder at the beginning of the season and hotter later on. As for tomatoes, here in the U.S. we have learned to make do with the cardboard-like tomatoes that are available year round, but no one cooks with them in Oaxaca. Your sauces will only taste truly Oaxacan if made in late summer and early fall when the local ones appear.

At one time most of these sauces would have been blended by hand, usually in a stone mortar (*molcajete*). If you have a good mortar and pestle, you might try some of the easier ones (for example, Salsa de Chile Jalapeño or Salsa de Tomate) by this method. But I have to say that blenders and food processors have carried the day in virtually all Oaxacan households with electricity. Once in a while restaurants and food stands will have signs proudly announcing that the sauces are *molcajeteadas* (pounded in a *molcajete*). The texture is still valued by some. If you want to compromise, experiment with reducing the blending or processing time to produce a chunkier, sturdier result rather than the finest purée.

Salsa de Chile Jalapeño

Roasted Jalapeño Sauce

This simple but delicious sauce appears on the table with almost everything at La Pereñita, one of the most famous restaurant stands in the 20 de noviembre market in Oaxaca City. The owner, Nicolasa Ramírez, insists that the secret is to boil and then cool the water—she swears it does not taste the same if you make it with plain tap or bottled water.

The sauce as I had it was thin, very smooth-textured, and hotter than hell from the good local jalapeños. If preferred, you can devein the chiles to reduce the heat. Or if yours aren't really *picante*, you can try substituting other fresh hot chiles for one or two of the jalapeños.

About 3/4 cup

8 large jalapeño chiles

2 garlic cloves

1/2 cup water, boiled and cooled to room temperature

1/2 teaspoon salt, or to taste

Griddle-roast the chiles by the directions on page 42. Place them in a paper or plastic bag and let sit for 15 minutes to loosen the skins. Peel and scrape off the blackened skin. Remove the tops; seed the chiles. Place the chiles and garlic in a food processor or blender. Adding the water a little at a time, process until smooth. Add the salt. It is best served at once, but will keep up to a day in the refrigerator.

Salsa de Chile Pasilla

Oaxacan Pasilla Chile Sauce

3 medium-small ripe tomatoes

1 Oaxacan pasilla chile or 1 dried chipotle or morita chile (pages 46 to 47)

1/2 small onion, coarsely chopped

1 garlic clove

1 teaspoon dried Oaxacan oregano or 1/2 teaspoon dried Mexican oregano, crumbled (page 38)

1/2 teaspoon salt, or to taste

*T*his is one of the most common table sauces in the state. It gets its haunting flavor from the Oaxacan pasilla chile, a smoked and dried type not to be confused with the regular Mexican pasillas that come from a different chile and are dried without smoking. Once unavailable in the U. S., the Oaxacan pasillas are starting to be imported by a few distributors. If you can't find them, dried chipotles or morita chiles are the closest substitute.

The sauce would go with any Oaxacan meal. I especially love it as an accompaniment to Molotes (page 67) and Bocaditos de Papa (page 57).

About 2 cups

Place the tomatoes and chile in a small saucepan, cover with water, and bring to a boil over high heat. Reduce the heat to low and cook, uncovered, for 15 minutes. Drain and let sit until cool enough to handle. Peel the tomatoes and remove the stem from the chile.

Place the tomatoes and chile in a blender with the onion, garlic, and oregano. Process until smooth. Season with salt to taste. The sauce will keep in the refrigerator, tightly covered, for up to 2 days.

Variation: *I have also seen this sauce metamorphosed into an appetizer called Queso con Salsa (cheese with sauce), as follows: Spread the sauce in a shallow ovenproof dish and cover thickly with shredded cheese of a good melting type such as Oaxacan string cheese (page 31); bake in a preheated 400°F oven just until the cheese is melted and serve at once with corn tortillas.*

Salsa de Chile Serrano con Limón

Lime and Serrano Chile Sauce

Here is another simple but delicious sauce from Nicolasa Ramírez at La Pereñita. This time the ingredients are finely chopped, not puréed. It goes perfectly with Pollo con Oregano (page 182) or any grilled meat. Use jalapeño chiles if you can't find serranos.

1/2 to 2/3 cup

4 large serrano chiles (page 45), tops and seeds removed

1 small onion

2 garlic cloves

Juice of 2 limes

1/2 teaspoon salt, or to taste

With a sharp, heavy chopping knife, finely mince the chiles, onion, and garlic. Combine with the lime juice and salt; let rest for at least 5 minutes before serving. This sauce will keep in the refrigerator, tightly covered, for up to 2 days.

Display of bread in a Oaxaca City storefront

Salsa de Aguacate
Avocado Sauce

Smoother and lighter than a usual guacamole, this is adapted from a *salsa* that arrives with the huge platters of sausages and roast meats at the outdoor restaurant La Capilla in Zaachila. It is the perfect accompaniment to robustly spiced meats like Cecina Enchilada (page 200) and Lomo de Puerco Adobado (page 206).

About 1 1/2 cups

1 jalapeño chile (page 45), top removed, coarsely chopped

4 large sprigs cilantro

1 ripe Hass or Fuerte avocado (page 28), peeled and seeded

1/2 teaspoon salt, or to taste

2 tablespoons distilled white vinegar

Process the chile and cilantro in a food processor until finely minced. Add the avocado, salt, and vinegar, and process to combine smoothly. Serve at once.

Variation: Salsa de Aguacate con Tomatillo *(Avocado Sauce with Tomatillos): For a slightly tarter, more vivid version, simmer 4 tomatillos (husks removed) in a small saucepan of water for 5 minutes. Drain and let cool to room temperature. Prepare the sauce as described above, but after puréeing the avocados add the tomatillos and process until smooth. Yields about 2 cups.*

Salsa Roja
Red Tomato Sauce

4 medium-size ripe tomatoes,
  quartered

1 large garlic clove, coarsely chopped

2 fresh green chiles such as
  jalapeños or serranos (page 45),
  tops removed, coarsely chopped

1/2 teaspoon salt, or to taste

*T*his is a good all-purpose sauce. I had it at some little *fonda* (food stand) in the Isthmus of Tehuantepec, but it's really a basic type that you find all over. Feel free to vary the flavor by adding herbs or spices; however, in Oaxaca it would be fairly unadorned so you taste the simple ingredients.

About 2 cups

Place the tomatoes, garlic, and chiles in a blender or food processor and process until smooth.

In a medium-size saucepan, bring the sauce to a boil over medium-high heat. Stir in the salt, lower the heat and simmer, uncovered, for 15 minutes, or until slightly concentrated. Serve either hot or cold.

Variation: *This sauce turns up with a few refinements that create new career opportunities for it. When enriched by frying, it's a great sauce for Chiles Rellenos (either the beef version on page 60 or the chicken version on page 62). Just heat 1 tablespoon lard or vegetable oil in a small, heavy saucepan; when almost smoking, pour in the tomato sauce and cook, stirring frequently for 5 minutes.*

Caldillo de Tomate
Soupy Tomato Sauce

*T*his is one of those great basic recipes that can be varied in many ways and that goes with all kinds of Oaxacan dishes from stuffed poblano chiles to roasted meats. I've had versions enlivened with different chiles (dried or fresh). It also works a great transformation on a simple chicken broth (see Caldo de Pollo, page 74).

In Oaxaca sauces of this kind work perfectly year round. In the U.S., I would make it only in the months when the local farm tomatoes are absolutely ripe. Do not attempt it with the usual store tomatoes. And don't skip the last step of "frying" the sauce in the hot oil. This is necessary for a really vibrant and concentrated flavor.

About 3 1/2 cups

2 1/2 pounds very ripe, juicy tomatoes, cut into quarters or large wedges

1 large onion, coarsely chopped

4 garlic cloves, coarsely chopped

1/2 teaspoon black peppercorns, coarsely crushed

4 whole cloves

3 large sprigs fresh thyme or 1/2 teaspoon dried, crumbled

2 large sprigs fresh Mediterranean oregano or 1/2 teaspoon dried Mexican oregano (page 38), crumbled

1 1/2 teaspoons salt, or to taste

1/4 cup vegetable oil

Place all the ingredients except the oil in a large, heavy saucepan and heat over medium heat, stirring, until the tomatoes are starting to cook in their juices, 5 to 10 minutes. Reduce the heat to low and simmer, partly covered, stirring occasionally, for another 20 minutes. Let cool until close to room temperature. Process in a blender—I don't recommend a food processor here—until thoroughly puréed (work in 2 batches if necessary).

In a wide, heavy saucepan, heat the vegetable oil over medium-high heat until it ripples. Add the tomato mixture, watching out for splatters. Stir vigorously to mix and reduce the heat to low. Cook, partly covered, stirring occasionally, for 20 minutes. Serve hot.

The sauce can be stored in the refrigerator, tightly covered, for up to 3 days.

Salsa de Tomatillo, Estilo Odilia

Odilia's Tomatillo Sauce

5 dried chipotle chiles (page 46)

3 árbol chiles (page 46)

1 guajillo chile (page 47)

12 large tomatillos, with husks

2 small garlic cloves, unpeeled

1 small onion, unpeeled

1 teaspoon salt, or to taste

On one of my visits to Juchitán in the Isthmus of Tehuantepec, I went to a great party at a restaurant called Bar Jardín. The chef, Odilia Román, gave me her recipe for this versatile sauce made with a combination of dried chiles. Odilia's version is quite hot. You could tone it down by lowering the amount of chipotle and árbol chiles and using more guajillos. I don't recommend the food processor; sauces with dried chiles are always best made in the blender.

About 3 cups

Rinse and griddle-dry the chiles by the directions on page 45. Place them in a deep bowl as they are done, cover with boiling water, and let soak for at least 20 minutes.

While the chiles soak, griddle-roast the tomatillos, garlic, and onion by the directions on pages 26 to 27. Set them aside in a bowl as they are done. When cool enough to handle, remove the husks from the tomatillos and peel the garlic and onion, saving the juices.

Drain the chiles. Working in batches as necessary, purée them in a blender together with the tomatillos, garlic, and onion. Stir in the salt.

The sauce will keep in the refrigerator, tightly covered, for up to 2 days, but it will set to a thick jell. If you wish, you can thin it by simply whirling it briefly in the blender—though I love to just spread the jelled sauce on a tortilla and eat it.

Salsa de Gusanitos

Maguey Worm Sauce

Perhaps you have seen a bottle of Oaxacan mezcal, the fiery liquor distilled from the agave or maguey plant, with a small object in the bottle that looks like a worm. It is. People in Oaxaca use every part of the maguey including the larvae of an insect that burrows into the roots and leaves. I have seen them being sold raw at the Etla village market in the Valley of Oaxaca, to be eaten as is with tortillas and a squirt of hot sauce or wrapped in corn husks and seared on a clay griddle. More often I have encountered the little *gusanitos* (worms) dried, salted, and strung on threads at places specializing in herbal cures (they are reputed to be an aphrodisiac).

I love the smoky flavor of the dried *gusanitos*, ground and used as a subtle seasoning for table sauces. As far as I know they are not imported now, but with the increase in Oaxacan products now being brought into this country, who knows? If you can travel to Oaxaca, be sure to bring back a string of them. They keep for a long time. This recipe, taken from my first book, is a fairly standard version of the useful *Salsa de Gusanitos*. I love it with seafood, boiled new potatoes, or Gorditas Infladas (page 58), but try it with any meat or vegetable. Go easy on the salt, since the maguey worms are already preserved with some.

About 3 cups

1 pound tomatillos, husks removed (about 10 to 12 large tomatillos)

2 Oaxacan pasilla chiles (page 47) or 2 dried chipotle chiles (page 46)

1/2 teaspoon salt, or to taste

1 small onion, coarsely chopped

1 garlic clove, coarsely chopped

1 tablespoon dried Oaxacan oregano or 1 teaspoon dried Mexican oregano, crumbled (page 38)

8 to 10 dried Maguey worms (page 35)

Place the tomatillos, chiles, and salt in a medium-size saucepan, cover with water, and bring to a boil over high heat. Reduce the heat to medium and cook, uncovered, until the tomatillos change color, about 5 minutes. Drain, reserving 1/2 cup of the cooking liquid, and let cool to about room temperature.

Place the tomatillos, chiles, and reserved cooking liquid in a blender with the onion, garlic, oregano, and maguey worms. Process until smoothly puréed. Taste the sauce and add more salt if desired. It can be stored in the refrigerator, tightly covered, for 2 or 3 days. It will jell when chilled, but can be restored to the original consistency by running it briefly in the blender.

Stopping for a shot of mezcal during the early morning shopping

Bebidas (Beverages)

For Mexicans, beverages can be not just thirst-quenchers and accompaniments to meals but meals on their own or exciting marriages of ingredients that U.S. consumers would not associate with drinks.

Since the local drinks often go off in directions surprising to non-Mexicans, they are usually slighted in Mexican cookbooks published in this country. The general assumption seems to be that nobody here would understand them or you couldn't get the ingredients anyhow. However, I feel that these beverages are a major keynote of the cuisine in Oaxaca (even more than other parts of Mexico) and nowadays U.S. cooks are not timid about embracing new ideas.

Easiest to embrace are the sweet, refreshing non-alcoholic cold drinks—*aguas frescas* or "cool waters" that restore body and soul in the tropical sun. We had *aguas frescas* in the North (they are made all over Mexico), but nothing like the profusion of different kinds I discovered in the Oaxacan markets. The basis is usually fruit juice; however, there are *aguas frescas* made with fruit rind alone, herbs, or even plants like alfalfa. When the drink is thickened with rice or ground nuts the name is usually *horchata* and the liquid will be milky. Though Oaxacans joyously consume *aguas frescas* the year round, there is a special day dedicated to them—the fourth Friday in Lent, when everybody in Oaxaca City drinks *aguas frescas* in memory of the Samaritan woman who met Jesus at the well in the Gospel of John.

I could not write about *aguas frescas* and *horchatas* without writing about Doña Casilda. No last name is necessary—to one and all in Oaxaca City she was Casilda *la horchatera* for more than fifty years, and her stand at the Benito Juárez market reigned above all other *horchaterías*. Casilda Flores Morales came from a long tradition, dating back to her great-grandmother, of people who have made their living calming the thirsts and delighting the palates of Oaxacans with a galaxy of *aguas* in great, cool-smelling earthen pots. She made the family business into a landmark as famous as the city churches. Of course she distributed free drinks to poor students and others every year on the Friday of the Samaritan. When asked the secret of her success, she said simply that she made things the way the customer liked it: "If you want it sweeter, I give it to you sweeter, if you want it with more fruit, I give you more fruit. I give you the *agua* as you wish it."

Doña Casilda's stand still flourishes, now run by her daughter María Teresa and granddaughter Socorro. I must have met one of them when I stopped by on a recent visit to discuss a recipe and a friendly, knowledgeable woman in her mid-fifties not only shared her expertise but treated me to a free *horchata*, saying, "Esto va de parte de Doña Casilda. Espero que le aproveche." (This is on behalf of Doña Casilda. I hope it does you good.)

Though bottled soft drinks now have a big following in Oaxaca, people still stop by the market for an *agua fresca* on hot afternoons, or pause at the carts set up on street corners. And people make and serve them at home, too, particularly with the lunch meal. It is a custom I highly recommend, especially now that markets with Latin American and southeast Asian clienteles regularly stock the frozen pulp of many tropical fruits that used to be unavailable here.

Atoles are more of an acquired taste for North Americans, but one that really isn't all that hard to acquire. The dictionary calls them "corn gruels," an unappetizing name for a delicious family of drinks that have been enjoyed since pre-Hispanic times. In one way or other the different *atoles* were traditionally based on corn cooked in liquid to bring out the starch. (After the coming of the Europeans the idea was applied to wheat and rice.) Since everyone in Mexico drinks *atoles*, I can't claim that they are uniquely Oaxacan—yet they are very deeply cherished in Oaxaca. People make them with loving care. The quickest-cooking commercial varieties sold in Mexico today use some type of pre-flavored cornstarch mix. Oaxacans seldom or never resort to that. They generally make *atole* with corn kernels, either plain or treated with natural alkali by the same method used for *masa*. The corn is cooked until soft enough to grind on a metate, then more water (or rarely, milk) is added and the mixture is cooked again until it thickens to a delicious gruel. An acceptable shortcut is the packaged *masa harina* now widely available in U.S. markets.

This drink, with different flavor variations, is a usual breakfast in most parts of Oaxaca. I recommend the breakfast *atole* to all visitors, for it is difficult to get a good cup of coffee in restaurants—more often than not, a waitress will unceremoniously plop a jar of Nescafé and a can of evaporated milk on the table. Nescafé is equally popular in the home. (This is a mystery to me, when piles of Oaxacan-grown coffee beans are displayed in many regional markets, either pre-roasted or green for home roasting.) You are better off with the corn drinks. In them you will find a world of flavors, sweet or savory.

The basic unsweetened *atole* is delicious in itself, but often you find it combined with other ingredients. Add chile and you have the eye-opening *chileatole*, which people claim is a great remedy for hangovers. On a muggy, oppressive day in the Isthmus I found *chileatole* being offered by a traveling vendor at the refreshing spring of Ojo de Agua near Ixtepec, rimmed with avocado and mango trees and reportedly the spot where Cosijoeza, the last independent Zapotec king of the Isthmus region, honeymooned with his Aztec bride Coyolicatzin. This version of the *chileatole* was new to me: it was sold with several small ears of fresh corn and you were supposed to strip the kernels into the drink. It was fantastic! There was the underlying blandness of the *atole*, the sprightly accent of the chile, and the crunch of the fat, starchy corn kernels. Unfortunately it can't be duplicated here without some strain of heirloom sweet corn that has more starch and less sugar than the preferred modern U.S. varieties.

The *atoles* are also made with the varied bounty of Oaxacan tropical fruits. I particularly love guava *atole* with its beautiful aroma and sensuous taste. Experiment with any preferred kind of fresh fruit (diced or puréed) or packaged frozen tropical fruit pulp. In all forms, you will find that an *atole* is a comforting drink and a nutritious meal rolled into one.

Chocolate is another favorite Mexican beverage that is made to perfection in Oaxaca. In pre-Hispanic times the equivalent drink of cacao diluted with water would have been drunk hot or cold, flavored with various wild herbs or seeds such as those of *pochote* (the kapok tree), and sometimes sweetened with the honey of native bee-like insects. From time immemorial it was beaten with a wooden contraption that the Spanish named a *molinillo* (little mill), a sort of whisk with carved wooden rings that revolve freely around a wooden shaft. The drink was placed in a narrow-necked pot or gourd and the device was whirled rapidly between the palms of the hands to make the rings dance, producing a luscious foam. Today chocolate is still whipped with the *molinillo*, but now the main ingredients are freshly roasted cacao beans, sugar, *canela* (Ceylon cinnamon), and sometimes almonds, usually ground by small milling shops to the taste of the individual consumer and formed into small tablets. (On special occasions dedicated cooks will do the grinding themselves at home on a metate.) These blends give more character and freshness to hot chocolate than the standard Mexican commercial chocolate brands like Ibarra or La Abuela. They make particularly fine *champurrado*, a combination of hot chocolate and *atole*.

Do not confuse the delectable but everyday *champurrado* with the specialty that officially bears the name *chocolateatole*, an elaborate preparation usually reserved for important ceremonial occasions. *Chocolateatole* belongs to an ancient family of Oaxacan beverages that consist of a liquid part and a frothy topping that is whipped separately. (These drinks crowned with foam must go back a long way in the region; an example is shown in the famous Mixtec manuscript known as the Codex Nuttall.) In the case of *chocolateatole*, the foam is produced by a specially treated white cacao called *pataxtle*. You cook a plain *atole*, fill it into individual cups, and top up each serving with an *espuma* or "foam" (*bichin* in Zapotec) made from *pataxtle* with ground toasted rice or wheat, ordinary cacao, *canela* (Ceylon cinnamon), and sugar, all mixed to a paste and thinned with enough cold water for whipping. I watched the grinding process at the home of my friend Zoyla Mendoza in the Valley of Oaxaca, as demonstrated with a pottery *comal* (griddle) and stone metate by Zoyla's beautiful cousin Jovita, and we drank the finished *chocolateatole* by stirring the thick and luscious *espuma* into the hot *atole* with specially carved wooden spatulas the shape of letter openers.

Pataxtle is only one of the foaming agents that Oaxacans use to make the much-loved frothed toppings. They can also be produced with several types of flowers including frangipani blossoms (*guie' chaachi'*) and a small, aromatic dried flower bud called *rosita de cacao* although it has no botanical connection with cacao. In *bupu*, the Isthmian version of *chocolateatole*, the *espuma* is prepared with the frangipani and sweetened with Oaxacan brown loaf sugar (*panela*). Another popular frothed specialty is *tejate* or *texate*, a refreshing drink that I regretfully had to omit from my recipes because the ingredients are unavailable here. It consists of an alkali-treated corn mixture—my informant, María Elena Sánchez López of the Juárez market in Oaxaca City, says to cook the dried corn kernels and the dried pit of the mamey sapote fruit (*Pouteria sapote*) with wood ashes and grind them to a paste with toasted cacao and *rosita de cacao*. Two thirds of this mixture is thinned with water and forms the liquid part of the drink; the rest is sweetened with sugar and beaten to a froth. You see women selling *tejate* out of metal tubs at market, serving it in colorfully painted gourds with an enticing crown of foam—but I have to say beware unless you know that it was made with purified water!

Oaxacans are also fond of various alcoholic drinks, ancient and modern. The well-known *tepache* is usually brewed with pineapple—sometimes other fruits—and a solution of the local brown loaf sugar. I have drunk it pleasant and mild, or frankly rather nasty-tasting and bitter with a strong dose of achiote. Because of the pineapple and sugar it must be a fairly recent invention, perhaps modeled on *pulque* or a similar drink made with the Mexican wonder plant, maguey.

Maguey and its daughter-products deserve a whole book to themselves. They are as much a part of the Mexican identity as chile and corn. Throughout the country different species grow wild and were domesticated in ancient times. Most belong to the genus of the agave or "century plant." The plant is not a real cactus, but people tend to assume that it is one since it thrives in arid conditions. It clothed, housed, and fed ancient Mexicans with the tough fibers of its sharp, pointed leaves (*pencas*) and the sweet nourishing central core that they sprout from. The Spanish who found people utilizing every part of the plant in some manner nicknamed it *el árbol de las maravillas* (the tree of marvels).

The kind of maguey that is now most important in Oaxaca is *Agave atrovirens*. The Zapotecs and other indigenous peoples had learned to tap the clear sap from the core and ferment it into a milky, mildly alcoholic drink called *pulque*. It is still made here and there in the state, but Oaxacans aren't really great *pulque* drinkers compared to the folks around Mexico City. The drink everyone thinks of when they say "Oaxaca" is mezcal, the distilled essence of maguey.

The technology of distilling liquor arrived only with the Spanish. Of course the most celebrated of all the many maguey liquors now made in Mexico is tequila, produced only in Jalisco and a handful of other states from an agave species that doesn't grow anywhere near Oaxaca. Abroad, mezcal is known more for the worm in the bottom of the bottle (a particular species that feeds on the maguey leaves and is highly sought for both cooking and medicinal purposes) than for any qualities of its own. But these days the mezcal makers are trying to follow up on the successful marketing of tequilas specially blended for the U.S. market—smooth-tasting products with none of the individuality of the locally produced Mexican varieties. Until recently, I hadn't tasted an exported mezcal that has the true smokiness of the Oaxacan versions. But now several premium blended mezcals are available for sale to restaurants in the Southwest. With interest increasing, it's likely that authentic mezcals will reach other areas of this country. In fact maguey and mezcal form one of the real Oaxacan success stories, a tale that has come full circle.

In ancient times people planted maguey in terraced fields on steep hills unsuited for other plants. It was a model of ecologically responsible plant use— food, cloth fiber, building material, and barrier against soil erosion all in one. Then the Spanish arrived with their own notions of planting, and for centuries the thrifty maguey was nearly ignored as a commercial crop. Beer and synthetic fibers eventually displaced *pulque* and maguey-based weaving until the plant almost became extinct. Now the popularity of mezcal has re-energized a whole industry around the "tree of marvels."

Today maguey farms flourish all along Highway 190 going from Oaxaca City to Tlacolula, some twenty miles southwest. (Visitors take note: There are mezcal shops all over Oaxaca City, but in my opinion anyone interested in the finest quality should head toward the Tlacolula neighborhood, where mezcal is mostly made to be consumed on or very close to the farm.) It is a beautiful sight, the tall spiky magueyes planted in perfect symmetry like a living quilt. The mezcal producers buy directly from the growers, who harvest the pineapple-shaped core (*piña*) and leave the fibrous *pencas* on the ground to be gathered by craftsmen from several towns of the Valley.

While the sweet *piñas* are ground in rudimentary stone pits—I saw this being done at the old-fashioned distillery of Casa Chagoya near Tlacolula, with a bored-looking donkey trudging round and round to turn a wooden wheel fitted with a sharp rotating blade—the *pencas* are being soaked and dried elsewhere. Through a rotting process the pulp of the leaves becomes stringy enough to be pulled apart into *ixtle* (maguey thread) and made into hammocks, bags, rugs, rope for bridles, and many other products. Once more the whole plant is being put to best ecological use.

The finest mezcal is made in home stills where the maguey cores are roasted over charcoal in a stone pit. This process gives mezcal its characteristic smoky taste and converts some of the carbohydrates into fermentable sugars. The roasted, ground pulp is then allowed to ferment at its own pace, which results in a smooth, velvety liquor. (Some commercial makers speed up the process with chemical additives that yield a harsher taste.) It is transferred to stills and—at the smaller, old-fashioned producers—put through a single distillation process. (The larger manufacturers now sometimes blend different batches and subject them to a second distillation process in an effort to produce a more neutral-tasting spirit.)

Mezcal can be drunk as is or with added flavorings like pineapple, almonds, blackberries, pecans, etc. Or it can be given a medicinal spin. Some Oaxacans steep it with fresh leaves of favorite folk remedies like the herbs locally called *damiana* (an ancient aphrodisiac and sedative) and *gobernadora* (which produces a resinous oily substance with a minty taste, believed to cure gastritis and rheumatism). Whether it cures you or not, by the time you drink a few shots of the mezcal you won't care about what ails you.

Agua Fresca de Guanábana (u Otra Fruta)

Soursop or Other Tropical Fruit Drink

This recipe—so simple I'm almost embarrassed to use the word "recipe"—is meant as a general model for the many *aguas frescas* based on Oaxaca's wealth of tropical fruits. When I first started visiting the area, I could never have duplicated these heavenly thirst-quenchers at home in New York. Now I can come close. Today some, though not all, of the fruits for the renowned Oaxacan *aguas frescas* can be bought in the form of frozen pulp imported from several Latin American countries. Look for these products in Latin and some southeast Asian markets, usually in 14-ounce plastic packets. The quality, though not on a par with fresh produce eaten in the regions where it's grown, is often better than that of the imported whole fruit. Among the varieties available are guava, mango, papaya, passion fruit, pineapple, tamarind, and—one of my favorites—the seductive, complex-flavored soursop, *guanábana*, a cherimoya relative that doesn't seem to have been discovered yet in the U.S. Experiment with any or all of these by the method given here, adding the sugar a little at a time until it is to your taste. If the flavor seems a little flat, add a dash of lime juice.

The labels are unfortunately a little vague on most of the frozen fruit-pulp packages, making it hard to tell whether you are getting sliced fruit or a purée. The *guanábana* is usually sold sliced, as it would appear in a typical Oaxacan *agua fresca*. If you do not like the slippery texture of the fruit, you can strain the juice through a medium-mesh sieve before beginning with the recipe (push down with a wooden spoon to extract as much juice as possible). Or whirl in the blender to purée, though in that case it would technically be known as a *preparado* rather than *agua fresca*.

Three servings (1 quart)

Place the *guanábana* pulp in a 1-quart measuring cup and fill up with water to the 1-quart mark. Add the sugar, 1 or 2 teaspoons at a time, tasting after each addition, until it achieves the desired sweetness. Stir to dissolve well. Chill thoroughly and serve over ice cubes.

1 package (14 ounces) frozen *guanábana* (soursop) pulp, thawed

2 to 2 1/2 cups cold water, or as needed

3 to 4 tablespoons granulated sugar, or to taste

Agua Fresca de Chilacayota
Spaghetti Squash Drink

1 *chilacayota* or spaghetti squash, about 2 to 2 1/2 pounds

1 pound *panela* or *piloncillo* (page 40), coarsely chopped or broken into chunks, or 1 pound dark brown sugar

One 3-inch piece *canela* (page 30)

2 quarts water

1 lime

1/2 small ripe pineapple, peeled, core removed, and finely diced (about 1 1/2 to 2 cups)

Ice cubes

*C*hilacayota is a kind of squash with a mass of "strings'" inside, much like U.S. spaghetti squash except that it is round instead of oval. I have seen them in Latin American stores in the boroughs of New York, but I assume that most people will be making the recipe with spaghetti squash.

This is one of the most beloved *aguas frescas* in Oaxaca City. Be sure to use fresh pineapple—the canned fruit is much too sweet.

5 to 6 servings (about 2 quarts)

Cut the unpeeled squash in half. Remove and discard the seeds and membranes; cut the squash halves into two or three pieces each. Place the squash in a large saucepan with the *panela, canela,* and water. Bring to a boil over high heat, then lower the heat to maintain a simmer for 30 minutes, partly covered.

Lift out the cooked squash pieces; remove and discard the rind. Return the squash to the pan and mash the flesh with a wooden spoon or potato masher to help separate the filaments. Let cool to room temperature, then refrigerate the squash and cooking liquid until very cold.

Just before serving, grate the rind of the lime into the chilled squash mixture, being careful not to include any of the white part. Stir to distribute it evenly. Divide the diced pineapple and the squash mixture among five or six 12-ounce serving glasses, placing about 1/3 cup of the pineapple at the bottom of each, adding ice cubes, and ladling the squash filaments and liquid on top. Oaxacans do not serve this with spoons, but don't hesitate to do so if you find it easier to negotiate.

Agua Fresca de Limón
Lime Drink

*M*exican limes are small, with a thick, very dark green skin and a refreshing flavor that is close to that of a U.S. lime but not quite the same. Only the rind of the fruit is used in this simple Oaxacan favorite, which I learned to make from Lucila Zárate de Fuentes of Oaxaca City. Her version differs from some in that the grated lime is added only at the very last moment before serving. When the drink is allowed to sit for a while before serving it turns a wonderful green-yellow color, but also develops a slight bitterness that Lucila does not like.

I prefer to sweeten the drink with a sugar syrup, which seems mellower, but plain granulated and superfine sugar is an acceptable substitute.

Four 12-ounce servings (6 cups)

6 cups cold water
1/2 cup Simple Syrup (below)
  or 1/3 cup granulated sugar
2 large dark-green limes

In a pitcher, combine the water and syrup or sugar, stirring to make sure the sugar is well dissolved. Refrigerate until very cold.

Just before serving, grate the rind of the lime into the pitcher, being careful not to include any of the white part. Serve over ice cubes.

Simple Syrup

1 cup

2 cups water
1 cup granulated sugar

Combine the water and sugar in a small saucepan. Heat gently, stirring constantly, until the sugar is completely dissolved. Bring to a boil over medium heat and cook until reduced to 1 cup. Let cool to room temperature; store, refrigerated, in a tightly covered container.

Atole Blanco
Plain Corn Gruel

1/2 cup *masa harina* (page 94)

7 cups cold water

1/2 teaspoon salt, or to taste

*I*f you want to make homesick Mexican friends happy, serve them *atole*. Those from the north might make it with milk replacing part of the water, but that is not the Oaxacan way. Any sort of fruit or fruit preserves can be used to flavor the *atole*. Up north my mother used to stir in a little of the peach marmalade she put up every year. In Oaxaca they use their incredible range of tropical fruits (see Atole de Guayaba, below, for a sample suggestion).

Here is a simple basic formula made with packaged *masa harina*, reasonably close to the more arduous originals that use home-ground corn. Please note that it is easy to scald yourself drinking hot *atole*, for it retains heat dangerously well. Allow a few minutes for it to reach a safe temperature.

5 to 6 servings (about 6 cups)

In a small bowl, combine the *masa harina* with 1 cup cold water and stir until smooth. In a medium saucepan, combine the paste with the remaining 6 cups of water. Bring to a boil, stirring often; reduce the heat to low and simmer for 25 minutes, stirring occasionally. It will thicken to the texture of a delicate gruel. Skim off any coagulated bits that may have formed on top. Stir in the salt, let sit to cool for a minute or two, and serve in mugs or breakfast cups.

Variation: Chileatole (Atole with Chile). *Follow the basic recipe for Atole Blanco, but when serving add 1 to 2 teaspoons Salsa de Chile Serrano con Limón (page 255) or any preferred fresh chile salsa to each cup; stir to combine.*

Variation: Atole de Guayaba (Guava Atole). *Follow the basic recipe for* Atole Blanco *through the step of combining the* masa harina *paste with 6 cups of water; add 1/2 cup granulated sugar and the thawed contents of a 14-ounce package of frozen guava purée. Cook as directed above.*

Atole Dulce
Sweetened Corn Gruel

A simple sweet *atole* is customarily flavored with *canela*. I prefer to bring out the cinnamon flavor by simmering sticks of *canela* in water, then adding the *masa harina* to the hot infusion as directed below. The mixture will not be as smooth-textured as an *atole* started with cold water, so I like to strain it before serving. If you wish to eliminate this step, let the *canela* infusion cool to room temperature and proceed as for Atole Blanco, adding the sugar and salt when you combine the *masa harina* mixture with the 6 cups of liquid.

5 to 6 servings (about 6 cups)

7 cups cold water
Two 3-inch pieces *canela* (page 30)
1/2 cup *masa harina* (page 94)
3/4 cup granulated sugar
1/2 teaspoon salt

Place 6 cups of water and the *canela* in a medium saucepan and bring to a boil over high heat. Reduce the heat to medium-low and simmer, covered, for 20 minutes. Remove and discard the *canela*.

Meanwhile, combine the *masa harina* with the remaining 1 cup of water in a small bowl and stir until smooth. Pour the *masa harina* mixture into the simmering *canela* infusion in a thin stream, stirring well to combine. Stir in the sugar and salt. Continue to simmer, uncovered, stirring occasionally, for 15 minutes; it will thicken to the texture of a delicate gruel. Remove from the heat and strain through a medium-mesh sieve into a heatproof pitcher. Let it sit for a minute or two to cool slightly; serve in mugs or breakfast cups.

Champurrado
Atole with Chocolate

For the atole

1/4 cup *masa harina* (page 94)

3 1/2 cups cold water

1/4 teaspoon salt

For the hot chocolate

3 cups milk

3 ounces (about 1/2 cup) Homemade Chocolate Mixture (see page 277), 1/2 cup Gazella chocolate mixture (see **Mail Order Sources**, page 320), or one 3-ounce tablet commercial Mexican chocolate (pages 277 to 279), broken in small chunks

*T*his delicious drink is like a morning cup of hot chocolate combined with breakfast porridge. How often I have begun the day with a fragrant, steaming cup of champurrado at La Pereñita, my favorite stand at the 20 de noviembre market in Oaxaca City! I love to accompany it with a sweet roll, preferably Pan de Yema (page 308).

5 to 6 servings (about 6 cups)

In a small bowl, begin the *atole* mixture by combining the *masa harina* with 1/2 cup of water and stirring until smooth. In a medium saucepan, combine the paste with the remaining 3 cups of water. Bring to a boil, stirring often; reduce the heat to low and simmer for 25 minutes, stirring occasionally. It will thicken into a light gruel.

While the *atole* is cooking, heat the milk in a small saucepan over medium heat. Before it starts to boil, add the chocolate. Continue to heat, stirring frequently, until the chocolate mixture is thoroughly melted and dissolved. Reduce the heat to low and simmer the hot chocolate, stirring frequently, for 3 to 4 minutes.

Pour the hot chocolate into the simmering *atole*, stirring vigorously to combine. Remove the mixture from the heat and beat with a whisk, eggbeater, hand-held electric mixer, or (best of all) Mexican wooden *molinillo* until a thick froth forms on top. Pour into mugs or breakfast cups, spooning some of the foam over the top of each serving.

Chocolate
Homemade Chocolate Blend

Scene: The backyard of my New York City house

Characters: Me (working furiously) and my twenty-year-old son Aarón (indoors, taking a shower before heading off to his restaurant job)

It is a hot, sticky summer afternoon and I am standing before my portable outdoor gas stove. Placed over the burner is a metate. This is my third attempt to make chocolate out of cacao beans. Having first tried simply grinding the beans in the food processor and adding the sugar and ground cinnamon, then varying the approach by first pre-warming the food processor and blade, I have "progressed" to the pre-Hispanic technique of grinding everything by hand on a stone metate. My fingers are sore and weary from peeling the beans, and we won't talk about the state of my nails. (By ill luck my manicurist just happened to stop by, and she almost had a breakdown on the spot.) However, I just had the bright idea of warming the metate over the outdoor gas stove. It's working! Back and forth I go with the heavy stone *mano* (pestle) rolling efficiently over the surface of the metate in a steady rhythm, watching the mixture turn satiny and glossy as the oils begin to come out of the ground cacao beans. The aroma of the mixture floats up like incense.

Aarón (suddenly interested, poking his still-dripping head out of the third-floor window and inhaling deeply): "Mom, are you making chocolate?"

Me (panting): "Yes."

Aarón (ecstatic): "Mom, that's HEAVY!"

Heavy does seem like the word for it. But I was determined to duplicate for myself the rich, deep-flavored chocolate mixtures with which I had seen people cooking in Oaxaca. Of course, the age-old grinding process has been speeded up even there. Most cooks go to the market, buy cacao beans, sugar, *canela*, and sometimes almonds, and head for the small shops called *molinos de chocolate* (chocolate mills) to have them prepared and custom-blended in all the desired ratios by a modern electric grinder with burr stones. There are *molinos* on one side of the Mercado Juárez in Oaxaca City and the smell of toasting cacao wafts down Las Casas street. I have often bought chocolate like this and brought it back to New York. It makes superb hot chocolate and a range of different beverages, but it is also an indispensable cooking ingredient, the secret of many a *mole* and other dishes. When I run out I fall back on the commercial Mexican chocolate tablets sold in any Mexican grocery in the U.S. They are adequate, but not remotely as luscious as the real thing.

But now there is good news for all who love cooking with real chocolate: I have found two mail-order suppliers of whole raw cacao beans, Hawaiian Vintage Chocolate in Honolulu and Gazella Mexican Chocolate in California (see Mail Order Sources, page 320). The beans—the dried and cured seeds of the cacao fruit—are not much to look at. They come covered with a thin brown skin and are about the size of large kidney beans, only not so shapely. The don't taste or smell much like chocolate until they are toasted to bring out the fragrant oils of the cacao butter. I have arrived at a home method that produces good results—but first let me describe the art of home chocolate-making as I saw it in the Valley of Oaxaca.

There are still people in Oaxaca who will go to the labor of grinding their own chocolate from scratch, and on one of my last visits I prevailed on my friend Zoyla Mendoza to show me the process all the way through, with the aid of her aunt Rufina Montoya. Early in the morning Zoyla set out for the market of her village, Teotitlán del Valle, to buy the necessary ingredients and a new *comal* (clay griddle) for toasting the beans. (*Comales* are wonderful cooking surfaces, but they break easily and have to be replaced frequently.) Before we began, she "cured" the surface by painting it with a mixture of *cal* (mineral lime; page 30) and water, using a bunch of dried corn husks instead of a brush. She then heated the *comal* over a wood fire in the courtyard of her house until the *cal* dried and cracked enough to be brushed off completely.

Zoyla bent over the prepared griddle, neat and serious in her tidy blue apron, her long glossy braids with matching blue ribbons falling gracefully down her back. One batch at a time, she placed the cacao beans on the surface and toasted them until the dark skin was a lighter brown, stirring almost constantly with the bunch of corn husks. The scent of roasting chocolate began to mingle with the smell of slightly charred husks. She removed them to a large, heavy basket as they were done and the rest of us—me, Rufina's daughter Jovita, and the trio of U.S. friends who had made the trip with me—started rubbing and peeling away the outer skin. This is a tedious chore, but you do have the intoxicating aroma of the toasted cacao to encourage you.

When the beans were all toasted, we clustered around the metate. Zoyla keeps a special one for this purpose only, so that the smell and taste of past *moles* or *adobos* will not invade the delicate chocolate. First she put some live coals in an old sawed-off jalapeño can and set it under the metate to heat it. Then under Rufina's supervision we all took turns with the rhythmic grinding, kneeling over the short-legged metate and making obvious jokes about pre-colonial aerobic workouts. It took about an hour of grinding. Rufina and Zoyla use only cacao, sugar, and ground *canela* in their chocolate mixture, never the almonds found in most versions. (The almonds add another flavor note and give a heavier body; I've cooked using mixtures made both with and without almonds, but for the homemade version I always follow Rufina and Zoyla in omitting them.) First the beans are ground to a dry powder that gradually becomes moist and shiny as the heat of the metate helps bring out the cacao butter. It is then easy to incorporate the sugar and *canela*, a little at a time, until it all becomes a velvety and glossy mixture that will keep its shape when formed into round tablets and air-dried for future use (though it can also be used as is).

Knowing that not one U.S. cook in a hundred thousand has a metate, I went through a lot of trial and error to produce usable cookbook directions. I have to say that the food processor won't do everything a metate or a commercial-scale Oaxacan chocolate grinder will. The processor has a cutting rather than a true grinding action. So it tends not to bring out the oil in the beans enough to make the mixture hold together. I get around this by finishing the grinding in a well-warmed Mexican *molcajete* or another heavy mortar. This fine grinding yields a smooth unctuous mixture compact enough to be pressed into tablets. But if you don't have a mortar big enough for the job—or if you just can't get the mixture to come together for shaping—the good news is that the chocolate-sugar blend will work just as well in recipes even in crumbly, uncompacted form.

The proportions given here are those of Zoyla and Rufina's recipe. In other places people prepare chocolate with much more sugar.

2 pounds, which translates roughly into roughly 9 to 10 cups of the powdered mixture (depending on how much it compacts in processing) or approximately thirty 1-ounce tablets.

1 pound (about 2 1/2 cups) *raw cacao beans* (page 277 to 279)

1 pound (2 cups) superfine sugar

1 tablespoon freshly ground *canela* (page 30)

If you have a large, heavy mortar and pestle for grinding, preheat the oven to 175°F or lowest possible setting and warm them while you toast the beans.

Select a heavy skillet (preferably cast iron) large enough to hold the beans in one layer, or use two skillets. Add the cacao beans and heat over medium-low heat. Toast the cacao, stirring constantly, for 40 minutes. (Shorter cooking over high heat does not bring out the cacao butter properly.) The medium-brown skin will become brittle and turn a lighter brown with darkened spots. Remove the toasted beans to a large heatproof bowl; when they are just cool enough to handle, peel off the skins by rubbing between the palms of your hands. They are easier to peel when they are still warm. (The beans can be kept warm in the preheated 175°F oven.)

Heat the blade and workbowl of a food processor by rinsing in very hot water for a few minutes. Dry very thoroughly before assembling the machine. Place the beans in the workbowl and process for 2 minutes, until the beans are finely ground. You should see the powder beginning to darken and look oily, a sign that the cacao butter is starting to separate; if not, continue to process for another 20 to 30 seconds. With the motor running, add the sugar and *canela* through the feed tube, a little at a time, and process until everything is evenly combined.

If you have no mortar, the mixture will probably remain too crumbly to hold together. This is perfectly acceptable. Let cool completely and store at room temperature in a tightly covered container.

If you are working with a mortar and pestle, remove them from the oven with padded mitts while you are processing the chocolate. Let cool enough to handle safely. Working in batches that will fit comfortably into your mortar, grind the mixture by hand until it glistens and begins to come together. This usually takes at least 15 to 20 minutes; rewarm the mortar as necessary. As the mixture becomes satiny and compact, press it firmly between your hands to form round cakes about 2 inches across and 1/4 inch thick. Set them aside on the counter as they are done and let sit 2 to 3 hours or until thoroughly dry. Wrap the tablets individually in aluminum foil and store at room temperature. The mixture will keep up to six months at room temperature.

Note: *See also Mail Order Sources, page 320.*

Chocolateatole

Atole with Chocolate Foam Topping

I have reluctantly omitted many important Oaxacan specialties because crucial ingredients cannot be found or even clumsily imitated in this country. Chocolateatole is one of only two recipes where I call for a principal ingredient that as far as I know can't be bought outside of Oaxaca. In this case it is a special form of cacao known as *pataxtle* or *patlaxle* which is the original "white chocolate."

I include this recipe because it is an important ritual drink, quintessentially Oaxacan and associated with the major festivals and rites of passage. Despite the name, it is not simply *atole* with chocolate, but one of the famous Oaxacan frothed beverages in which a special *espuma* (foam) is prepared separately and served on top of a drink. The froth is so rich that it remains stable for a long time instead of disappearing like the foam on plain whipped hot chocolate.

The secret of the foaming action is the *pataxtle*, of which I have heard different descriptions. Some say that it is just ordinary cacao (*Theobroma cacao*) that has been specially treated, others that it is a wild cacao or a separate *Theobroma* species. In any case, the beans are fermented differently from those for usual purposes. They are soaked in water for about a week, then buried in a pit in the ground, with alternating layers of cacao beans and sand. They ferment there for four to five months, during which time they are watered twice a day and periodically dug up, washed clean, and reburied. At the end of the process the thin skins have become shrunken, half-split black shells around a pure white, chalky-textured interior. They are most dramatic-looking, a little like "tiger-eye" stones.

To make Chocolateatole, the *pataxtle* is combined with regular cacao and some form of ground toasted grain (wheat, rice, or both). The mixture is very finely milled on a metate—an electric coffee grinder and a food processor make everything much easier—and chilled before being thinned with just enough cold water to enable it to whip. It becomes a thick foam, somewhat like beaten egg whites but with less body. Meanwhile, you have prepared a plain *atole*. The hot *atole* is served with the cold *espuma* on top, like Viennese coffee with whipped cream.

6 ounces (1 cup) *raw* cacao beans
(page 277 to 279)

3 ounces (1/2 cup) *pataxtle*
(see headnote)

1 cup raw rice (any variety)

1 cup raw wheat berries (I use Laxmi
brand from India)

2 tablespoons freshly ground *canela*
(page 30)

Ice water for mixing (about 2 cups
in all)

Atole Blanco (page 274)

2/3 cup granulated sugar, or to taste

Sometimes the *atole* is sweetened; I prefer to sweeten the foam and leave the *atole* plain. Serve it as a breakfast beverage, or at teatime with a selection of little Mexican sweets.

6 cups before whipping; serves 10

Select two medium-size heavy skillets (preferably cast iron). Place one over medium-low heat and add the cacao beans. Roast the beans, stirring often, for 40 minutes; the skin will become brittle and turn a lighter brown with darkened spots.

While the cacao toasts, place the second skillet over medium heat and add the *pataxtle*. Toast, stirring frequently, for 5 minutes. The black husk will split away and the chalky interior will start to break up. Set aside on a plate to cool; remove and discard the husks. Add the rice to the same skillet and toast, stirring often, until golden, 7 to 10 minutes. If the rice starts to pop, reduce the heat slightly and remove any popped grains. Set aside on a separate plate to cool. Add the wheat berries to the same skillet and toast, stirring often, until slightly darkened and nutty-smelling, about 5 minutes. Set aside on a separate plate to cool.

When the cacao is thoroughly toasted, let cool until just safe to handle and peel off the skins by rubbing them between the palms of your hands.

In an electric coffee or spice grinder, grind the toasted rice until it is very fine, almost like flour. Set aside and grind the toasted wheat to the same consistency. (This step is necessary because the food processor won't grind the grains fine enough.)

Place the toasted *pataxtle* and cacao beans in a food processor and process for 2 minutes. The pulverized mixture should darken slightly and look damper as a little of the cacao butter starts to separate from the beans. Add the rice, wheat, and *canela* and process until thoroughly combined. With the machine running, add ice water through the feed tube, 1 tablespoon at a time, until the mixture is a heavy paste like beaten fudge. The amount depends on the moisture content of the rice and wheat; I generally use up to 1 cup.

Scoop out the mixture into a deep, narrow bowl and pour enough additional ice water over it to cover by 1 inch. Refrigerate, uncovered, until it is thoroughly chilled, preferably overnight.

About half an hour before you are ready to serve the Chocolateatole, prepare the *atole* and keep warm over low heat or a heat-diffusing device such as a Flame Tamer. Working in batches as necessary, place the chocolate mixture and the water in the blender; process until thoroughly smooth. It should have the consistency of an icing mixture; add more ice water if necessary, one tablespoon at a time.

Have ready a large, deep chilled mixing bowl. Place half of the mixture in the bowl. With a Mexican wooden *molinillo*, chilled rotary eggbeater, or hand-held electric mixer (set on medium-low speed), beat in 1/3 cup sugar (or to taste) and whip until a thick, stable foam forms on top, about 15 minutes. Lift the foam off with a spatula or soup skimmer and set aside in a small bowl. Continue to whip, lifting off the foam as it forms, until all of this portion of the mixture has been used.

Fill large mugs or breakfast cups about three-quarters full with the hot *atole* and top with the foam. Serve at once.

Repeat with the rest of the mixture if desired. (If you do not wish to use the full amount at once, store the other half of the cacao-*pataxtle* mixture in the refrigerator, tightly covered, for up to 3 days or frozen for 3 weeks.)

Note: *See also Mail Order Sources, page 320.*

Different flavors of nieves

Desserts, Sweet Breads, Confections, Ices

One of the happier results of the Conquest can be seen every time you walk into a bakery in Oaxaca or buy a candy on the street. The local art of baking and confectionery dates from the arrival of the Spanish missionaries.

There were religious as well as culinary reasons for the emphasis placed on baking. Communion wafers were among the first baked foods tasted by the indigenous peoples; the Dominicans who were sent to convert them made wheat-growing a priority on the farms attached to their new Oaxacan convents and built flour mills to ensure a reliable source of materials. Dome-shaped brick and adobe ovens on Spanish models were among the first European cooking installations built in Oaxaca. (Known as *calabaceros* from the rounded "pumpkin" shape, they are still in use today.)

Wheaten loaves were introduced at the same time. The new yeast breads won prompt acceptance. From a few simple kinds that members of the religious community at first made for their own use, the range of varieties soon increased dramatically. Today the breads of Oaxaca are many and excellent. But not all are easy to reproduce outside Oaxaca. Those that I have been able to duplicate—like Pan Resobado and Pan de Yema—are rich and sweet, somewhat resembling egg breads like brioche or challah that I often suggest as alternative sources for bread crumbs in recipes. Sweet, eggy doughs of this general type are always used for the most famous bread of all: the colorfully decorated loaves called *pan de muerto* that are made for the Days of the Dead.

The craft of breadmaking is not the only one that goes back to religious origins in Oaxaca. The Spanish nuns who arrived during the sixteenth and seventeenth centuries came prepared to transplant to the new land a long-standing tradition of convent-made sweets, one of the main sources of income for some orders.

It was as revolutionary a change as the breads. Not only had the indigenous people never known wheat flour before the Spanish armies marched in, they had never known sugar, butter, or domestic chicken eggs—or the fruits and nuts regularly used in European desserts. Now dozens of cakes, cookies, pastries, custards, jellies, meringues, preserves, and candies were introduced, and hybrid European-American specialties came into being (for example, New World fruits such as the hawthorn-like *tejocote* candied in sugar syrup). There was a big family, now diminished, of extravagantly sweet confections based on sugar (the cane had been brought over and planted in low-lying areas of Oaxaca) and incredible quantities of egg yolks. For a long time, sugar-based foods were considered expensive delicacies, and old descriptions of fanciful tinted and shaped sweets set forth in lavish arrays for banquets to celebrate saints' days and other solemn occasions have an aura of aristocratic glamour.

During the colonial period confectionery, like breadmaking, eventually came under the control of secular artisans' guilds and today is a lay occupation (though even now some convents continue to make special cakes and sweet-meats). Formerly costly candies and pastries are now inexpensive enough to be sold by street vendors. This is also true of the beautiful Oaxacan *nieves*, or ices, which were originally a fantastic luxury.

Though I did not find any Oaxacan desserts requiring up to two hundred egg yolks like some in the old convent recipe books, I confess that the egg-and-sugar specialties are often too cloying for me. In recording the sweet things I have encountered in the state, I have included only a few of the richest and most elaborate desserts (in slightly lightened versions) and tried to point to some of the simpler, more unusual dishes like griddle-roasted plantains, cookies made from ground toasted corn (Pimpo), and rice flour bread with cheese (Quesadilla de Arroz).

Lechecilla
Plain Custard or Custard Filling

2 1/2 to 3 cups whole milk
   (see headnote)

1/2 cup or 1/2 cup plus 2 tablespoons
   granulated sugar

One 1 1/2-inch piece *canela* (page
   30), left whole or thinly slivered
   (see headnote)

3 tablespoons cornstarch

8 large egg yolks, lightly beaten

*T*his plays the same roles as a simple boiled custard or pastry cream in European cooking. In one version it is eaten as a pudding; when made thicker it is a filling for cakes and pastries. The method of cooking is identical expect that the pudding uses the larger amounts of milk and sugar suggested below and often contains the stick of *canela* broken into thin, delicate slivers that are left in rather than removed.

Strain the beaten egg yolks if you're worried about stringy bits remaining in the custard, but I've never had any problem.

About 3 cups (4 servings as a pudding)

Combine the milk and sugar in a medium-size saucepan. Add the *canela*; bring to a boil over medium-high heat, stirring to dissolve the sugar. Reduce the heat to low and cook for 7 minutes. Remove the *canela* if making a pastry cream filling. Adjust the heat to low.

In a small pitcher or measuring cup with a spout, mix the cornstarch with 1/2 cup cold water until smoothly dissolved. Add the egg yolks and whisk gently to combine well without creating too much foam. Pour the mixture into the simmering milk in a slow stream, whisking rapidly to incorporate the egg-cornstarch mixture. Cook, stirring constantly, until it thickens to a custard, 3 minutes or longer. Remove from the heat and let cool; if using as a pudding, apply a sheet of plastic wrap to the surface to prevent a skin from forming. Serve chilled as a pudding, or use in Sopa Borracha (page 291) or Empanadas Dulces (page 298) as a filling.

Marquesote
Sponge Cake

*M*arquesote differs from our version of sponge cake in being made with wheat starch, the part of the flour that is left when the gluten is removed. You may have tasted wheat starch in the delicate wrappings for some types of Chinese dim sum; it can usually be found in Asian markets. Cornstarch is an acceptable substitute. In the Isthmus of Tehuantepec they use rice flour.

Marquesote can be eaten plain, but it is best known as the basis of layered cakes like Sopa Borracha (page 291) or Ante de Almendra (page 290). An electric mixer gives the best results. In Oaxaca, I have usually eaten it as a loaf cake, but I prefer to bake it a shallower pan.

One 9×13×2 1/2-inch cake, or 8 servings as plain cake

Preheat the oven to 375°F.

Line a 9×13-inch ovenproof glass baking dish with wax or parchment paper cut to fit the bottom. Butter and flour the paper and the sides.

In a large mixing bowl, beat the egg whites to stiff peaks. Add the yolks, one at a time, beating well after each addition.

Sift together the dry ingredients and carefully fold into the egg mixture, in several additions. Add the butter, stirring to incorporate thoroughly.

Spoon the batter into the prepared pan and sprinkle evenly with the sesame seeds. Bake for 40 minutes, or until a toothpick inserted in the center comes out clean. Let cool in the pan (set on a rack) before removing and peeling off the waxed paper.

8 large eggs, separated

1/2 cup granulated sugar

1 teaspoon baking powder

1/4 teaspoon salt

1 cup plus 2 tablespoons wheat starch or cornstarch

1/2 cup (1 stick) unsalted butter, melted and slightly cooled

2 tablespoons sesame seeds

Ante de Almendra
Layered Cake with Almond Filling

2 1/2 cups blanched slivered almonds

3 1/2 cups whole milk

2 3/4 cups granulated sugar

One 2-inch piece *canela* (page 30)

1 cup sweet sherry

1 Marquesote (page 289)

1/4 cup dark raisins

*A*ntes are one of the great Spanish-descended traditions in Oaxaca. They are very, very sweet layered compositions based on the sponge cake-like Marquesote and every kind of filling—preserves of sapote and other tropical fruits, candied coconut, or the almond mixture given here.

This can be made in 6 layers as suggested for Sopa Borracha (page 291).

10 or more servings

Preheat the oven to 350°F.

Spread 1/4 cup of the almonds on a baking sheet and bake for 10 to 12 minutes, or until fragrant and toasted. Remove and set aside.

Place the remaining almonds in a food processor and process until finely ground but not pasty. Combine the milk with 1 3/4 cups of the sugar in a medium-size saucepan set over medium heat and stir to dissolve the sugar well.

Reduce the heat to low before the milk can boil up, and add the ground almonds. Cook, stirring frequently, until it is as thick as porridge, for about 30 to 35 minutes. Let cool while you make the syrup.

Place the remaining sugar and the *canela* in a small heavy saucepan and add 2 1/4 cups water. Heat to a boil, stirring to dissolve the sugar thoroughly. Reduce the heat to medium and cook, uncovered, for 15 minutes, or until the syrup is thick enough to coat the back of a spoon. Remove from the heat, remove and discard the *canela*, and stir in the sherry.

With a long, sharp knife, slice the Marquesote horizontally into 3 layers, taking care not to break them. Place the bottom layer on a suitably sized serving plate. Brush one third of the sherry-syrup mixture over it, then spread one third of the almond filling over the cake. Top with a second and then a third layer, brushing each with the syrup mixture and spreading with the almond filling as before. Cover the sides with the almond mixture. Decorate with the raisins and reserved toasted almonds.

Sopa Borracha
Layered Cake with Custard Filling

Sopa Borracha strictly translates as "Drunken Soup"—*borracha* referring to the sherry and *sopa* to the "sopping" or soaking-up action that was part of the old Spanish concept of soups. It is very similar to Ante de Almendra (page 290). If desired, soak the raisins briefly in the sherry to plump them, but Oaxacan cooks don't bother with this refinement. If you prefer to make a smaller cake with more layers, cut the Marquesote crosswise into two 9×6 1/2-inch pieces before slicing horizontally into 3 layers; make a stack of 6 layers, topping each with a sixth of the sherry mixture and the custard.

10 or more servings

1/4 cup blanched slivered almonds

1 cup plus 2 tablespoons granulated sugar

One 2-inch piece *canela* (page 30)

1 cup sweet sherry

1 Marquesote (page 289)

Lechecilla (page 288, made with 2 1/2 cups milk)

1/4 cup dark raisins

Preheat the oven to 350°F.

Spread the almonds on a baking sheet and bake for 10 to 12 minutes, or until fragrant and toasted. Remove and set aside.

Place the sugar and *canela* in a small, heavy saucepan. Add 2 1/4 cups water and heat to a boil, stirring to dissolve the sugar thoroughly. Reduce the heat to medium (or just enough to keep it from boiling over) and cook for 15 minutes, or until the syrup is thick enough to coat the back of a spoon. Remove from the heat and stir in the sherry. Remove and discard the *canela*.

With a long, sharp knife, very carefully slice the Marquesote horizontally into 3 layers. Place one layer on a suitably sized serving dish and brush one third of the sherry-syrup mixture over it. Spread one third of the Lechecilla over the wine-soaked cake. Top with a second and then a third layer, brushing each with the syrup mixture and spreading with custard as before. Decorate the top layer of custard with the raisins and reserved toasted almonds.

Panque de Almendra

Almond "Pound Cake"

4 large eggs, separated

1/2 cup granulated sugar

2/3 cup finely ground blanched
    almonds

2/3 cup wheat starch (page 41)
    or cornstarch

1/4 teaspoon salt

1/2 cup whole milk

*P*anque is apparently a phonetic spelling of "pound cake," though it really isn't very similar. The texture is somewhat more like a sponge cake. My recipe is an adaptation of one by María Concepción Portillo de Carballido.

I like to pair this simple cake with Nieve de Aguacate (page 317).

4 to 6 servings

Preheat the oven to 350°F.

Butter and flour an 8 × 5-inch loaf pan or an 8-inch Bundt cake pan.

In a large bowl, beat the egg yolks and sugar together until the mixture is thick and lemon-colored and falls from the beaters in a ribbon. Stir in the ground almonds.

Sift the starch and salt together. Beat into the almond mixture alternately with the milk, in 3 additions.

In a deep bowl, beat the egg whites to stiff peaks; fold into the almond batter. Spoon the batter into the prepared pan. Bake for 25 to 30 minutes, or until a toothpick inserted into the center comes out clean.

Pan de Chocolate
Chocolate "Bread"

The first time I visited Oaxaca City, I was wandering from the Presidente Hotel (now the Camino Real) toward the big *Zócalo* without really knowing where I was going when I found Evangelina García sitting on a stoop selling small loaves of this pan de chocolate baked in the oval sardine cans called portolas. I stopped to buy one and it was so good I asked for the recipe. The following version is close to hers but not identical. Evangelina used the inimitable Mexican *crema*, a delicious, lightly cultured product not exactly equivalent to either plain cream, crème fraîche, or sour cream. The recipe I give here has been worked out substituting a mixture of heavy cream and buttermilk. If you are a skilled baker and can find *crema* in a store catering to a Mexican or Salvadoran clientele, by all means try it. But be aware that because of the lower moisture and higher butterfat content of *crema*, other factors like the amount of flour and butter may be slightly out of balance and the result may be heavier or greasier.

The name "pan" (bread) is confusing. These are actually delicious little cakes. Since I was unable to duplicate the original oval portolas here, I like to bake the batter in the form of cupcakes.

Thirty 3-inch cupcakes

2 cups heavy cream

1 cup cultured buttermilk

3 1/2 cups unbleached all-purpose flour, sifted before measuring

1/2 teaspoon salt

4 1/2 teaspoons baking powder

1 cup unsweetened cocoa

1 1/4 cup (2 1/2 sticks) unsalted butter

2 1/4 cups granulated sugar

1 cup egg whites (about 7 large)

Preheat the oven to 350°F.

Butter and flour thirty 3-inch muffin cups, or line muffin tins with paper cups.

Combine the cream and buttermilk in a small pitcher or glass measuring cup. Set aside.

Resift the flour with the salt, baking powder, and cocoa.

Cream the butter in a large mixing bowl. Add the sugar, a little at a time, and cream until light and fluffy. Gradually beat in the cream-buttermilk mixture. (Don't worry if the mixture looks curdled.) Add the dry ingredients in two batches, beating well after each addition.

In a large mixing bowl, beat the egg whites to stiff peaks. Mix about 1/3 of the whites into the batter, using the beaters or a whisk. Carefully fold the remaining whites into the batter with a rubber spatula. Spoon the batter into the prepared muffin tins and bake until a toothpick inserted in the center of a cupcake comes out clean, about 35 to 40 minutes. Set on a wire rack to cool completely before removing from the pan.

Beating the frothed topping

for Chocolateatole

Quesadilla de Arroz
Sweet Rice-Flour and Cheese Bread

*T*his *quesadilla* is not related to the familiar snack of the same name that consists of a folded tortilla or envelope of *masa* enclosing a melted cheese filling. It's a cake-like bread or bread-like cake made with rice flour and given a zestful accent with air-dried cheese of the *cotija* type. In Ixtaltepec, the town of the Isthmus where I encountered this unusual specialty, I found it being baked in round wooden cheese molds or dark metal loaf pans and served in wedges. In my adaptation the loaf is baked in a Pyrex pan and cut into squares for serving like a U.S. corn bread. In Ixtaltepec it would be eaten either as a breakfast bread to go with hot chocolate or as part of the *merienda* (the Mexican equivalent of British teatime).

The rice flour used in this recipe should be a Latin American brand such as Goya. Asian rice flour gives a totally wrong texture. Actually, people usually grind their own from soaked and sun-dried rice.

8 servings

One 2 1/2-inch piece *canela* (page 30)

1/2 cup (1 stick) unsalted butter, at room temperature

3/4 cup vegetable shortening

1 cup granulated sugar

4 large eggs

1 pound (roughly 3 to 3 1/2 cups) rice flour (page 39)

1 1/2 teaspoons baking powder

2 cups (8 ounces) finely grated aged cheese such as *cotija*, *queso añejo* (page 31), Parmesan, or Romano

Grind the *canela* in an electric coffee or spice grinder. Set aside.

Preheat the oven to 425°F.

Butter a 13×9-inch ovenproof glass baking dish.

In a large mixing bowl, cream the butter and shortening to combine well. Add the sugar and cream until light and fluffy. Add the eggs, one at a time, beating well after each addition.

Sift together the rice flour and baking powder. Beat into the creamed mixture a little at a time. Stir in the grated cheese and *canela*; beat until thoroughly combined.

Spoon the batter into the prepared baking dish and bake on the center shelf of the oven for 20 to 25 minutes, until the cake is golden brown and a toothpick inserted into the center comes out clean. Set the pan on a wire rack to cool. Serve warm or at room temperature, cut into squares.

Carlitos
Coconut-filled Meringue Cookies

3 cups Dulce de Coco (page 297)

4 large eggs, separated

1 cup cornstarch

1 cup confectioners' sugar

*T*hese pretty little sandwich cookies are served at baptisms in Oaxaca. The mixture is not a true meringue since it contains egg yolks and cornstarch, but something between a meringue and the kind of egg batter used for ladyfingers. An electric mixer will give best results.

The candied coconut mixture is versatile and delicious. It shows up in layered cakes (*antes*) and other small pastries such as Empanadas Dulces (page 298). A similar type of coconut jam is made in the Middle East.

About 2 dozen filled cookies

Prepare the Dulce de Coco and set aside to cool.

Preheat the oven to 350°F.

Grease 2 baking sheets and line each with greased parchment paper.

In a large mixing bowl, beat the egg whites to stiff peaks. Add the egg yolks, one at a time, beating well after each addition.

Sift the cornstarch and confectioners' sugar together. A little at a time, fold the mixture into the beaten eggs.

Drop the mixture by tablespoons onto the prepared baking sheets, flattening each with the back of a spoon to make a neat round the size of a silver dollar. Bake until firm and well set but not browned, about 7 minutes. Remove and let cool on the baking sheet. Sandwich the cookies together by placing about 2 teaspoons of the candied coconut on the flat side of one and pressing the flat side of another over the filling.

Note: *Both the cookies and the filling keep well separately. You can store the filling in the refrigerator indefinitely, tightly covered. The cookies can also be stored indefinitely at room temperature in a tightly sealed container.*

Dulce de Coco

Candied Coconut

I've made this recipe many times and I find that a candy thermometer is absolutely essential. The coconut tends to crystallize unless you cook it to the exact temperature.

About 3 cups

1 1/4 cups granulated sugar

2 cups grated fresh coconut (from half of an average-size coconut)

Place the granulated sugar in a small, heavy saucepan. Add 1/4 cup water, stirring to dissolve well. Bring to a boil over medium heat. Watching carefully to see that it does not boil over, cook to the soft-ball stage (234°F on a candy thermometer), occasionally washing down the sides of the pan with a pastry brush dipped in cold water. (This helps to keep the syrup from crystallizing.) The syrup takes about 10 minutes to reach the correct temperature and will thicken slightly. Stir in the coconut and reduce the heat to low. Cook, brushing down the sides as before, until it is transparent, 6 to 8 minutes. Set aside to cool.

Empanadas Dulces

Sweet Turnovers

Masa para Empanadas (page 299)

1 1/2 cups (approximately) Lechecilla (page 288, made with 2 1/2 cups milk) or Dulce de Coco (page 297)

Savory empanadas such as Empanadas de Sardina (page 66) are popular in Oaxaca, but sweet empanadas, both fried and baked, are more common. Some are associated with particular religious holidays. The usual fillings are very rich and sweet: Two typical ones are the candied coconut used in Carlitos (page 296) and the classic pastry cream, Lechecilla (page 288).

24 empanadas

Preheat the oven to 400°F.

Make the dough as directed (page 299).

To shape the empanadas, use a sharp or serrated knife to slice the cylinder of dough into 24 equal pieces. (Lightly mark off into eighths, then cut each eighth into 3 slices.) With well-floured hands or rolling pin, pat or gently roll out each slice into a 4-inch circle, placing them side by side on the counter or (if you don't have the counter space) stacking them 3 or 4 at a time with plastic wrap separating each piece. Cover the rounds of dough with a damp towel as you work to keep them from drying out. (If desired, the dough rounds can be refrigerated overnight before baking.)

Crimp the edges firmly to seal and bake on 1 or 2 baking sheets for about 12 minutes or until golden. Place about 2 to 3 teaspoons of the chosen filling on one side of each round and fold over into a half moon.

Masa para Empanadas
Pastry Dough for Turnovers

I had a terrible time trying to reproduce this rich, soft pastry dough with its unusual whorled pattern. At last I called the home of my first Oaxacan culinary mentor, María Concepcíon Portillo de Carballido, only to discover that she had just passed away, But luckily I was able to talk to her daughter, Lolis, who steered me in the right direction Nina Gannon helped fine-tune the proportions for U.S. kitchens.

Enough dough for 24 four-inch turnovers

3/4 cup plus 2 tablespoons vegetable shortening

3 1/2 cups unbleached all-purpose flour, or as needed

1/4 teaspoon salt

7 large egg yolks

1/2 to 3/4 cup ice water, or as needed

Cut 3/4 cup of the shortening into bits. Sift together the flour and salt. Place in a large mixing bowl or the work bowl of a food processor. Add the bits of shortening; cut in thoroughly with a pastry blender or process until the fat is evenly distributed. Add the egg yolks one at a time, mixing well with a wooden spoon or pulsing in the processor after each addition. Stop occasionally to scrape down the sides of the processor bowl. Have ready 3/4 cup ice water. Continuing to mix vigorously or with the motor running, slowly begin adding the water. Use only enough to make a smooth but not sticky dough.

Test the consistency of the dough. It will be soft and easily stretched. If it is slightly sticky, knead in a little flour by hand. Form the dough into a ball, wrap well in plastic wrap, and refrigerate for at least 1 hour.

Generously flour a large pastry board or other work surface. Using a rolling pin covered with a floured stockinet, roll out the dough into a rectangle 8×12 inches. Cover with plastic wrap and let rest for 10 minutes.

In a metal measuring cup or small saucepan, gently melt the remaining 2 tablespoons shortening and let stand in a warm place.

Meanwhile, pull the dough into a larger rectangle, sliding your fingers underneath the edges and very gently tugging from the center to enlarge it to 10×15 inches. Using a small, sharp knife, trim any thick or rounded edges to make the corners neat. Spread the partly cooled shortening evenly across the surface with a pastry brush. Let it rest until the shortening has completely solidified. As if rolling up a jelly roll, roll up the dough into a tight cylinder. Trim the edges to make a length of about 10 inches.

Fill, fold, and bake as directed.

Bocadillos de Garbanzo
Chickpea Fritters in Syrup

1 1/4 cups (8 ounces) dried chickpeas

1/2 teaspoon salt

4 ounces young *queso cotija*
(about 1 cup; page 31) or aged
ricotta salata cheese, crumbled

2 large eggs

1 pound Mexican brown loaf sugar
(*panela* or *piloncillo*; page 40),
broken into chunks, or 1 pound
dark brown sugar

One 3-inch piece *canela* (page 30)

Vegetable oil for frying

*T*hese flavorful "little mouthfuls" (the literal meaning) of ground chickpeas are unusual in both texture and flavor. The heavy brown sugar syrup plays unexpectedly against the tang of the cheese.

Dried chickpeas—I don't recommend canned in this case—vary a lot in moisture content, depending on how long they have been in storage. The more dried-out they are, the longer they will take to cook. The cheese should be of the *cotija* type, but young enough to be crumbly, not aged to the hardness of *queso añejo*.

About 2 dozen fritters

Place the chickpeas in a deep bowl. Cover generously with water and let soak overnight. Drain, place in a medium-size saucepan, and add water to cover by 2 inches. Bring to a boil, reduce heat to medium-low, and cook, partly covered, for about 1 hour and 15 minutes. Test for doneness by eating one; if necessary, continue to simmer until they are tender. Drain and set aside to cool. When you can handle them, remove the skins by rubbing the chickpeas between your palms, a handful at a time.

Place the chickpeas in a food processor and process until smoothly puréed. Add the salt, crumbled cheese, and eggs; process until the mixture is completely smooth.

Roll the chickpea mixture between your palms to form walnut-sized balls. Flatten into small, compact cakes.

Make a syrup by combining the broken-up loaf sugar with 4 cups water in a medium-large saucepan and heating to a boil, stirring to dissolve thoroughly. Add the *canela*; adjust the heat to medium and cook for 15 minutes, or until it thickens to the consistency of thin honey. Set aside.

Pour the oil into a deep, heavy medium-size skillet to a depth of 1 inch. Heat to 375°F. Fry the chickpea cakes, a few at a time, until they swim to the top and turn golden (about 30 seconds). As they are done, place them on paper towels to drain.

Return the sugar syrup to the stove over medium heat. Puncture the chick-pea fritters on all sides with a toothpick, to help them absorb the syrup. Add them to the hot syrup and let it return to a boil. Cook for 5 minutes; if the fritters are not well covered with the syrup, turn them frequently and spoon syrup over them. Serve hot or at room temperature, with some of the syrup spooned over each serving.

VARIATION

Antojito de Garbanzo

This delectable sweet also is served as a savory appetizer. Omit the syrup of sugar and *canela* and replace the young *queso cotija* with the aged equivalent, *queso añejo* (page 31), or with aged goat cheese. Serve with Salsa de Chile Pasilla (page 254) or Salsa de Chile Serrano con Limón (page 255).

Buñuelos
Sweet Pastry Fritters

1 pound Mexican brown loaf sugar
  (*panela* or *piloncillo*; page 40),
  broken into chunks, or 1 pound
  dark brown sugar

One 3-inch piece *canela* (page 30)

2 teaspoons aniseed

1 tablespoon granulated sugar

Husks of 6 fresh tomatillos (page 41),
  if available

2 pounds (about 7 1/2 cups)
  unbleached all-purpose flour

1 teaspoon baking powder

1/2 teaspoon salt

4 large eggs

1/2 cup commercial lard or vegetable
  shortening, at room temperature

Vegetable oil for frying

I included this recipe in my first book, *Food From My Heart*, but I feel obliged to repeat it here, for it is one of the signature dishes of Oaxaca. *Buñuelos* are eaten all over Mexico, but in Oaxaca City they are especially associated with the Christmas season and the July festival of the *Guelaguetza*. At these times food-sellers appear all around the cathedral, many of them offering *buñuelos* served in pottery bowls with a light sprinkling or a generous dousing of brown sugar syrup. (The lightly sprinkled version is called *roseado*, or "bedewed"; the heavily doused is *ahogado*, or "drowned.") When you have finished you break the bowl by throwing it against the cathedral wall while making a wish.

If you prefer not to bother with the syrup, sprinkle the hot fritters with real cinnamon sugar made with freshly ground *canela* (page 30) instead of commercial powdered U.S. cinnamon, which is really a misnomer for the cheaper cassia.

This is one case where I would not use home-rendered lard, or at least not the soft and intensely flavored kind appropriate in other Oaxacan dishes. A fluffier consistency is necessary here.

20 buñuelos

Make a syrup by combining the broken-up loaf sugar with 4 cups water in a medium-large saucepan and heating to a boil, stirring to dissolve thoroughly. Add the *canela*; adjust the heat to medium and cook for 15 minutes, or until it thickens to the consistency of thin honey. Set aside.

In a small saucepan, bring 2 cups of water to a boil with the aniseed, granulated sugar, and tomatillo husks. Reduce the heat to medium and simmer until reduced by half. Strain and let cool.

Sift the flour, baking powder, and salt into a large bowl. Make a well in the center and put in the eggs, anise tea, and lard. Work together with your hands until the mixture begins to form a dough. Knead vigorously on a lightly floured surface, lifting the dough and slapping it down several times until smooth and blistered. Cover with a damp cloth and let rest at room temperature for 2 hours.

Lightly flour a rolling pin and work surface. Shape the dough into 20 balls and let rest for 10 to 15 minutes. Keeping them covered with a damp cloth before and after working with them, roll out each into an 8- to 10-inch circle.

Gently reheat the *canela* syrup and keep warm.

Pour oil into a large, heavy saucepan or deep-fryer to a depth of 2 to 3 inches. Heat to 375°F and deep-fry the *buñuelos*, one at a time, until golden, about 1 to 2 minutes for each. Be careful to keep the temperature of the oil as constant as possible while working. Drain the *buñuelos* on paper towels; serve warm, sprinkled with the syrup. (If using the cinnamon sugar and omitting the syrup, serve at room temperature.)

Pimpo
Toasted Corn-Flour Cookies

One 1 to 1 1/2-inch piece *canela* (page 30)

3 cups dried dent-corn or flour-corn kernels (page 91)

3/4 cup (1 1/2 sticks) unsalted butter, cold

1/2 cup grated Mexican brown loaf sugar (*panela* or *piloncillo*; page 40), packed before measuring, or 1/2 cup dark brown sugar, packed

I was walking through the crowded marketplace at Juchitán, the capital of the Isthmus, when I nearly stumbled over María Ruíz sitting daintily on the ground with two small children in the shade of an arch, next to a basket lined with a snowy embroidered cloth. I was already attuned enough to the region to think that this pretty young woman did not look quite like the flamboyant *juchitecas* around her, and sure enough I learned that she was from the town of Tehuantepec some twenty miles distant, where they specialize in making *totopos dulces*, sweet crackers of fine corn flour and dried coconut. I could not replicate María's *totopos*, which require a tandoor-like sunken clay oven, but she gave me her recipe for these little cousins that can be made like cookies in a regular oven.

To grate the sugar, use the fine side of a standard straight-sided grater. The recipe requires a starchy type of corn.

About 3 dozen 1-inch cookies

Preheat the oven to 375°F.

Grind the *canela* in an electric coffee or spice grinder. Set aside.

Spread the corn on a large baking sheet and bake until the kernels are bright yellow, about 25 to 30 minutes. Remove and let cool completely while keeping the oven set to 375°F.

The corn must now be ground to a fine powdery flour. I prefer to do this in an electric coffee or spice grinder, about 1/2 cup at a time. (You can also grind the kernels in several batches in a food processor, but the flour will not be as finely or evenly ground.) Three cups whole kernels should yield about 2 1/2 cups flour; if your yield is greater, use only 2 1/2 cups. Mix well with the ground *canela*.

In a large bowl, cream the butter well and add the sugar; continue to cream until light and fluffy. Gradually add the toasted corn-flour mixture, beating well after each addition. It will form a somewhat stiff dough.

Roll out the dough on a lightly floured board to about 1/3-inch thickness. With a cookie cutter, cut into 1-inch rounds. Reroll leftover scraps of dough for cutting until all has been used. Place on a greased baking sheet and bake for 10 to 12 minutes.

Plátanos Asados
Griddle-Roasted Plantains

This very simple dessert requires ripe but not super-ripe plantains and the unique Mexican cultured cream called simply *crema*. If you can't find *crema*, don't try the dish—no other form of sour cream has the right flavor. You will understand when you taste it.

4 servings

2 large yellow plantains (page 39), beginning to blacken but not yet heavily darkened

1 to 2 cups *crema* (page 33)

2 teaspoons freshly ground *canela* (page 30; optional)

Leave the plantains whole in the skin. Heat a heavy griddle or large cast-iron skillet over medium heat until very hot. Place the plantains on the griddle and cook for about 25 to 30 minutes, turning once or twice to sear evenly on both sides. The skin will become slightly papery and may split; this doesn't matter.

Remove the plantains to a plate and let cool only until cool enough to handle. With a sharp knife, cut each in half crosswise. Make a lengthwise slit from the cut end to the tip of each half and pull back a flap of skin. (Alternatively, completely skin each half.) Serve with a pitcher or bowl of *crema*, which each diner ladles over his or her portion. If desired, place the ground *canela* in a clean salt shaker and pass around the table.

Pan Resobado
Rich Spiced Sweet Bread

One 3-inch piece *canela* (page 30)

1 teaspoon aniseed

4 envelopes dry yeast (1 ounce total)

8 1/2 to 9 1/2 cups unbleached all-purpose flour, or as needed

3/4 cup granulated sugar

1 teaspoon salt

3/4 cup (1 1/2 sticks) unsalted butter, melted and kept slightly warm

4 large eggs, at room temperature

4 large egg yolks, at room temperature

1/2 cup dark raisins

This is typical of the sweet yeast breads that are made in the Valley of Oaxaca for the Days of the Dead, November 1 and 2. Often they are simple round loaves that are inset after baking with cameo-like images done in colored sugar and special decorative materials—for example, a woman's face with golden earrings.

Gabriel Cruz Aguilar, a master baker in the town of San Antonino in the Valley of Oaxaca, uses this dough for his Days of the Dead loaves. In his wood-burning brick oven he bakes up to a thousand loaves a day for the celebration (compared with the normal three hundred), and while I was in the shop several women came by with meter-high baskets to pick up orders of a hundred loaves each! (Families pay many ceremonial visits to each other at this time, and both the hosts and the guests offer gifts of food, including decorated loaves of Pan Resobado, to place on the family altar.) But Gabriel also makes plain loaves of Pan Resobado the year round.

Resobado means "specially kneaded" or "extra-kneaded," and the soft, rich dough does require very thorough and careful kneading. This recipe is a loose home-kitchen translation of Gabriel's original, which began, "Take three sacks of flour . . ." Allow yourself some leeway on the flour. The dough may require more or less.

Three 8-inch loaves or 22 to 24 rolls

Place the *canela* and aniseed in a small saucepan with 3 cups water and boil rapidly until reduced to 1 1/2 cups. Strain the infusion; place 1 cup in a medium-size bowl, reserving the rest. Let cool to warm (110°F). Dissolve the yeast in the liquid. Stir in 1 cup of the flour and 1/4 cup of the sugar; mix to a smooth batter. Let stand in a warm place until foamy, about 10 minutes.

In a large mixing bowl, combine 7 cups of the remaining flour with the remaining 1/2 cup sugar and the salt. Make a large well in the center. Stir down the prepared yeast mixture and add along with the melted butter. Add the whole eggs, egg yolks, raisins, and reserved spice infusion to the well. With the fingers of one hand, break the yolks; begin combining the liquid ingredients in the well and gradually working in more of the flour from around the sides until you have a uniformly mixed dough. At this stage it will be very loose and sticky.

Use some of the remaining flour to generously flour a work surface. Turn out the dough and begin kneading it, working in more flour as necessary to produce a soft, yielding, but kneadable consistency. Knead for about 20 minutes, until the dough is silky and elastic. Place in a greased bowl and let stand in a warm place, covered with a damp towel or plastic wrap, until doubled in volume, about 30 to 40 minutes.

Punch down the dough and shape into three 6-inch round loaves or about 22 to 24 rolls. Place on greased baking sheets and let stand in a warm place, loosely covered with damp cloths or greased plastic wrap, until doubled in volume, about 45 minutes.

Preheat the oven to 375°F.

With a very sharp small knife or razor blade, make 3 parallel slashes across the top of each loaf or roll. Bake about 35 to 40 minutes for the loaves, 15 to 20 minutes for rolls. Check after 10 to 15 minutes and tent with aluminum foil if the crust is darkening too quickly.

Pan de Yema
Egg-Yolk Bread

4 envelopes dried yeast (1 ounce total)

8 1/2 to 9 1/2 cups unbleached all-purpose flour, or as needed

3/4 cup granulated sugar

1 teaspoon salt

1 cup (2 sticks) unsalted butter, melted and slightly cooled

6 large eggs, at room temperature

10 large egg yolks, at room temperature

I was driving from San Antonino—a great town for bakers—to Oaxaca City when I gave a lift to a man who turned out to be an ex-baker. He shared his recipe (in industrial-size quantities) for this bread, which I'd become familiar with in the form of breakfast rolls. Whenever I stay in Oaxaca City I love to wander down to the 20 de noviembre market first thing in the morning and enjoy a steaming cup of Champurrado (page 276) or Mexican hot chocolate in the popular stand called La Pereñita. But they buy their rolls from a professional baker, so I'd never been able to ask them for the recipe.

You will notice that many of my sauce recipes are thickened with the crumbs from a chunk of stale brioche or challah. These are substitutes for what would authentically be used in Oaxaca—Pan de Yema. It contributes a definite sweetness and flavor as well as body. If you make the recipe and have leftovers, by all means use them for sauce-thickeners in preference to the brioche and challah. Incidentally, the dough is equally good baked in large loaves.

22 to 24 rolls or two 9-inch round loaves

In a medium-size bowl, dissolve the yeast in 1 cup warm (about 110°F) water. Let stand until the mixture is frothy, about 5 minutes. Add 1 cup of the flour and 1 tablespoon of the sugar; mix to a smooth batter. Cover with a damp towel or plastic wrap and let stand in a warm spot until spongy and doubled in size, about 15 minutes.

Combine 7 cups of the remaining flour in a large bowl with the remaining sugar and salt. Make a large well in the center. Stir down the prepared yeast mixture and add along with the melted butter, 5 of the whole eggs, and the egg yolks. (Reserve the remaining whole egg for the glaze.) With the fingertips of one hand, break the yolks and begin combining the liquid ingredients in the well. Gradually work in more and more of the flour until you have a uniformly mixed dough of a somewhat loose, sticky consistency.

Use some of the remaining flour to generously flour a work surface. Turn out the dough and begin kneading it, working in more flour as necessary to produce a soft but kneadable consistency. Knead for 15 minutes, or until the dough is silky and resilient. Place the dough in a large greased bowl, cover with a damp towel or plastic wrap, and let stand in a warm draft-free place until doubled in volume, about 45 minutes.

Punch down the risen dough and transfer it to a lightly floured work surface. Shape into 22 to 24 rolls or 2 round 7-inch loaves . Place on 1 or 2 greased baking sheets, cover with slightly damp towels or greased plastic wrap, and let stand in a warm place until roughly doubled in volume, about 45 minutes.

Preheat the oven to 375°F.

With a very small sharp knife or razor blade, make 3 slashes across the top of each roll or loaf. In a small bowl, beat the remaining whole egg with 1 to 2 tablespoons cold water and brush the mixture over the loaves or rolls. Bake until golden, about 15 to 20 minutes for the rolls or 45 minutes for the loaves. To guard against over-browning, check the bread after 10 to 15 minutes and tent with aluminum foil if the crust is darkening too quickly.

Hojaldre
Flaky Yeast Rolls

5 to 5 1/2 cups (approximately) unbleached all-purpose flour

1/2 cup granulated sugar

1/4 teaspoons salt

2 envelopes dried yeast (1/2 ounce total)

1 1/4 cups vegetable shortening

Colored sugar crystals for decoration

The name *hojaldre* may confuse Spanish-speakers who recognize it as a standard term for puff pastry. Though I've never seen an explanation, I suspect that these tender, highly shortened rolls came by their title because they have a flaky, layered crumb a little like some versions of mock puff pastry.

The baker Gabriel Cruz Aguilar shared his method of making *hojaldre*. Like other professional bakers I've talked to in Oaxaca, he combines the yeast and other main ingredients without going through a proofing stage. The recipe requires an electric mixer fitted with a dough hook.

20 to 22 rolls

In a mixing bowl, combine 3 1/2 cups of the flour with the sugar, salt, and yeast. Have ready 1 to 1 1/2 cups warm (about 110°F) water. With a wooden spoon, stir in the water a little at a time, just until you have a stiffish dough; do not thin the mixture beyond this point. Cover the dough with a cloth or plastic wrap and let sit until doubled in bulk, about 30 to 40 minutes.

Stir down the dough and place in a workbowl of an electric mixer fitted with the dough hook. Beat in 1/2 cup of the shortening, a tablespoonful at a time, then about 3/4 cup of the remaining flour. Scrape down the bowl occasionally with a rubber spatula. Repeat the process with another 1/2 cup shortening followed by another 3/4 cup flour. The dough should be springy and somewhat firm.

In a small saucepan, gently melt the remaining 1/4 cup shortening and keep it slightly warm.

Have ready 1 or 2 greased baking sheets. Divide the dough into 20 to 22 golfball-size portions. Flatten each into a circle about 1/2 inch thick and pull together the dough at the center to form a peak (a little like the point on a Hershey's Kiss). Place the rolls on baking sheets. Brush with the melted shortening and decorate with the colored sugar crystals. (Red and white are what Gabriel Cruz Aguilar uses.) Let stand, loosely covered with damp towels or greased plastic wrap, for 25 minutes or until nearly doubled in bulk.

Preheat the oven to 350°F.

Bake for 30 minutes.

Gollorías
Cinnamon Pecan Pralines

These irresistible candies certainly justify their Spanish name, which means something like "luscious morsels." Needless to say, the cinnamon used in this recipe is the same true cinnamon (*canela*) called for throughout the book, not the harsher-tasting cassia sold as cinnamon in U.S. markets. This is another recipe where a candy thermometer is essential.

About 12 to 14 candies

One 2-inch piece *canela* (page 30)

1 1/3 cups granulated sugar

1 cup water

2/3 cup (one 3 1/2-ounce package) pecan meats, broken in pieces

Grind the *canela* very fine in an electric coffee or spice grinder. Mix it with the sugar. Combine the sugar mixture and water in a small saucepan. Stir to dissolve the sugar thoroughly. Bring to a boil over medium-high heat. Cook the syrup to the hard-ball stage, 260°F on a candy thermometer. Stir in the pecans. Working quickly, drop the mixture by tablespoons onto sheets of buttered waxed paper. Let stand until completely cooled. They will keep 3 to 4 weeks in a tightly covered container.

Calabaza en Tacha
Sweet Preserved Pumpkin

One 7- to 8-pound pumpkin

1/2 to 3/4 cup *cal* (slaked lime; page 30)

4 or 5 short chunks (3 to 4 inches) fresh sugarcane (page 40), optional

3 1/2 pounds Mexican brown loaf sugar (*panela* or *piloncillo*; page 40) or 3 1/2 pounds (about 8 cups) dark brown sugar

2 teaspoons allspice berries, bruised

One 6-inch piece *canela* (page 30)

The Days of the Dead (November 1 and 2) are not only one of the most dramatic of Oaxacan fiestas but among the most family-centered. Altars dedicated to *los difuntos* ("departed ones") appear everywhere—outside churches, on shop premises, and especially at family grave sites and in the home, where everyone is preparing for the annual reunion with late friends and relatives. At this time every marketplace in Oaxaca blazes with piles—absolute mountains—of fuschia-red cockscombs and intense orange marigolds. Tall sugarcanes with long fronds and huge banana leaves tower like jungles nearby. The flowers will be used to adorn the altars and the giant fronds to mark arched entries for the souls of loved ones to pass through.

People buy their late cousin's favorite kind of cigarettes or their departed father's usual beer to place on the home altar. The other offerings usually include fresh fruit, candies in all kinds of macabre *memento mori* shapes, decorated breads made from a sweet egg-enriched dough like that for Pan Resobado (page 306), and this traditional spiced preserved pumpkin. Every home altar holds a plate of Calabaza en Tacha—an offering that represents about four days' labor of love.

The pumpkin—I use a regular Halloween pumpkin or sometimes the green West Indian type—is soaked first in a solution of the same *cal* (slaked lime) used to treat corn for tortillas. The alkali makes it firm enough to absorb the sugar without disintegrating. Oaxacan cooks like to make the preserve very sweet; I have slightly reduced the amount of sugar. It may not be traditional, but I like to serve it with vanilla ice cream.

I find that using fresh sugarcane as a support on which to arrange the pieces of pumpkin is a handy and flavorful trick (though not an indispensable part of the recipe). Look for it at Latin American and other tropical groceries; it can also be found as a specialty produce item in some large supermarkets.

12 servings

Cut the pumpkin into 6 equal wedges. Remove and discard the seeds and stringy pulp, then cut each wedge in half crosswise. Prick the rind all over with the tines of a fork to help the slaked lime solution and sugar penetrate.

Pour 5 quarts cold water into a stainless-steel or heavy-duty plastic bucket. Add 1/2 cup of the slaked lime and stir with a wooden spoon to dissolve thoroughly. Taste the solution; it should have a noticeably astringent "bite." If not, stir in more lime a tablespoon at a time. Add the pumpkin wedges and loosely cover the bucket. Let stand overnight (about 10 hours) in a cool dark place.

The next day, remove the pumpkin and rinse well under cold running water. The texture should now be firm.

Prepare a large heatproof earthenware vessel or non-reactive stockpot. You have to make a sort of prop in the center to lean the pieces of pumpkin against. For flavor as well as support, use the optional chunks of sugarcane placed together in a bunch. Or simply place one of the curved pieces of pumpkin in the center. In either case, rest the wedges of pumpkin, skin side out, against the supporting "platform," arranging them like petals coming out from the center.

Using a hammer, break up the loaf sugar into small pieces (no larger than 1/2 inch) and scatter over the pumpkin. Add the allspice and *canela*. Add enough water to cover the pumpkin by 2 inches. Bring to a boil over high heat; cover the pot loosely and simmer over very low heat for 5 hours. Remove from the heat and let stand overnight, uncovered or just loosely covered.

The next day, return the pumpkin to a simmer over low heat and cook for 5 hours. Let stand again overnight. On the third day, return to a simmer; this time any remaining syrup should be absorbed after 2 to 3 hours. Watch very closely as the syrup disappears, since the dish tends to scorch easily at this point. Let cool completely before serving; it will keep in the refrigerator, tightly covered, for up to 1 week.

Las Nieves
Frozen Desserts

Oaxaca City is one of the world capitals of ices. The general name is *nieves*—"snows"—and the city has been famed for them for many generations. I have read that snow actually used to be brought down from the mountains to make *nieves* before there were ice-cream freezers, and they were served to aristocratic Spanish families in exquisite crystal goblets. Today they are made in more flavors that anyone can count. Oaxacans have passions for different kinds. People flock to their favorite *nieves* stands in the market, hoping to find some particular flavor. Or in the evening they gather in the most famous spot of all for ices, the plaza of La Soledad church. The Virgin of Soledad is the patron saint of Oaxaca, and the shady terraced plaza is said to have the most cooling breezes of any place in the city. Here young and old linger over *nieves* made in every color imaginable—pale pink, spring green, ivory white, pastel yellow-green, lemon-yellow, rich brown, exotic greenish-black, rusty brown, brilliant crimson.

They taste as wonderful as they look, and the secret is in the ingredients. The Oaxacan *nieves* are a showcase for every kind of tropical fruit at its local best—papaya, guava, mamey sapote, black sapote, lime, *tuna* (the delicious fruit of the prickly pear cactus), *jiotilla* (the even better fruit of another cactus), mango, tamarind. I wish I could bring you the full rainbow including the prized, exquisite *nieve de rosa* made from fragrant pink rose petals. I'm afraid you have to go to Oaxaca for this and a few others.

But there is good news: many ingredients that were unavailable in the U.S. when I first tasted Oaxacan *nieves* are now regularly carried here in hundreds of Latin American groceries. Look in the freezer section for the frozen pulp (either puréed or in chunks) of many delicious fruits. Usually it is of better quality than the whole fruit would be if shipped across the same distance.

The three recipes I give are meant to be the preface to your own experiments. Keep in mind that the texture you want is not that of a rich, silky ice cream. The classical Oaxacan *nieve* is more like a milk sherbet or an ice milk and is usually quite simple—fruit purée, milk, and sugar syrup. The flavor should be very clean. My directions for Nieve de Tamarindo can serve as the model for other versions made with guava, mango, mamey, and so forth.

I don't usually try to plug special pieces of hardware, but I have had outstanding results making Oaxacan-style ices in the Donvier ice-cream maker from France. It is a non-electric device consisting of a metal container that fits inside an insulated plastic housing with a crank handle. First the metal insert is chilled in the freezer for several hours, or preferably overnight. Then you add the prepared ice-cream mixture, fit the insert into the insulated bucket, and turn the handle twice every three minutes over a twenty-minute period to agitate the mixture. The only disadvantage to this method is that the *nieve* has to be eaten that same day. If left in the container overnight it will freeze rock-solid. I heartily recommend this device, but in the interest of flexibility I have written the recipes to allow for either following the manufacturer's directions for whatever machine you own or still-freezing the mixture in a container such as a stainless-steel mixing bowl.

Nieve de Tamarindo (u Otra Fruta)

Tamarind or Other Fruit Ice

One 14-ounce package frozen
tamarind pulp, thawed

2 cups whole milk

1 cup (approximately) Simple Syrup
(page 273)

*T*amarind is not native to Oaxaca but was brought by the Spanish from Asia. It has a tart, invigorating flavor that is extremely refreshing in hot weather. The puréed frozen pulp is stocked in Latin American and many Asian groceries.

The recipe will work equally well with any kind of fruit pulp from peach to papaya, but always taste to adjust the amount of sugar syrup according to the natural sweetness of the fruit.

1 quart

Combine all the ingredients in a mixing bowl, adding the sugar syrup last so that you can use more or less to taste. Stir to mix thoroughly. Freeze by manufacturer's directions for your ice-cream maker. Or to still-freeze, pour into a 1-quart container (preferably stainless steel), place in the freezer, and freeze for 2 hours. Remove and beat the mixture until it is a fine-textured slush, using a chilled rotary beater or hand-held electric mixer (with beaters chilled). The aim is to break up the ice crystals and aerate the mixture for a fluffier texture. Return to the freezer for 1 more hour; remove and beat in the same manner. Return to the freezer until ready to serve.

Nieve de Aguacate

Avocado Ice

$\mathcal{T}$he idea of making ice cream from avocados is not strange or outlandish to Oaxacans. In many Latin American countries, avocados are eaten as dessert. (Brazilians make them into a sweet mousse.) *Nieve de Aguacate* is one of the perennial favorites at Oaxaca City ice-cream stands. It is naturally creamier than the usual fruit-based *nieves*; but some acid is necessary to offset the blandness of the avocado. Fresh lime juice is the perfect complement.

About 1 quart

2 ripe Hass avocados, peeled and seeded

2 cups whole milk

1 cup (approximately) Simple Syrup (page 273)

1/4 cup (approximately) freshly squeezed lime juice

In a blender or food processor, process the avocados and milk to a perfectly smooth texture. Add the syrup and lime juice, starting with a little less than the suggested amount of each and adding more to taste.

Freeze by manufacturer's directions for your ice-cream maker. Or still-freeze by placing in a 1-quart container (preferably stainless steel) and freezing as directed on page 316 for Nieve de Tamarindo—i.e., beating with chilled beaters after 2 hours of freezing, beating again after an additional 1 hour's freezing, and returning to the freezer until serving time.

Nieve de Leche Quemada
"Burnt Milk" Ice

1 quart whole milk

One 3-inch piece *canela* (page 30)

1 1/3 cups granulated sugar

4 large egg yolks

*T*his is one of the most famous and characteristic of the Oaxacan *nieves*. Actually it has two versions, one more distinctively Oaxacan than the other but also harder to approximate here. To add to the confusion, in other parts of Mexico the term *leche quemada* refers to a rich caramel made by cooking down milk and sugar together to an intensely flavored syrup (it also goes by the name *cajeta*). Neither of the Oaxacan *nieves* exactly matches this. In the simpler one, the sugar is caramelized and then briefly cooked with the milk before being combined with a custard mixture. In the other, the milk is literally burnt—put in a saucepan over high enough heat to actually scorch the bottom. (I was unable to achieve this with commercial U.S. milk without it boiling over.) The scorched flavor is communicated to the whole dish—another example of the Oaxacan fondness for burnt flavors that shows up in some *moles* and other savory dishes.

In Oaxaca City, Nieve de Leche Quemada is always served with a dollop of crimson preserves from the cactus fruit called *jiotilla* (*Escontria chiotilla*). The tart flavor is a wonderfully refreshing contrast to the sweetness of the ice cream. If desired, try a substitute such as a spoonful of tart strawberry or raspberry preserves.

The terminology of frozen desserts in Oaxaca can get a little complicated. Some would refer to an egg-enriched ice cream like this as a *sorbete* or *sorbete de nieve*, as distinguished from the simple fruit- and milk-based *nieves*.

About 1 quart

In a small saucepan, heat 2 cups of milk with the *canela* over medium heat until just boiling. Remove before it boils over and keep warm over a Flame-Tamer or other heat-diffusing device while you caramelize the sugar.

Put 2/3 cup of the sugar in a 1 1/2-quart heavy saucepan and heat over medium-low heat. At first nothing will happen, then the sugar will rapidly darken and liquefy. At once—while it is still medium-light rather than dark brown—pour in a little of the boiled milk, stirring rapidly to start dissolving the sugar. Watch out—it will splatter up furiously at first. Quickly add the rest of the hot milk and cook, stirring, over low heat until the caramelized sugar is completely dissolved and the milk pale brown, about 5 minutes. Keep warm while you make the custard.

In a mixing bowl, lightly whisk the egg yolks and add the remaining 2 cups milk and 2/3 cup sugar. Whisk or stir to combine well and dissolve the sugar without creating too much froth. (Alternatively, process the egg yolks, milk, and sugar together in a blender for 20 to 30 seconds.) Pour the mixture into a medium-size saucepan and place over very low heat; or for still gentler cooking with less danger of curdling, use a double boiler top set over simmering water. Stirring constantly with a wooden spoon, heat until the custard thickens enough to coat the spoon, 3 to 5 minutes (or a little longer in a double boiler). Be careful—too high heat or long cooking will curdle the mixture. Add the caramelized sugar mixture and stir to combine smoothly with the custard. Remove from the heat and let cool completely. Discard the *canela*.

Freeze by manufacturer's directions for your ice-cream maker. Or still-freeze by placing in a 1 1/2-quart container (preferably stainless steel) and freezing as directed for Nieve de Tamarindo (page 316)—i.e., beating with chilled beaters after 2 hours of freezing, beating again after an additional 1 hour of freezing, and returning to the freezer until serving time.

Mail Order Sources

CALIFORNIA

Gazella Chocolate, 3200 Corte Malpaso #108, Camarillo, CA 93012, telephone 818-991-8224. Raw cacao beans and a powdered Oaxacan-style chocolate.

Frieda's by Mail, P.O. Box 58488, Los Angeles, CA 90058, telephone 800-421-9477. Wide spectrum of chiles including some Oaxacan varieties.

Herbs of Mexico, 90 Whittier Boulevard, Los Angeles, CA 90023, telephone 221-261-2521. Wide assortment of dried herbs and spices.

Tierra Vegetables, 13684 Chalk Hill Road, Healdsburg, CA 95448, telephone 707-837-8366; fax 707-433-5666. Locally grown chiles including chilhuacle negro and costeño.

FLORIDA

Burns Farms, 16158 Hillside Circle, Montverde, FL 34756, telephone 407-469-4490. Frozen huitlacoche and fresh *hoja santa* in season.

HAWAII

Hawaiian Vintage Chocolate Company, 4614 Kilauea Avenue, Suite 435, Honolulu, HI 96816, telephone 808-735-8494; fax 735-9640. Raw cacao beans. Though this company does not currently sell cacao commercially, it will accommodate readers of this book. Please mention the book when ordering at 800-429-6246.

MASSACHUSETTS

María and Ricardo's Tortilla Factory, P. O. Box 1763, Jamaica Plain, MA 02130, telephone 617-524-6107; fax 617-524-4826. Slaked lime, blue corn, dent corn, and frozen masa.

The Oriental Pantry, 423 Great Road, Acton, MA 01720, telephone 800-828-0368, or 508-264-4576; fax 617-275-4506. Wheat starch (ask for "wheat flour").

NEW JERSEY

The CMC Company, P.O. Drawer 322, Avalon, NJ 08206, telephone 800-CMC-2780; fax 609-624-8414. Large selection of Mexican ingredients and equipment, though at high prices. Carries cast-aluminum tortilla press, cast-iron comal, dried avocado leaves, epazote, shrimp, Mexican oregano, and canned huitlacoche.

Chile Today-Hot Tamale, Inc., 919 Highway 33, Suite 47, Freehold, NJ 07728, telephone 800-468-7377; fax 908-308-1717. Occasionally carries Oaxacan amarillo chiles in addition to anchos and guajillos.

NEW MEXICO

The Chile Guy, 206 Frontage Road, Rio Rancho, NM 81244, telephone 800-869-9218 or 505-891-0291; fax 505-891-8241. Chilhuacle negro, chile pasilla de Oaxaca, and may carry Oaxacan oregano. Wholesale only.

Old Southwest Trading Co. P.O. Box 7525, Albuquerque, NM 87194, telephone 505-836-0168. Oaxacan chiles including chilhuacle negro, chilcosle, costeño, and pasilla de Oaxaca. May carry Oaxacan oregano.

NEW YORK

Kitchen Market, 218 Eighth Avenue, New York, NY 10011, telephone 212-243-4433. Wide assortment of Mexican ingredients including Oaxacan chiles, canela, Mexican oregano, and canned huitlacoche.

OHIO

Lehmans Non-Electric Catalog, One Lehman Circle, P.O. Box 41, Kidron, OH 44636-0041, telephone 216-857-5757; fax 216-857-5785. Manual corn grinder.

TEXAS

Don Alfonso Foods, P.O. Box 201988, Austin, TX 78720-1988, telephone 800-456-6100; fax 800-765-7373. Selection of Mexican chiles and seasonings.

Golden Circle Farms, 1109 North McKinney, Rice, TX 75155, telephone 214-2225-0500. Fresh epazote and *hoja santa*.

It's About Thyme, 11726 Manchaca Rd., Austin, TX 78748, telephone 512-280-1192; fax 512-280-6356. *Hoja santa* and epazote plants.

The Mozzarella Co., 2944 Elm St., Dallas, TX, telephone 214-741-4072 and 800-798-2954; fax 214-741-4076. Queso blanco, queso fresco, and Oaxacan string cheese.

Pendery's, 304 E. Belknap St., Fort Worth, TX 76102, telephone 817-332-9896. Oaxacan pasilla chiles and chilhuacle negro.

WISCONSIN

Penzey's, P. O. Box 1448, Waukesha, WI 53187, telephone 414-574-0277; fax 414- 574-0278. *Canela* (ask for Ceylon or soft-stick cinnamon), dried epazote, and Mexican oregano.

Shopping Sources

CALIFORNIA

Los Angeles area

La Guelaguetza 3337 1/2 West 8th Street, Los Angeles, CA 90005, telephone 213-427-0601. Best single source of ingredients called for in this book, including fresh and dried herbs, chiles, and even chapulines (grasshoppers) and gusanitos de maguey (maguey worms)! If you don't see something you want on display, ask for it, they almost surely have it in the storeroom.

Top Valu. Chain with several stores in the area; call store # 8 in Santa Ana, Orange County (714-957-2529) for locations. Large selection of Mexican ingredients and chiles.

Valley Food Warehouse, 14530 Nordhoff, Panorama City, CA 91402, telephone 818-891-9939. Frozen chepil, banana leaves in addition to other Mexican and Central American ingredients.

San Francisco

Casa Lucas Market. 2924 24th Street, San Francisco, CA 94110, telephone 415-826-4334. Mexican seasonings and chiles.

La Palma Mexicatessen, 2824 24th Street, San Francisco, CA 94110, telephone 415-826-4334. Mexican seasonings and chiles.

Tierra Vegetables. A branch of the Healdsburg company (see California Mail Order Sources, above) is open at the Ferry Plaza Farmers' Market on the Embarcadero held on Saturday and Sunday mornings.

ILLINOIS

Jiménez Enterprises, Inc., 2140 North Western and 3850 W. Fullerton, Chicago.

Supermercados Cárdenas, 3922 N. Sheridan and 2153 W. Roscoe, Chicago. Mexican seasonings and ingredients.

NEW JERSEY

Mi Bandera Supermarket, 518 32nd Street, Union City, NJ, telephone 201-348-3660. Wide assortment of Latin American ingredients including Mexican-style cheeses.

NEW YORK

Fiesta Mexico, 87-21 Roosevelt Avenue, Jackson Heights, NY, telephone 718-779-2198. Excellent source of Mexican ingredients including frozen chepil, frozen fruit purées, and Mexican cheeses.

Kaufman Pharmacy, Lexington Avenue & 50th Street, New York, NY, telephone 212-755-2266. Slaked lime (calcium hydroxide powder) by special order.

Kitchen Market (see New York Mail Order Sources).

Plaza Piaxtla, 898 Flushing Avenue, Brooklyn, NY, telephone 718-386-2626. Good source from Mexican ingredients and equipment including wooden tortilla press.

Stop 1 Supermarket, 210 W. 94th Street, New York, NY, telephone 212-864-9456. Large selection of Mexican chiles and seasonings including dried avocado leaves, *hoja santa*, epazote and canela.

Tortilleria Piaxtla, 913 Flushing Avenue, Brooklyn, NY, telephone 718-381-4527. Fresh *masa*, nixtamal, and slaked lime.

Bibliography

José Alcina Franch, *Calendario y Religión Entre los Zapotecos*. Universidad Autónoma de Mexico City, 1993

Luis Rodrigo Alvarez, *Geografía General del Estado de Oaxaca*. Carteles Editores, Oaxaca City, 1994

Luis Rodrigo Alvarez, Historia General del Estado de Oaxaca, Carteles Editoriales, Oaxaca City, 1995

Helen Augur, *Zapotec*. Doubleday & Company, Inc., Garden City, NY, 1954

Ralph L. Beals, *Ethnology of the Western Mixe*. Cooper Square Publishers, Inc, New York, 1973

Sybille Bedford, *A Sudden View: A Mexican Journey*. Harper and Brothers, Publishers, New York, 1953

Heinrich Berlin, Ed. *Idolatría y Superstición Entre Los Indios de Oaxaca*. Gonzalo de Balsalobre, Diego de Hevia y Valdés, Ediciones Toledo, Mexico City, 1981

John Bierhorst,*The Mythology of Mexico and Central America*. Quill, William Morrow, New York, 1990

José María Bradomín, *Historia Antigua de Oaxaca*. Oaxaca City, 1993

José María Bradomín, *La Gran Incógnita*, Oaxaca City, 1992

José María Bradomín, *Leyendas y Tradiciones Oaxaqueñas*. Oaxaca City, 1990

José María Bradomín, *Oaxaca en la Tradición*. Oaxaca City, 1991

José María Bradomín, *Toponomía de Oaxaca* (Crítica Etimológica). Oaxaca City, 1992

María Concepción Portillo de Carballido, *Oaxaca y su Cocina*.Litoarte, S.A. de C.V., Oaxaca City, 1987

Andrés Cecero, *El Vuelo de la Gente Nube* (Narraciones Zapotecas). Secretaría de Educación Pública, Mexico City, 1988

Ana María Vásquez de Colmenares, *Tradiciones Gastronómicas Oaxaqueñas*. Comité Organizador del CDL Aniversario, Oaxaca City, 1982

Miguel Covarrubias, *Mexico South: The Isthmus of Tehuantepec*. Alfred A. Knopf, New York, 1946

Wilfrido C. Cruz, *Oaxaca Recóndita*. Talleres Linotipográficos "Beatriz de Silva," Mexico City, 1946

Directorio Nacional Gastronómico. Secretaría de Turismo, Mexico City, N. D.

Dr. Eulogio G. Gillow, *Apuntes Históricos*. Imprenta del Sagrado Corazón de Jesús, Mexico City, 1889

Andrés Henestrosa, *Los Hombres Que Disperso La Danza*. Organización Editorial Novaro, S.A., Mexico City, 1975

Gilberto Hernández Díaz y Roberto Acevedo Escamilla, *Los Primeros Panaderos de Oaxaca*. Proveedora Escolar, S. de R.L., Oaxaca City, 1992

Barbara Hopkins, *Oaxaca: Crafts and Sightseeing*. Minutiae Mexicana, Mexico City, 1992

Etzuko Kuroda, *Bajo el Zempoatepetl: La sociedad mixe en las tierras altas y sus rituales*. CIESAS - Instituto Oaxaqueño de las Culturas, Oaxaca City, 1993

El Maguey: "el arbol de las maravillas." Gobierno del Estado de Hidalgo, Museo Nacional de Culturas Populares, Mexico City, 1988

Prof. Maximino Martínez, *Catálogo de Nombres Vulgares y Científicos de Plantas Mexicanas*. Fondo de Cultura Económica, Mexico City, 1994

Prof. Maximino Martínez, *Plantas Utiles de la República Mexicana*. Talleres Linotipográficos de H. Barrales Sucr., Mexico City, 1928

Alejandro Méndez Aquino, *Noche de Rabanos (Tradiciones navideñas de Oaxaca)*. Dirección General de Educación, Cultura y Bienestar Social del Gobierno del Estado de Oaxaca, Oaxaca City, 1990

Gilberto Orozco, *Tradiciones y Leyendas del Istmo de Tehuantepec*. Published by the author, Oaxaca City, 1995

Luis Ortíz Macedo and Jose Pablo Fernández Cueto, *Los Hijos del Sol*. Seguros America, Mexico City, 1989

Ana Rosaura de Paola y Luna, *Las Recetas de la Tía Rosaura*,.Carteles Editores, Oaxaca City, 1994

Velma Pickett et al, *Vocabulario Zapoteco del Istmo*. Instituto Lingüístico de Verano, Mexico City, 1988

Kimball Romney and Romaine Romney, *The Mixtecans of Juxtlahuaca*. Robert E. Krieger Publishing Company, Huntington, New York, 1973

Ursulino Rueda Saynez, *De Juchitán Oaxaca: Leyenda, Tradición y Poesia*. Editorial del Magisterio "Benito Juárez," Juchitán, Oaxaca, 1987

Ursulino Rueda Saynez and Ma. Magdalena Rueda Jiménez, *Juchitán: Un Pueblo Típico Zapoteca*, Editorial del Magisterio "Benito Juárez," México, D.F., 1988

Alberto Sánchez López, *Oaxaca: Tierra de Maguey y Mezcal*, Instituto Tecnológico de Oaxaca City, 1989

Santamaría, Francisco J., *Diccionario de Mejicanísmos*. Editorial Porrua, S.A., Mexico City, 1992

Chloë Sayer, *The Costumes of Mexico*. University of Texas Press, Austin, Texas, 1985

Chloë Sayer, *The Mexican Day of the Dead*. Shambhala Redstone Editions, Boston and London, 1994

Barbara Howland Taylor, *Mexico: Her Daily and Festive Breads*. Latin American Books, Volume V, The Creative Press, Claremont, California, 1969

Gutierre Tibón, *La Ciudad de los Hongos Alucinantes*. Panorama Editorial, S.A., Mexico City, 1985

Frances Toor, *A Treasury of Mexican Folkways*. Bonanza Books, New York, 1947

Las Tradiciones de Días de Muertos en México. Secretaría de Educación Pública, Mexico City, 1987

Jack Weatherford, *Indian Givers*. Fawcett Columbine, New York, 1988

Whitecotton, Joseph W., *Los Zapotecos: Principes, Sacerdotes y Campesinos*. Fondo de Cultura Económico, México, 1985

Marcus Winter, *Oaxaca: The Archeological Record*, Minutiae Mexicana, Mexico City, 1989

Index

Page numbers in *italics* refer to photos.

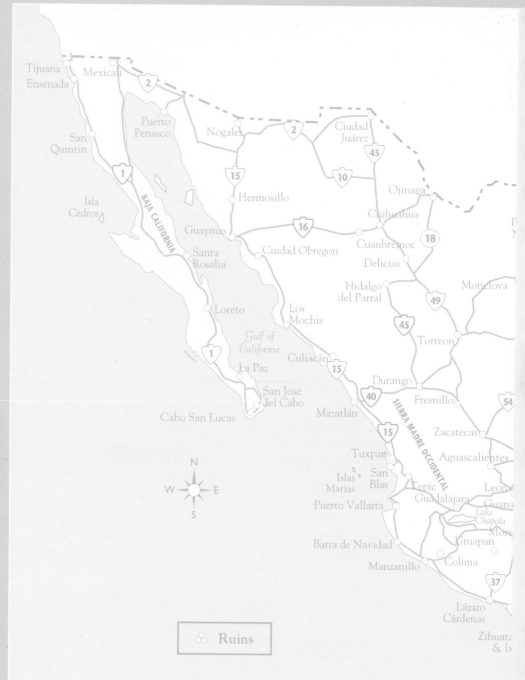

Ruins

Pacific Ocean